Praise for *The Beijing Consensus*

"China's rising influence has real-world consequences, and one of the many virtues of *The Beijing Consensus* is the way that it describes exactly what they are.... Halper is undeniably a sure-footed guide to modern China and what its rise means to the world. In brisk, readable prose—enlivened by pop culture references to Bruce Springsteen, Tom Clancy, and Star Trek—he sees through China's confounding contradictions, the way its imposing strength is balanced by surprising fragility."   —*Asia Times*

"Halper cogently rejects the 'conventional wisdom' that suggests America's relationship with China is 'on track' in this lucid, probing text.... [Halper] concludes this sobering, excellently argued book with concrete policy recommendations."
                                                               —*Publishers Weekly*

"Halper is right to criticize the triumphalist argument that China would inevitably become more democratic and aligned with the West once it entered the international economy. It has done neither. He is correct that China is not shy about buying off dictators to obtain natural resources and political support—efforts that have undercut American policies. And, he is certainly right that America has to do a better job of standing up for the benefits of its system and values in the developing world."   —*American Spectator*

"In this deeply researched and well-written book, the challenge posed by China, as Dr. Halper sees it, is not fundamentally military, but political and economic. China's example of rapid economic growth and authoritarian rule may well have greater appeal in the developing world with the result that developing nations increasingly reject democratic values, transparency, and rule of law in favor of a dynamic market-authoritarian model that delivers growth but limits many freedoms we cherish. Among the results are trends that leave this country increasingly isolated.   —James R. Schlesinger, former
Secretary of Defense and Energy

"Stefan Halper has written a thoughtful and provocative book that challenges us to rethink the conventional wisdom about the impact of China's ascendance on the world order. It should be required reading the policy community."
                                                        —Professor Minxin Pei,
                                        Senior Scholar, The Carnegie Endowment,
                                      Professor of Political Science, Claremont College

"Stefan Halper provides a thoughtful, refreshing analysis of the strategic and economic enigma that is China, carefully avoiding the fallacy of seeing China as either a mortal military and commercial threat to the United States or as a benign strategic partner for this country. Halper demolishes an assortment of myths and may well have written the most important book to have appeared in the past decade on China and U.S. policy toward that emerging great power."

—Ted Carpenter, Executive Vice President
for Defense and Foreign Policy, The CATO Institute

"Twenty years of mismanaged diplomacy and deterrence enabled an avoidable world war in the Pacific. If Stef Halper had been writing then it might have been different. Today a similar pattern of inadequate strategy carries the seeds of another Pacific war involving America and China, but Halper has provided a timely book to help avoid history repeating. His concepts and logic, delivered in lucid, even elegant, prose are overwhelmingly persuasive, setting a positive new framework for debate in Washington."

—John Lehman,
former Secretary of the Navy

"This brief but richly detailed and annotated volume is an excellent and helpful handbook for the foreign-policy professional as well as the serious student of Sinology."

—*Washington Times*

"Stefan Halper has analyzed and given historical perspective to probably the greatest issue we face in the 21st century, the rise of China and the role of the United States. China and the U.S. must cooperate, cautiously, for the sake of mankind but this must be accompanied by a clear-eyed view of a military/strategic balance. This is a wide-ranging book, challenging and well-written and researched, and should be read by people who have an interest in the outcome of the 21st century."

—James R. Lilley, former U.S.
Ambassador to China and South Korea and
Chief of the U.S. Mission in Taiwan

"In this deeply researched and well-written book Stefan Halper challenges Washington's conventional wisdom, arguing powerfully that the strategic battle will not be primarily over territory or even markets. It will be over values, a contest between the liberal values of the Enlightenment and the Chinese model of market authoritarianism. This book does not pretend to suggest that there is an easy answer, much more valuably it lays out the issues clearly and sets the stage for an informed and rational debate. —James B. L. Mayall, University of Cambridge, Emeritus Professor of International Relations and Departmental Chairman

"Halper served in the White House of Presidents Nixon, Ford, and Reagan. His understanding of Washington's policymaking community is therefore excellent. . . . His plea is for the world's last remaining superpower to 'get China right.'"
—Kerry Brown, Senior Fellow in the Asia Programme, Chatham House, and author of *Friends and Enemies: The Past, Present and Future of the Communist Party of China*

"This is an excellent book. Halper provides a fine analysis of the foundations of Chinese foreign policy and Beijing's highly effective policies in developing nations."
—*Choice*

"Despite Halper's portrayal of 'the problem' as one of insurmountable complexity, he insists there is reason 'to be optimistic.' And it would seem his optimism warrants a recommendation of his book for anyone who is interested in matters of contemporary geopolitical gamesmanship."
—*Post & Courier* (Charleston, SC)

"Halper has written a worthwhile and stimulating book. He well diagnoses the problems inherent to the complicated U.S.-China relationship.
—*American Spectator* online

"In *The Beijing Consensus*, [Halper] argues that the rising 21st century superpower is suppressing the yuan, exporting unemployment, and even standing in the way of America's lagging recovery from the global recession. In the process, Halper writes, 'China is also exporting its overall philosophy of economics and governance at the expense, pardon the pun of our own.'"
— AlterNet

THE
BEIJING
CONSENSUS

LEGITIMIZING
AUTHORITARIANISM
IN OUR TIME

With a New Preface by the Author

STEFAN HALPER

BASIC BOOKS
A Member of the Perseus Books Group
New York

Copyright © 2010 by Stefan Halper
Hardcover first published in 2010 by Basic Books,
A Member of the Perseus Books Group
Paperback first published in 2012 by Basic Books

Books published by Basic Books are available at special discounts for bulk purchases in
the United States by corporations, institutions, and other organizations. For more information, please contact the Special Markets Department at the Perseus Books Group, 2300
Chestnut Street, Suite 200, Philadelphia, PA 19103, or call (800) 810-4145, ext. 5000, or
e-mail special.markets@perseusbooks.com.

Designed by Pauline Brown

The Library of Congress has catalogued the hardcover as follows:

Halper, Stefan A.
  The Beijing consensus : how China's authoritarian model will dominate the twenty-first
century / Stefan Halper.
    p. cm.
  Includes bibliographical references and index.
  ISBN 978-0-465-01361-6 (alk. paper)
  1. United States—Foreign relations—China. 2. China—Foreign relations—United
States. 3. China—Foreign relations. 4. China—Foreign economic relations. 5. China—
Politics and government. I. Title.
  JZ1480.A57C653 2010
  327.51—dc22
                                                                              2009050659

Paperback ISBN: 978-0-465-02523-7
E-book ISBN: 978-0-465-02826-9

10 9 8 7 6 5 4 3 2 1

With love to Lezlee, the light of my life,
my partner and guide in thought and deed

CONTENTS

PREFACE TO
THE PAPERBACK EDITION

WHY WRITE A BOOK?

There were certain points I wished to make in writing *The Beijing Consensus:* First, China had risen more rapidly and in different ways than most had anticipated just a few years ago, and this has had profound and now visible effects on the West and the concept of the West. Second, China will not become a member of the club—as Roosevelt had hoped for Stalin. Third, the market will not, inexorably, lead to democracy, as many in Washington have thought since the 1980s. Fourth, China's example of a "developing nation" now approaching the pinnacle of world power and soon to have the world's largest economy has legitimized authoritarianism in our time. And last, reflecting the view that "it's not whose army wins, it's whose story wins," China will *not* confront the West on the battlefield, but rather in the global information space, where Beijing seeks to frame the public's understanding of unfolding events in a China-friendly way.[1] (Here, success for Beijing would mean delegitimizing the West's version of events and enfranchising China as an increasingly authoritative arbiter of global affairs—particularly among those in the world beyond the West.)

The Beijing Consensus describes a China challenge arriving in several dimensions. It explores a range of economic and security questions and, importantly, addresses a quite serious challenge found in a different dimension. This challenge is ideational. There has emerged a battle of ideas about governance that will have far-reaching consequences.

The Chinese have refined the Asian growth model to develop a fast-growth, stable, "market-authoritarian" governance that is admired in the world beyond the West and particularly among Third World leaders.

Regime leaders in Africa, Latin America, and elsewhere see governance without contentious legislatures or challenging media. Such governance provides the people with employment, housing, and the hope of a better future. Crucially, these governments do not promise an open public square or the rights of speech, belief, or political association. The public is asked to respect the authorities and stay out of politics.

Non-Western views of China's example are important: The words *envy* and *admiration* come to mind. With China's rise, a newly developed country has charted a course that demonstrates how authoritarian governments can benefit from the power of the market. China offers not just an alternative path to development, but also an alternative to the Western-authored, liberal international order—rejecting, for example, the concept of universal human rights.

The People's Bank of China—now six times the size of the World Bank—is financing infrastructure and energy development with low-interest loans across Africa, Latin America, Central Asia, and the Near East, including loans to outliers and pariah states. With these hard-currency loans, China, in effect, provides a path around the West—making Western standards and institutions less relevant.

For thirty years, the Chinese have been our economic partners. Now, they are our political—and rising military—rivals. Successful market reforms indicate the Communist Party is not about to crumble. And it is certainly not melting into democracy.

That China has crafted a distinct posture since the Soviet collapse—neither conforming to the U.S. worldview, nor confronting (until recently) the U.S.-led system—begs the question of what these trends mean for the West and the idea of the West.

Since *The Beijing Consensus* was written in 2009, the recession brought a new assessment of China. Double-digit growth, trade surpluses, huge and growing hard-currency reserves, moderate inflation, a growing middle class, and a generally improving quality of life—it seemed China's market-authoritarian system was managing the global crisis remarkably well.

Moreover, from America's distress, there arose an uncomfortable new norm in the way Washington perceived its relationship with Beijing. Economic interdependence muted America's voice on certain values and issues that had underpinned the U.S.-led liberal order—values such as progress on human rights, minority rights, the rule of law, and free speech.

Recall that in Beijing in 2009, Hillary Clinton told journalists and officials that pressing China on "other issues," like transparency, Tibet, and human rights, "must not interfere with addressing the global economic crisis." The same message was conveyed in November 2009, when President Obama visited Beijing, and in his low-key, non-televised meeting with the Dalai Lama at the White House in February 2010.

In the long tradition of Chinese strategic thought stemming from Sun Bin and others in the fourth and fifth century BCE, leaders of the Communist Party and the People's Liberation Army (PLA) analyzed Washington's changed posture and concluded that there was potential for gain. Hard-line factions in both organizations, encouraged by the change, generated heightened tensions in U.S.-China relations. The chairman of the People's Bank of China captured the moment when, referring to the housing bubble and poorly regulated banks, he announced in London, "Now the teachers have problems," but as Sun Tzu emphasized (also in the fourth century BCE) such strategic judgments must be "accurate in every factor," and this time, the Mandarins may have read too much into the moment.[2]

A CHANGED VIEW IN WASHINGTON

Just as we frequently have difficulty deciphering the meaning of Beijing's statements and initiatives, so have the Chinese miscalculated America's capacity to manage the economic downturn, which, while not always pretty and certainly controversial, has seen the nation muddle through the worst of the storm with 3 percent GDP growth. With the equity markets showing growth in 2010, inflation moderate, unemployment stubbornly high, productivity increasing and the Congress struggling to put a deficit-reduction program in place, progress has been uneven but the picture of America's decline is no longer so clear.

Some in Beijing now say that events in the United States may simply have reflected poor management and inadequate regulation, rather than a crisis for market democracy as some had hoped. And, of course, this is all the more poignant for as

2011 concludes China now confronts its own difficulties: a property bubble rapidly rising (perhaps uncontrollable), local and provincial government debt, inadequate bank reserves against bad loans, rising social unrest, and inflation linked to an artificially low Renminbi estimated at 5.8 percent.

During his recent Washington visit, President Hu discovered that American attitudes toward China have hardened. When Obama took office in 2009 and tried to embrace China as a partner in tackling the financial crisis and other global issues, China misread American motives. This led to missed opportunities for better relations. The Chinese took American proposals for cooperation as weakness. Moreover, Beijing's more aggressive tone had a profoundly negative effect in Washington.

China has moved on from the late Deng Xiaoping's *taoguang yanghui*, which can be translated as "biding our time and building up our capabilities"—to the aggressive self-awareness described in U.S. Ambassador Jon Huntsman's recent cables (courtesy of WikiLeaks). In these communiqués, Huntsman refers to China's "muscle-flexing, triumphalism and assertiveness."

Among other things, the carefully constructed China story that has knit corporate America together with senior policy makers, with the encouragement of Henry Kissinger and Brent Scowcroft, has begun to unravel. Important assumptions made about China over the last two decades have proven wrong.

Contrary to Robert Zoellick's soothing reassurance, for example, that China is a "stakeholder" in the global commonweal, the reality is more complex. China has been helpful on certain matters—North Korea, piracy in the Gulf of Aden, providing UN peacekeepers in many places—and has been a spirited, though often difficult, participant in the World Trade

Organization (WTO) and the United Nations. But over time, it has become plain that China's actions are guided by a distilled pragmatism that serves the country's direct interests rather than an embrace of global norms or the ethics that have informed the post–World War II global architecture. This phenomenon is particularly pronounced in China's dealings with the resource-rich developing world.

Here *The Beijing Consensus* examines China's calculus, which is rooted in what has been called China's growth trap. China must grow at a minimum of 8 percent to ensure stability and provide jobs and housing to migrant workers flooding into and out of the east coast cities (and to recent university graduates as well). Failure to achieve this growth rate carries the risk of chaos—a nightmare in a country of 1.5 billion.

To grow, Beijing must find and secure steady, long-term sources of energy, copper, iron, zinc, cobalt, and timber. A latecomer to these markets and spurred by unprecedented demand, China must offer better terms than the established players—which it does in several ways.

Beijing uses its $3 billion in hard-currency reserves to provide low-or no-interest, long-term loans or grants to resource-rich governments. It normally commits to road and rail construction to move the resources to a port; sometimes agrees to build schools and hospitals that otherwise might not be built; and makes large, private payments to chiefs of state, to be sure that all goes smoothly.

Most importantly, Chinese decision-makers pledge non-interference in internal affairs. They are not concerned about Western ethics and norms, good-governance issues, the rule of law, transparency, environmental questions, or labor conditions. They are concerned about one thing: extracting the resources needed for growth and stability in an efficient and timely way. And because ensuring growth and stability conditions the party's survival, China will not become a stakeholder, contrary to Zoellick's prediction, in the norms and ethics of the global community—except when it benefits them.

THE CHINA EFFECT

The so-called China effect is seen in several dimensions: It is quietly remaking the landscape of international community and politics. And it is doing so in ways that progressively limit the projection of Western influence beyond the NATO bloc. This process is most pronounced in the Third World, but Second World nations like Syria, Indonesia, and Iran also have regional influence (I call them pivot powers) and are also adopting elements of China's example.

Over time, one effect of China's embrace among Third World nations has been to marginalize the principles that have informed Western governance and progress. This is seen in China's assiduous support for a number of authoritarian regimes across sub-Saharan Africa. Another aspect of the China effect has been the selective rejection of precedents enshrined in international law and custom. This is found in the declaration that the South China Sea is a "core interest." In people terms, the China effect means that for those ruled by governments admiring or seeking to replicate China's market-authoritarian example, the prospects of a democratic civil society are remote—perhaps nonexistent.

A separate dimension of the China effect is a casual approach to the rule of law. China accepts a lax application and adjudication of the law among foreign business partners just as it does at home. Thus, in an anything-goes business culture, Chinese contractors complete projects rapidly, but the results are often substandard. *The Economist* gives a striking example: "A hospital in Luanda, the capital of Angola, was opened with great fanfare but cracks appeared in the walls within a few months and it soon closed. The Chinese-built road from Lusaka, Zambia's capital, to Chirundu, 130 km (81 miles) to the southeast, was quickly swept away by rains."[3]

The China effect also touches the technologies that might function as instruments of change in developing countries. It has developed technical antidotes designed to identify and locate Internet users and suppress the range of social media—Twitter, Facebook, and texting are not permitted in China—that have contributed to change in the Near East.

In yet another dimension of the China effect, the environment, as well as workers' rights and safety, are routinely ignored—again reflecting China's domestic standards. When added to the incipient racism often reflected in the violence employed by Chinese owners managing African workers, many Africans ask whether the Chinese are making their lunch or eating it.

China is, in effect, catalyst in chief for a profound and far-reaching process. Just as globalization is shrinking the world, China is shrinking the West—its values, principles, and standards—a point underscored in yet another realm by its success in persuading nineteen countries to skip the Nobel ceremonies for Liu Xiaobo in 2010.

NOW A COMMENT on the dog that didn't bark. In 1989, American political theorist Francis Fukuyama claimed that we had entered a new era embracing the Western model of free-market democracy. But that era failed to materialize. Instead, new ideas about capitalism brought wealth without democracy.

Put simply, many leaders in the world beyond the West, reflecting a broader global trend, are replacing the free-market democratic model. They are substituting it with a market-authoritarian model that opens the economy to investment and market development and allows the ruling party to control the government, the courts, the military, and information.

These developments—new centers of economic autonomy beyond the West and the growing appeal of illiberal capitalism—are the dual engines for the diffusion of power *away* from the West. When added to Beijing's continuing currency manipulation, they are the key force-multipliers in the global rise of China.

Of course, some of China's progress is a function of the failure of the Washington Consensus in the late 1980s and early 1990s. Countries across Africa and Latin America were worse off for following the World Bank and International Monetary Fund (IMF) one-size-fits-all prescriptions for growth. Lax oversight and poor management left many countries with stagnant literacy rates, job loss, and declines in per-capita income. As disillusion rose, the door was left open for China to gain traction using policies that adroitly combined the timely provision of hard-currency support and noninterference in internal affairs. Here, China essentially provides an exit option for Third World governments seeking loans—and relief from World Bank and IMF moralizing and hectoring demands for government reform—and has greatly benefited from it.

China has built on these commercial relationships to exert political leverage in international bodies, creating a group of grateful and compliant acolytes, but not in the Cold War sense. There are no voting blocs within the United Nations or in other global institutions that take instructions from a bloc leader (though Beijing expects support on Taiwan, Tibet, sovereignty, and human rights issues). Rather, we see nations loosely connected by an admiration for China, a desire to capture the power of international markets, and an equal desire to remain autonomous from Western concepts of global civic culture and liberal development economics.

While there is no Chinese model per se (and indeed, Beijing is recently sensitive to the term *model*, now preferring the word *case*), a complex set of developments and reforms in China over the last thirty years has owed its success to China's unique culture, demography, geography, and governing philosophies. In this sense, there is no model to speak of that can be replicated in, or exported to, places like Latin America or sub-Saharan Africa.

But in ideational terms, China is exporting something simpler, and indeed more corrosive, to Western preeminence. This is the basic idea of *market authoritarianism.*

Beyond everything else that China sells to the world, the country functions as a global billboard for "going capitalist and staying autocratic." Thus, Beijing provides a compelling demonstration of how to liberalize economically without surrendering to liberal politics. In this respect, China presents the challenge of a new type of corporate state.

China has, in effect, legitimized authoritarianism in our time.

HENRY KISSINGER makes the point that we must revitalize the democratic story, demonstrating to ordinary people in the world beyond the West the promise of democratic government, transparency, and good management. We must underscore our social contract guaranteeing an open public square and the freedoms of speech and belief. Most important, we must show that by maximizing individual opportunity, we improve the prospects for wealth and a stable future.

The United States and China approach these matters of civil organization and the social contract in different ways. The essential question as the twenty-first century opens is whether it will be the American story or the Chinese story that seizes the world's imagination and frames the future.

CHINA'S CHALLENGE TODAY

Though comforted by China's notable progress in bringing millions out of poverty, creating the largest middle class in the world, fashioning a modern military force, practicing strong fiscal and trade management, and producing an economy that rivals the largest in the world, China's leaders confront serious challenges—foreign and domestic—for which solutions are not now apparent.

Domestically, inflation is *primus inter pares.* China faces rampant, so-far-uncontrollable inflation. The situation is spurred by local government spending, loose bank lending policies, an artificially cheap yuan, and the 60 percent of the economy controlled by largely unregulated entrepreneurs who often pay usurious interest rates for loans. Many local governments are selling land or spending money loaned from state-owned banks or using property tax revenues to invest in housing or commercial development that often remains unoccupied for extended periods—or are doing some combination of these things. While attempts to reform local governments have been largely unsuccessful, recent steps to increase bank lending rates, boost loan-loss reserves, and tighten the criteria for acceptable loan collateral have slowed bank lending.

Today the inflation rate is thought to range between 6 and 10 percent. Without local government reform, a more rapid rise in the value of the yuan, and continued progress in reigning-in bank lending, China's inflation may be unstoppable.

What is at stake? First, failure to control inflation will see wage rates rise, which will lead to unemployment and instability. This will bring about a further emphasis on domestic security with a resulting increase in social tensions. Higher production costs will also make exports less competitive (a trend that began in June), reducing China's hard-currency earnings. A measure of the seriousness of the problem is the widely held belief among economists that the European sovereign debt problem and China's inflation are the two problems most likely to trigger a global financial crisis.

A second serious challenge to the Beijing leadership is the problem of fully integrating China's fifty-five minorities. The Tibetans, the Uighurs in Xinjiang Province, and the Mongolian minorities are particularly unsettled and, in the case of the Tibetans, have experienced the systematic deconstruction of their culture and society. Unrest in Tibet and among the Uighurs has led to crackdowns and subsequent criticism of China in the global media. This set of problems parallels others, including the stubborn income disparity between the coast and the interior; China's struggle to fashion a new, post-Marxist identity; the slow acceptance of the rule of law; and the increasingly serious shortage of fresh water. These matters, while beyond the scope of this preface, are addressed in the book.

Third, China's increased military budget—up 17.4 percent this year—makes it the third-largest in the world. Certain of Beijing's initiatives threaten to cast China as an adversary, not just of the United States, but also to its neighbors, from Japan to India.

Still, the most prominent security issue on Beijing's political-military table is the potential formation of a U.S.-Japan-Korea military alliance and the link this may have to India with its concerns about the Indian Ocean. This underscores the age-old threat of containment China faces from the sea.

In recent years, with strong trade balances, double-digit growth, huge hard-currency accumulations, and an adroit avoidance of the worst of the financial crisis, Beijing has assumed a markedly aggressive posture in the region, advancing territorial claims from the Ryukyu Islands to the South China Sea to Arunachal Pradesh (which Beijing calls "Southern Tibet") on the Indian border. China's new "Blue Water" navy is of particular concern to the Philippines, Vietnam, Singapore, and Taiwan, all of whose disputes with Beijing center on the South China Sea.

Among the effects of China's new posture has been an express welcome of President Obama's return to Asia strategy, which has brought comfort to those facing a less predictable China. China has attempted to balance this by emphasizing its strong trading relations within the region its role as an engine for growth and infrastructure development and as a source of hard-currency investment. Beijing emphasizes that of China's ten largest trading partners, six are regional neighbors. Yet, commentary from bloggers and other Internet sources clearly suggests that even with the Association of Southeast Nations (ASEAN) Free Trade Area formally established in 2010, Beijing feels vulnerable to the mounting U.S. presence—most recently manifested in the U.S.-South Korea Trade Agreement.

The Korean peninsula remains a leading problem for China. Beijing fears that potential chaos there may cause the Japanese to rethink their security situation and revitalize their military capacity. Relations have been strained with South Korea, which, until the fall of 2010, had been a rapidly expanding market for Chinese exports and direct investment. Moreover, the unpredictable Pyongyang regime invited a larger U.S. military profile by attacking the South Korean frigate *Cheonan* in international waters, with the loss of forty-six lives, and a nearby South Korean island, with the loss of four lives. Washington was quick to act with naval exercises in the Yellow Sea and a reiteration of its support for Japan's claim to the Ryukyu Islands.

The renewed U.S. presence in the Western Pacific is a response to a range of Chinese actions—many of which go beyond China's claims of Japanese territory or its unwillingness to join the UN in condemning North Korea. China left the door open in recent months to a larger presence in the Western Pacific, and the United States stepped through.

ONGOING DISPUTES

In addition to the various challenges discussed above, China faces several ongoing disputes. First, it has planted its flag on the floor of the South China Sea, claiming a 200-mile territorial limit that effectively closes the sea lines of communication. Beijing has warned the world that the South China Sea is a "core interest," not a transit area. Seven of twelve nations attending the July 2010 ASEAN Regional Forum in Hanoi cited the principle of "freedom of navigation" and the global commitment to "open sea lanes" and rejected Beijing's claims. The United States, Japan, Australia, India, and others have, accordingly, resolved to proceed with naval and commercial transits through the area.

Second, China has claimed the mineral and energy rich Ryukyu Islands, which have been a part of Japan since 1879. The United States conquered the islands during World War II and returned them to Japan in May 1972.

Third, China refuses to discuss ongoing disputes over the Paracel Islands, the Spratly Islands, and Mischief Rocks. These are claimed by the Philippines, Vietnam, and Taiwan; Singapore, Malaysia, and Indonesia also claim one or more of them.

Fourth, Beijing has, without explanation, made public a plan to subdue these territories in which the Chinese air force, working in tandem with air combat units of the navy, would stage surprise bombing runs over military ports and ships based at targeted islands. The plan calls for eliminating the enemy's combat capability over the course of about an hour and followed by amphibious landings.[4]

Fifth, as if rising tensions along China's east coast were not enough, tensions in the China's own west—namely, East Turkestan (Xinjiang) and Tibet—along with the very long border with Islamic Central Asia, are growing problems. They are not flash points today, but smolder zones. They receive little coverage, but Islamic militants are active in Central Asia and in confronting Han oppression in China itself. Afghan veterans—some al-Qaeda trained, others former Taliban jihadists—are gradually filtering into the Uighur community in Xinjiang. They are embittered, alienated, and militarily able to pose real problems, as will the weapons flow in from Tajikistan, Uzbekistan, Iran, and elsewhere.

And finally, fresh border disputes and troop buildups on the Indian border at Kashmir and Arunachal Pradeshhave alarmed Delhi. The border is believed to be among the most heavily militarized in the world.

CLOSER TO HOME

Turning to a different arena, a stealth attack by China, employing an artificially cheap yuan and heavily subsidized Chinese exports, has effectively undersold U.S. manufacturers in U.S. markets, helping to limit U.S. GDP growth while China's remains at 7.5 percent.

Reacting to China's currency policy, the U.S. Congress recently passed legislation that would (in violation of WTO regulations and unsigned by President Obama) allow the imposition of tariffs on Chinese imports. Moreover, China's currency manipulation was a high-profile issue in the 2010 congressional elections and in more than thirty individual races.

There is a growing consensus—clearly expressed at the IMF and in Washington—that by subsidizing export industries and suppressing the value of the yuan to make exports cheap, China's beggar-thy-neighbor approach has exported unemployment to the West, where 30 million have lost their jobs since 2007. Widespread unemployment among trading partners has slowed recovery from the recession. Considering the 9.1 percent unemployment at home and the Democratic losses in the House of Representatives, it is small wonder that President Obama, in discussions with Premier Wen Jiabao last year, indicated that U.S.-China relations would remain uneven until

China allowed its currency to rise more rapidly. Progress on this has been slow however. The yuan has risen 4.5 percent against the dollar since June 2010, but has fallen by 4.3 percent since that time, against a trade-weighted basket due to dollar weakness.[5]

China thus confronts several difficult domestic and foreign challenges. But rather than hiding its capabilities and biding its time in keeping with Deng Xiaoping's counsel, China's leaders now believe there is benefit in highlighting the nation's resources and capabilities.

This change in presentation, no doubt spurred by surging pride in all that China has accomplished in the last decade, has been accompanied by the belief that with China's rise will come competition—and confrontation with the West, particularly the United States. Military confrontation with the United States is unlikely—at least not in the early stages. Rather, the principle battle space, the place where disputes between China and the West will be joined and where each will seek advantage, is the global information space. Here Chinese planners, embracing the realities of post–Cold War conflicts, have taken a leaf from Harvard's Joe Nye, who makes the point that it is not whose army wins, it's whose story wins.[6]

To be sure, the China story "wins"; Beijing invested $6.8 billion in 2010 to create a global network with daily news and commentary in fifty-six languages on television, on radio, and in print. The objective is to frame developing stories in a China-friendly way. Beijing is determined to move beyond the days when international opinion could blame China for the collision of a Chinese fishing boat and a Japanese Coast Guard vessel in the Ryukyu Islands, or allow the Tibet story to diminish and embarrass China on the front pages of the world's press.

Li Congjun, the president of Xinhua in Beijing, announced that "CNC will present an international vision with a Chinese perspective."[7] He emphasized that the focus is on "improving our ability to guide international opinion."

CNC will have to work hard to convince viewers of its legitimacy however. Xinhua was originally the Red China News Agency, later becoming the Chinese Communist Party's propaganda arm; the new CNC will not be available for viewers in China. In addition to censoring Twitter, bloggers, Facebook, e-mails, texting, and even karaoke, Beijing still limits much of the West's media reporting. Moreover, even while the *People's Daily* says, "those of us in control of the modern media should play the role of a 'cheerleader' to enhance our national charm," Wu Jincai, controller of CNC World, insisted in an interview with the BBC's Chinese Service that CNC was a "news channel, not a propaganda station."[8]

Significantly, this initiative is not simply a public relations effort. It derives from a strategic calculation that China's progress in global affairs must address China's broadly negative image among Western metropolitan audiences.[9]

Yet, seemingly absent from Beijing's analysis of China's global presentation is any consideration of the effects of the credibility deficit. Because CNC serves at the pleasure of a one-party authoritarian regime, the commentary and reportage are correctly seen as serving the regime's objectives. The news agency has set for itself an impossible task; as if the leopard can change its spots, CNC World seeks to compete for legitimacy and authority with independent news organizations such as the BBC, CNN, and Deutche Welle that are guided by established ethical standards requiring the unbiased reporting of events as they unfold. One must wonder at how this will unfold.

WHAT LIES AHEAD?

Beijing's planners know that in this time of multidimensional change, China must frame the Asian story going forward. China will either be seen as Asia's engine of growth, delivering growth, investment, trade, and markets to smaller Asian nations, or it will be defined a hegemon — a large nation seizing oil, gas, and mineral deposits, a rogue requiring obeisance from others — asserting its interests wrapped in a muscular diplomacy. Cheng Li of the Brookings Institution makes the point that regardless of how it is perceived, "China now wants a seat at the head of the table. Its leaders expect to be among the key architects of global institutions."

China has global influence, yet public opinion at home in China is increasingly combative — sometimes jingoistic. So with one eye on China's interests and the other on domestic critics who accuse the leaders of coddling the West, Beijing has begun to push harder to reshape the international system to make it more China-friendly. We see this push in Beijing's global media program and its determination to redesign the Web, where China wants to vastly increase its share of the trillions of new Internet addresses to be distributed 2011–2012.

We can expect a major Chinese initiative in space — not just tests of antisatellite weapons, but also a full-up moon program leading to a landing in 2013. The objective? Potential energy sources like helium-3, technical and commercial spin-offs, minerals needed to sustain economic expansion, and, the opportunity to showcase China's advanced technical capacity.

IN SUMMARY, although China has recently generated regional and global tensions with aggressive trade and currency policies and territorial claims, of greater concern is its ideational challenge. China's present-day approach to governance and civil society informs a new generation of leaders and global strategists beyond the West. Its market authoritarianism has brought a new form of corporate state that challenges the progressive social contract underpinning Western society and thought in the global information space. And that is here, that China's "story" confronts the Western narrative and where twenty-first century preeminence will be determined.

ACKNOWLEDGMENTS

THERE ARE MANY who have inspired my interest in China and the ever delicate U.S.-China relationship—far too many to name here. While serving in the White House as a young staff assistant to President Richard Nixon, the Nixon-Kissinger team electrified Washington by opening relations with Mao's China. Years later, I learned more of the reality of U.S.-China relations from Secretary of State Henry Kissinger in conversations in New York and Cambridge, England, and from former National Security Advisor Col. Robert "Bud" McFarlane, who accompanied Kissinger to China. Colonel McFarlane conducted top-secret talks in the basement of the Great Hall of the People, detailing the troops, armaments, and capabilities of the Soviet divisions confronting China across the Amur River and thus providing the key substantive element on which the new U.S.-China relationship was built. I am grateful to both Henry Kissinger and Bud McFarlane for their generosity, perceptive intellect, and balanced perspective on China's rise and its implications for the United States.

I am especially grateful to Ambassador Jim Lilley, a friend and an anchor to windward on a turbulent issue; his nuanced understanding of China and appreciation of the Chinese mind is without parallel in Washington today.

I wish to thank Gen. Brent Scowcroft (U.S. Air Force, ret.); Sir Richard Dearlove, former Director of MI-6 and now Master of Pembroke College, Cambridge; the late Dr. Ray Cline; former National Security Advisor Richard Allen; Dr. George Carver; former Secretary of Defense James Schlesinger; Admiral James Stark (U.S. Navy, ret.); Captain Robert Mercker (U.S. Army, ret.); Hon. Jerry Leach, The American University, Cairo; Professor George Joffe, University of Cambridge; Professor James Mayall of the Royal College of Defense Studies; John Sherer, Publisher, Basic Books, New York; William Frucht, Editor, Yale University Press; Admiral Ronald Christenson (U.S. Navy, ret.); the late Dr. Peter Rodman; Minister Massimo Ambrosetti, Italian Ministry of Foreign Affairs; Herman Pirchner, President of the American Foreign Policy Council; Dr. Clyde Prestowitz, former U.S. Trade Representative; former Secretary of the Navy John Lehman; and Andrew W. Marshall of the U.S. Department of Defense for their encouragement and for taking the time and effort to talk through—on several occasions—the enigma of today's China and its impact on world affairs.

Thanks are also due to Ambassador Winston Lord; Dr. Nicholas Eberstadt of the American Enterprise Institute; Professor Harry Harding of George Washington University; Ed Timperlake, author and former Defense Department official; Hon. Sven Kraemer; John B. Henry of the Committee for the Republic; and to Dr. Olaf Corry, my Cambridge colleague, for his help in tracing the etymology of the term "Beijing consensus" used by Joshua Ramo and others in the 1990s.

A special thanks to Deputy Chief of Mission Xie, Minister

Counselor Ruan and staff of the Chinese Embassy in Washington, the Ministry of Foreign Affairs in Beijing, Admiral Ye at the National Defense University in Beijing, and the helpful staff at the Academy of Military Sciences in Beijing.

The Master and Fellows of Magdalene College, Cambridge, have provided the perfect counterpoint to my academic immersion in the *new* China. A wonderfully entertaining, sometimes enigmatic, but always challenging High Table has, for me, been the soul of Cambridge. I thank each of them.

Dr. Tarak Barkawi of Cambridge; Dr. Ted Galen Carpenter of the CATO Institute; Dr. Philip Towle of Cambridge; Ben Tyree of the *Washington Times*; Al Regnery of the *American Spectator*; Dr. Joel F. Rogers of Cambridge University; and the Hon. Robert Dean read the manuscript—often several times—offering invaluable suggestions and improvements.

INTRODUCTION

SECRETARY OF STATE HILLARY CLINTON'S decision to visit China within weeks of assuming office in 2009 provided evidence of the importance Washington now attached to Sino-American cooperation.[1] Clinton called for a "deeper" and "broader" U.S.-China partnership, saying that cooperation between the United States and China on global issues such as the economy was "imperative."[2] In similar tones, Chinese Premier Wen Jiabao told former U.S. President Jimmy Carter shortly before Clinton's arrival that the only path for China and the United States was to "strengthen mutual trust and cooperation, and pass through the difficulties together."[3]

Wen's words were a perfect iteration of the so-called new China that we've seen emerging on the world stage over the last decade. Long gone are the ideological crusades of the 1960s—crusades that took Maoism to Africa, spread revolution in Southeast Asia, and sought to overthrow the great powers of the West. On the contrary, capitalism is now a global phenomenon—with China among its greatest champions. And since this new incarnation has embraced the capitalist road, the country has come to rely on international markets, global institutions, and free trade to achieve economic growth. This has allowed living standards to rise, contributing to political stability at home. In the process, China has progressively engaged with the international community it once spurned, showing a willingness to cooperate on a range of priority issues. In so doing, its leaders have taken great pains to craft a new personality for China in the world, which explicitly avoids the historical imagery of a rising power.

Would that this were so. It is not. The discussion that follows makes the case that China's fresh global face belies a profound challenge to America and the West. This threat is partly hidden by a nuanced and pragmatic Chinese foreign policy. It allows Beijing at once to cooperate on current economic challenges, to promote nonproliferation objectives, disaster relief, peacekeeping operations, antipiracy, and more—all underscoring its support for the global good. In the process, China has carefully avoided direct challenges to the United States, preferring to avoid crises.

But while its leaders follow a path of progressive engagement with the liberal international order, Beijing's leaders are also leading a formidable assault on this order. As the following pages convey, China is the protagonist in a clash of values, governance, and two versions of modernity in the twenty-first century. On one side are the Western liberal founders of the global marketplace. These actors take for granted their political and economic preeminence in the world they constructed after 1945. On the other side are the new non-Western market converts, from Asia to Latin America, which have learned how to extract the best from both market capitalism and one-party government, thus shattering the illusion that capitalism begets democracy.

Thus, new centers of wealth in the developing world are diminishing the traditional leverage and centrality of Western economic power; meanwhile, today's emerging markets are increasingly drawn to a new and compelling doctrine of state-managed capitalism. They are learning to combine market economics with traditional autocratic or semiautocratic politics in a process that signals an intellectual rejection of the Western economic model. According to this doctrine, the government maintains central control over a partly liberalized economy, and the people accept a very non-Western kind of civic bargain: political oppression in the public square in return for relative economic freedom and a rising quality of life. Both of these trends have a powerful cheerleader in Beijing.

What's more, the Chinese have become a critical source of financial autonomy for smaller countries as well as a beacon of ideas and management expertise about capitalism in a less Western, less liberal format. Taken together, these trends suggest that China is set to have a greater impact on the world in the next two decades than any other country.[4]

The net effect of these developments is to reduce Western and particularly American influence on the global stage—along both economic and ideational axes. My purpose is to recast our understanding of this challenge, for its strategic importance cannot be overstated and will have vastly greater impact than will the tactical military and economic "China threats" concerning Washington today.

TWO MYTHS: THE END OF GLOBALIZATION . . . THE BURSTING OF CHINA'S BUBBLE

Finally, two popular ideas have developed in parallel with the recent economic crisis. The first is that the global recession might have slowed the rate of globalization, and the second is that this same phenomenon has burst the bubble of China's rising. Both are mistaken.

Global economic integration has been under way for decades, and while the downturn has upset its tempo, the recession won't derail it. The global economic system has become so deeply connected, for example, that neither Washington nor Beijing can afford to backslide into heavily protected fortress economies. This realization was apparent from the second half of 2008, when both governments made repeated calls to avoid protectionism. Premier Wen Jiabao used his speech at the World Economic Forum in Switzerland in early 2009 to emphasize the need for Washington and Beijing to "stick to a policy of opening up and co-operation."[5] Weeks later, the Obama administration removed passages from its domestic stimulus bill that referred to a "Buy American" policy advanced by members of Congress. As Obama told journalists, "we can't afford to send a protectionist message."[6]

Admittedly, the following months saw subtle forms of creeping protectionism among various members of the G20. In February 2009, the World Bank announced that it had identified forty-seven measures "that restrict trade at the expense of other countries" between November 2008 and February 2009, including bans on certain Chinese toys in India and Chinese tariffs on Belgian chocolates.[7] As the recession's grip tightened in mid-2009, China was featured on the front pages of the *New York Times* for quietly adopting policies that encouraged exports and curbed imports. Authorities were, according to the *Times,* assisting exporters with larger tax rebates and generous loans from state-owned banks while prohibiting provincial government agencies from buying imported goods except where no local substitute existed.[8] Notwithstanding these infractions, however, there was a broad commitment to free-flowing international trade—a commitment not present during earlier economic crises such as the Great Depression. This new collective fear of serious and sustained protectionism was evident after the London G20 summit of April 2009, which saw renewed pledges to avoid such policies.[9]

Declining world trade and the falling price of food and fuel in 2008 may have taken the wind out of the global export boom for countries like China, Russia, and India. But beyond the balance sheets for 2009, a broader shift in the world economy remains intact. When India, China, the former Soviet bloc, and other regions joined the capitalist world, the global labor pool grew by over three billion. Never again will the West live in a world with so little global competition as it did in the late twentieth century.[10] Beyond the facts and figures of the recent economic slowdown, we continue to witness the broad emergence of a new economic order, in which great economic powers such as the United States will continue to wield immense influence, but where new economies such as China can demand an ever-greater say.

Premier Wen has, perhaps predictably, used the crisis as a platform to talk about the need for a novel world order.[11] On a trip to Moscow in November 2008, he spoke of the importance of building a new international financial order by attaining new levels of financial and industrial cooperation among China, Russia, and other groups, like the Shanghai Cooperation Organization. Wen also stressed the need to give developing nations more say in global institutions such as the International Monetary Fund (IMF) so that these nations could play a bigger role in international regulatory mechanisms and supervision over financial institutions in countries whose currencies are held as reserves around the world—namely, the United States.[12]

CHINA'S RISE DERAILED?

On the domestic front, some commentators have suggested that the global recession has derailed China's rise and set the scene for economic and political meltdown inside the country.[13] Futurology has great scope when it comes to China, from predictions of impending collapse to inevitable democratization. Suffice it to say, Beijing has so far overseen three decades of staggering growth without losing political control. The recent economic crisis has failed to undermine the seemingly magical blend of economic liberalization and political oppression.

Without question, rising unemployment, factory closures, and a slowdown in exports presage more difficult times. This is a clear problem for a country that has, at times, depended on international trade for up to 80 percent of its GDP.[14] But important details in the current downturn have kept the leadership optimistic about the continuity of its system.

The slowdown in the G8, for example, has not been mirrored by the fastest-growing developing economies. The two largest, China and India, expect high, single-digit growth in the next two years, albeit less than in 2000–2007.[15] Countries like Brazil, China, and India have also benefited from large foreign-exchange reserves that can be used to cushion domestic shortfalls with accelerated public spending. If the global recession concludes in 2011–2012, we can reasonably expect Chinese, Brazilian, Russian, and Indian economic growth to accelerate.[16]

China's semiplanned economy can comfortably maintain growth of 7 percent or more, propelled by state-led investment in infrastructure, while it waits for global consumer markets to recuperate. Which, of course, they will.

Speaking politically, although the downturn has caused serious concern within the politburo, it doesn't come anywhere near the convulsions of 1989, when students and workers led a nationwide protest from Tiananmen Square over racing inflation, economic hardships, and political oppression. While this is a testing time for the ruling party, the odds are clearly in Beijing's favor. Many Chinese people today feel a sense of gratitude for the economic reforms that have lifted millions out of poverty and brought the thrills and comforts of modernity to Chinese towns and cities. The protests are small compared with what Beijing has seen before—and more importantly, they remain uncoordinated, a crucial detail in a place as expansive and difficult to organize politically as China.[17] New China also has a larger role—socially, politically, and economically—for the new middle classes. This distinguishes China from the country it was twenty years ago. Today's middle class is meritocratic, individualistic, committed to education and thrift—yet lured by the consumer culture.[18] The downturn is unlikely to change its outlook radically. Middle-class Chinese are accustomed to their new position in society and are more likely to worry about keeping their children in private school by spending less in the supermarket, than they are about running into the square and building Statue of Liberty models to the sound of Bruce Springsteen. The global recession could actually become a source of confidence for the ruling party in the longer run. As the government staves off significant, coordinated protest, it will mark a milestone for the party's ability to suffer turbulence and manage a robust, durable system, as new China passes its thirtieth birthday.

In the process, a global economic architecture for tomorrow is being quietly constructed today, and when the current economic turbulence has passed, global capitalism will no longer proceed from the old Western formulae. David Rothkopf, a Commerce Department official in the Clinton administration, has mused that "the balance of power shifts quietly during times of crisis."[19] The economic preeminence of the West is being increasingly moderated by the new norms and networks of the rest; the "invisible hand" of free markets around the globe is being balanced by the notably more visible hand of central governance.[20] In the following chapters, we look at China's pivotal role in this emerging future.

CHAPTER 1

CHINA AND THE GLOBAL SHIFT

BEATING THE WEST AT ITS OWN GAME

In January 2009, as legislators in Washington and London wrangled over where to find the cash to pay for expensive stimulus plans, the Chinese government unveiled an ambitious budget of 45 billion yuan (then approximately US$6.8 billion) for a new project called *waixuan gongzuo*, literally "overseas propaganda."[1] The *South China Morning Post* called it Beijing's new "global media drive," with plans to create a network of overseas bureaus that would present the modern face of China to every country in the world. Proposals included English editions of Chinese newspapers to suit a more international readership and a twenty-four-hour Asian television network to rival the successful Al Jazeera channel.[2]

Behind the eye-catching budget was an equally big idea. As official media sources suggested, events now presented an opportunity to tell the world about the "China model"—the perfect antidote to the unbridled capitalism that had underpinned the recent crisis.[3] As the government newspaper *Xinhua* reported, the excesses and failures of free-market fundamentalism had emphasized the superiority of the Chinese way of doing things under President Hu Jintao's "scientific theory of development." This was the official name given to the ruling party's policy of promoting welfare for the masses under the strict guidance of the central government.[4] In other words, *state capitalism.*

The Chinese public information chief, Li Chang-Chun, explained his government's view that the global information space now ranks among the crucial battlegrounds for power in the twenty-first century. As he told an audience of executives at China Central Television (CCTV) in similar terms, "Communications capacity determines influence. . . . Whichever nation's communications capacity is strongest, it is that nation whose culture and core values spread far and wide . . . with the most power to influence the world." Previous attempts to present China's case internationally, Li admitted, had reached only a limited audience; they also proved inadequate in countering Western criticism of the Chinese government during the protests in Tibet and the Olympic Torch Relay in 2008. Under the new project, he said, China would "try to produce news the way that Western media do" and beat the West at its own game.[5]

Li's words highlight an important theme. America and the West face a serious challenge from the East, but not according to conventional definitions of the China threat. Over the past two decades, U.S. analysts have viewed China's actions in the Taiwan Straits and South China Sea, the purchase of U.S. Treasury debt, and the hugely unfavorable trade balance with varying degrees of concern. It seems scarcely a week goes by when one of the networks or a prominent think tank doesn't point to an emergent peril from China in one or another of these areas. This book makes a different case, however. It says that while the problems of the Taiwan straits, the purchase of U.S. debt, and China's rising military capacity are very important, they can be managed.

Beijing does present a clear and gathering threat to Washington, but the terms of the challenge remain unformed in the public mind and, indeed, in policy circles. Eschewing confrontation, China's true challenge arises in a separate realm, namely, Beijing's transformative, leading role in the rise of a Chinese brand of capitalism and a Chinese conception of the international community, both opposed to and substantially different from their Western version. In a global battle between different visions of the future and different versions of capitalism, China is the protagonist. As traditional hubs of Western power — like the International Monetary Fund (IMF) and the World Bank — are circumvented and undermined by readily available Chinese capital, these new non-Western champions of the free market are *beating the West at its own game.*

MYTH AND REALITY IN THE "CHINA THREAT"

First, let's turn to the most common perceptions of the "China threat" and clarify the challenges that they do, and do not, pose for Washington.

THE MILITARY THREAT

Many in the national security community and beyond have been concerned about China's growing military power for two decades, warning that China is catching up with America's military lead in ways that may soon challenge American military supremacy in the Western Pacific and, possibly, elsewhere.

Clearly, this threat requires serious and sustained attention at Washington's highest policy levels. The speed and degree of Chinese military modernization has increased in tandem with the nation's emergence as a global economic player. Rapid economic growth has enabled the government to channel ever-greater resources into a range of programs and research and development (R&D) without leaving gaping holes in the broader national budget.

The overall budget for the People's Liberation Army (PLA), for example, doubled in recent years, from $27.9 billion in 2000 to $60.1 billion in 2008.[6] This period was actually the second half of a long, two-decade trend of double-digit-percentage increase in the Chinese military budget. R&D spending has similarly grown at an annual rate of 19 percent since 1995. By 2005, the annual figure was $30 billion—the sixth-largest in the world. The Pentagon, moreover, has estimated that in terms of *actual military expenditures,* the total military-related spending for 2008 was more likely between $105 billion and $150 billion.[7]

It is clear, then, that Beijing takes the question of military modernization very seriously. Fast-paced development can be seen in each section of military capacity. Beijing is working hard to make the same progress in deterrence that Western powers made in the 1960s, from vulnerable, land-based intercontinental-range ballistic missiles (ICBMs) to submarine-launched ballistic missiles (SLBMs). Accordingly, nuclear-powered ballistic missile submarines (SSBNs) have seen considerable investment, alongside their hunter-killer variants. *Kilo*-class diesels have come from Russia, while the nuclear-powered *Shang*-class is being developed domestically.[8] A steady flow of submarine-faring experience is also trickling over the border from old-timers of the Soviet Silent Service, arguably unrivaled among their Cold War peers in the dead-quiet arts of sprint and drift—despite what Tom Clancy might say.

You can add to this shopping list a variety of aerospace products, including such items as Russian jets, precision weaponry, and destroyer-based anti-air missile systems, plus the domestic development of multirole fighters to match the capabilities of the new Joint Strike Fighter currently in its final stages of development by the United States and other NATO allies.[9]

The fast-developing theater of cyberspace has seen similar levels of attention. An example of Chinese capabilities in this area is found in the sophisticated espionage program recently directed at the Dalai Lama, the Tibetan leader in exile. In early 2009, Information Warfare Monitor (IWM), a Canadian-based think tank that specializes in cyberspace analysis, published the findings of a ten-month investigation into alleged Chinese cyberspying against Tibetan institutions. The IWM found an extensive system that blanketed Tibet's activities worldwide with a network of 1,295 infected computers across 103 countries. A third of these targets were considered "high value": The "infected" computers were found in government ministries in Iran, Bangladesh, Latvia, Indonesia, the Philippines, Brunei, Barbados, and Bhutan and embassies in India, South Korea, Indonesia, Romania, Cyprus, Malta, Thailand, Taiwan, Portugal, Germany, and Pakistan. China's cyber-espionage network also penetrated the ASEAN Secretariat (Association of Southeast Asian Nations), SAARC (South Asian Association for Regional Cooperation), and the Asian Development Bank, plus news organizations and "an unclassified computer located at NATO headquarters." This new generation of cyberattackers had taken complete control of computers, not only searching and stealing documents, but even covertly controlling Web cameras and activating audio inputs.[10]

The investigation concluded that Beijing has been working to develop its cyberspace capabilities since the late 1990s as part of its military modernization program.[11] This has coincided with an increase in recent allegations of China-based hackers making high-level penetrations of computer systems in Europe, North America, and Asia.[12] Attackers have infiltrated government computers in the United States, Britain, France, Germany, South Korea, and Taiwan. They've stolen data from commercial and financial institutions, and the Pentagon reports that it is "continuously targeted by Chinese attackers, most notably in the series of attacks since 2003 known as 'Titan Rain,' which targeted the Department of Defense and numerous defense companies."[13]

As we see in Chapter 6, these facts and figures can be used to paint a grim picture of Chinese military development, which is expanding its global reach to threaten American military power across the Pacific and beyond. This would be the case had Chinese military development not proceeded on a different logic.

In reality, Chinese leaders want neither the strain on finances nor the negative and potentially costly atmospherics that would accompany a genuine arms race with the United States. This helps to explain the continued and yawning gap between American and Chinese defense budgets. The statistics of Chinese military development might sound impressive, but they are dwarfed in comparison with their American counterpart. The official base budget for the U.S. Department of Defense in 2009 was $515.4 billion, showing an almost 74 percent increase since 2001. Behind this sits another $70.0 billion in "emergency allowance" to support "activities related to the Global War on Terror into 2009."[14]

A more accurate description of Chinese military development would be a just-in-case capacity to "puncture" the American battle space. China has sought to leapfrog American military hardware with the development of high-tech, close-in weapons, which target American vulnerabilities, principally its reliance on communications and intelligence technology. These weapons are intended to provide an "area of denial" around mainland China and Taiwan without purchasing millions of tons in new hardware to reach parity of force projection with Washington. As Rear Admiral Yang Yi told me in 2008, "The navy will move faster in researching and building new-generation weapons to boost the ability to fight in regional sea wars under the circumstance of information technology."[15]

Susan Shirk, a former deputy assistant secretary of state responsible for Sino-American relations, explains that the nature of Chinese military developments over the last decade demonstrates recognition that the United States will always have superior firepower. The Chinese government has focused accordingly on asymmetric capabilities that it calls its "assassin's mace," which specialize in informational warfare to exploit "Goliath's" offensive capabilities in the theater around Chinese borders.[16] China's priority here is to disrupt U.S. command, control, communications, computers, intelligence, and reconnaissance in the requisite battle space. For these reasons, Secretary of Defense Robert Gates has referred to Chinese military development as giving cause for concern about U.S. interests in the Taiwan Straits, but not for panic about expansive Chinese ambitions.[17]

As important as China's military initiatives are, each is
being addressed in turn as a tactical challenge. China has made
wide-ranging territorial claims along the Indian border, in the
South China Sea, and in the Sea of Japan, revolving mainly
around mineral and gas deposits. China has also sought to extend its defense perimeter to the east of Taiwan. In the case of
the latter, the Pentagon has developed a raft of sophisticated
countermeasures and intelligence capacity to address Chinese
force projection.

Among these countermeasures are antisubmarine warfare
(ASW), including subsea warfare countermeasures such as
sensors, relays, sea-bed-launched missiles, and submarine-
launched missiles. Steps have been taken for protection against
Chinese space-based laser technology, space mines, and satellite-
based battle management systems. The Pentagon has also taken
measures for protection against Chinese cyber warriors seeking
to penetrate U.S. information systems, particularly defense and
intelligence facilities, and has been carefully tracking PLA air
force advances in refueling. Other countermeasures the U.S.
military is undertaking include long-range force projection
and unmanned vehicles (drones).

Meanwhile, defense planners are confident that the Seventh
Fleet remains able to support Taiwan in the event of an attack
by the mainland and capable of projecting decisive force into
all areas of the Western Pacific to ensure that sea lines of communication remain open and that nations such as the Philippines, Vietnam, Malaysia, and Singapore can resist Chinese
claims to islands or shoals in their territories. Close coordination with the armed forces of Japan, Singapore, Australia, and
India are also deemed essential to ensure a balance of power
in the Western Pacific and Indian Oceans.[18]

Washington's interest in stronger relations with India in particular has grown rapidly in recent years as U.S. strategic planners have seen a convergence of U.S. and Indian interests regarding China, extending from the Indian Ocean to Afghanistan.[19] Both the United States and India have, for some time, noted the construction of China's "string of pearls," naval bases across the Indian Ocean, from Pakistan to the Malaccan Straits. In the fall of 2009, the reality of Beijing's muscular political-military policies and the potential benefit of stronger relations with Washington became increasingly clear to Delhi.

Throughout October, the Indian press carried front-page reports of Chinese claims to the northern Indian state of Arunachal Pradesh, warnings to Indian Prime Minister Manmohan Singh not to campaign there during the recent election (which he won), demarches from Beijing demanding that the Dalai Lama not visit the state as planned, and Chinese maps that showed the Indian state of Jammu and Kashmir not to be a part of India. News editors often placed these stories adjacent to reports of U.S.-Indian joint naval exercises in the Indian Ocean, U.S.-Indian joint air force exercises, and the provision of special "search and recovery" training to the Indian army by U.S. special forces. The business pages of mass-circulation newspapers like the *Hindu* and the *Deccan Chronicle* carried stories about U.S. defense contractors moving to replace the long-standing Soviet/Russian relationship with new licensing, sales, and maintenance agreements.[20]

China has been adept at cloaking its objectives with ambiguity but, in the case of India, has renewed latent fears and opened the way for fresh U.S. diplomatic, military, and commercial initiatives that have provided confidence to Delhi, which is still smarting from its 1962 defeat at China's hands. Further, Indian coordination with the United States and the seagoing nations of the Western Pacific, mentioned above, helps, at a minimum, to ensure that China's regional initiatives are balanced and that the sea lines of communication remain unencumbered.

THE TAIWAN THREAT

Here we meet another popular iteration of the "China threat." As much as any location in Asia, the Taiwan Straits are a focus of concern; they have all the traditional makings of a great power flashpoint. But, reflecting the mainland's shift from Maoism to market authoritarianism, the prospect of conflict between the United States and China over Taiwan, displayed in primary colors for a half century from 1950, is now seen in pastels.

Against the backdrop of periodic diplomatic friction, cross-strait economic ties have blossomed over the last decade. China has become Taiwan's largest trading partner while Taiwan has become one of China's biggest investors. Taiwan's trade with mainland China totaled $102.3 billion in 2007, rising 16.1 percent from the previous year. Its exports to China in 2007 totaled to $74.28 billion, an increase of 17.3 percent, reaching a new high in the last three years.[21] Thus, the economic effects of a war between the two sides today would be catastrophic for both sides.

There are similar trends in the social sphere. Over a million Taiwanese now live and work on the mainland. Many refer to the "Shanghai heat" to describe how Taiwanese entrepreneurs have opened or purchased businesses in China and invested in farms and other fixed assets—and how the Chinese authorities have treated them without prejudice. A retired colonel in the Taiwanese army, whose sister owned a grape winery near Shanghai, relayed the latter point with some degree of amazement. He thought her background and his line of work would surely attract the attention of the local authorities and lead to extortion—or worse. But for fourteen years, this has never came to pass, contributing instead to a growing folk wisdom surrounding the direction of China-Taiwan relations, now underscored by direct mail and charter flights.

Thawing cross-straits relations were further apparent in 2008 with the resounding victory of the Kuomintang Party (KMT), led by Ma Ying-jeou in a campaign that centered on improving relations with the mainland. General Brent Scowcroft (USAF, ret.), former national security advisor to Presidents George H. W. Bush and Gerald Ford, speaks for many in Washington when he describes what he sees as an historical evolution taking place in the relationship as more of the Taiwanese economy is integrated with the mainland and ever more exchanges take place.[22]

Yet, the straits and the Taiwan question often expose raw nerves in Washington, Beijing, and Taipei. Missteps in any of these places—putting sovereignty or pride on display—could still trigger bellicose rhetoric and the kind of angry public reactions that exert pressure on the various leaders. Economic interdependence doesn't make war impossible.[23]

But the point is that today's stability draws on a more subtle context. The United States, China, and Taiwan are bound by a set of agreements grounded in an artful diplomacy that uses ambiguity to sustain what has been a successful arrangement for some three decades. The United States has pledged to provide Taiwan with the arms and the support it needs to defend itself; both the United States and China have agreed that China will not attempt a forceful unification with Taiwan, and both sides have also agreed that there is only "one China."[24] These arrangements allow China to retain its honor with irredentist claims and threats of military intervention; they also allow the United States to uphold an established alliance with a democratic ally and maintain credibility in the region. And finally, they allow Taiwan to sustain its de facto independence.

The continuity of this arrangement was assured by the Obama administration. After the president assumed office in January 2009, his administration quickly intimated that it favored continuing the present policy, understood the value of ambiguity, and, barring the unexpected, would pursue a "talk and do less" approach to cross-strait relations.[25] The gradual improvement in atmospherics over the straits was further confirmed in a defense-policy paper published by the Chinese government in the same month. The paper claimed that separatists in Taiwan had been "thwarted" and relations had taken a "significantly positive turn" of historic proportions.[26]

The Economic Threat

Aside from the issue of China's ownership of very large amounts of U.S. debt, which we will come to in a moment, the United States has also seen an emerging chorus of alarm about the effects of Chinese direct investment in the U.S. economy. Without question, U.S.-China economic relations are the most complex of the various renditions of a China threat. Moreover, relations in this area have been unusually susceptible to simplification and misconception.

Chinese investment has proceeded through a range of public and private entities, including high-profile, government-owned organizations such as the $200 billion Sovereign Wealth Fund, the China Investment Corporation (CIC), and the China National Offshore Oil Corporation (CNOOC), the last of which attempted to purchase the U.S. oil firm Unocal in 2005 before the move was blocked by Congress. Critics have argued that Chinese ownership of important U.S. economic assets could present a serious national security threat. This is true, but it depends on the industry, the scope of the follow-on effects, and the dimensions of the investment (Chapter 6 discusses China's perceived threats to national security further). Another dimension in which China possesses ominous leverage over the American economy is its rising surplus of dollars, which it reinvests in American debt.

As Americans have purchased large quantities of Chinese exports, China has used significant parts of the profit to reinvest in American bonds and shares. This has given rise to a popular theme in our formulation of the China threat, which warns that Beijing could heavily damage Washington by slowing its ongoing purchases of U.S. Treasuries, thereby injecting doubts about the dollar's continued strength, or selling a portion of its U.S. securities. Either step would see interest rates—hence mortgage, credit card, and loan rates—climb and the value of the dollar fall.

This is a significant liability. China's position as an American creditor, however, is not simple and is better assessed in less apocalyptic terms. The large amount of credit Beijing has extended to Washington also represents a serious liability for China.

In fact, a measure of stability is found in what has become a marriage of liabilities; China's "threat" to the United States is mitigated by the U.S. "threat" to China. The Chinese have as much interest in keeping the U.S. economy and the U.S. dollar stable as do Americans themselves. The Chinese government has purchased American debt for the simple reason that such purchases sustain the macroeconomic engine the Chinese people rely on. Chinese investment in American assets such as bonds and mortgage-backed securities has helped to keep American interest rates low, made credit easier to obtain, and generated a pool of capital for Americans to continue buying consumer products—that is, *Chinese* consumer goods. Low interest rates have also been crucial in enabling American businesses to expand. Lower mortgage rates help more people to buy houses and push up the value of real estate. With higher house prices, consumers have borrowed against the increase in equity in their homes and spent the difference.[27] The huge supply of foreign money has enabled the U.S. government to fund large deficits that have stimulated the U.S. economy, allowing for lower taxes and more jobs created by government spending.

China doesn't fund American borrowing because it wants to humble or hinder the United States; it does so because the United States remains the largest overseas market for an economy that relies on exports.[28] American consumers are the lifeblood of the Chinese economy. American entrepreneurs are one of China's most important sources of foreign direct investment. Beijing buys American assets to maintain the value of the dollar, which both protects the value of its Treasury bond investments and makes Chinese goods cheaper and easier to buy. Beijing also buys these assets (Treasury bonds) to keep its own currency stable. The yuan's exchange rate is loosely pegged to the dollar.[29] At the time of writing, roughly 70 percent of China's giant foreign exchange portfolio is held in liquid

U.S. dollar assets such as Treasury bonds. If the Chinese government allowed the dollar to fall significantly against the yuan, this would wipe out billions of dollars of value in its coffers.[30]

China's acute insecurity on these matters was apparent in March 2009, for example, as the U.S. recession grew worse. At the time, Chinese Prime Minister Wen Jiabao said his country was "worried" about its holdings of U.S. Treasuries, and called on the United States to provide assurances that the investments were safe.[31] Beijing's fear was that its approximately $800 billion investment in U.S. Treasuries (up from $767 billion in the first quarter of 2009) was being jeopardized by the extraordinary amount of money being borrowed by Washington to finance stimulus and bailout packages. Borrowing on such a large scale could, it was thought, spur inflation that would reduce the value of China's $1.6 trillion in dollar holdings.

Paradoxically, this insecurity was also on display when Zhou Xiaochuan, the governor of China's central bank, seemingly called for a new reserve currency. As Zhou announced in March 2009, "the desirable goal of reforming the international monetary system" should be "to create an international reserve currency that is disconnected from individual nations."[32] His American audiences immediately shuddered at the thought that China might be seeking to displace the dollar in favor of a new rival.

But in this instance, Zhou's purpose was more political than economic. His objective was to mark Washington the culprit as the global atmosphere clouded over. Was Zhou seeking to take advantage of the new administration's economic difficulties? Yes. Was he seeking to destabilize the dollar? Most probably not, for the reasons given above. But he was opening a discussion that was to serve as a warning to U.S. policy makers:

China would not tolerate a loss in the value of its dollar holdings, and though expanded use of the IMF's Special Drawing Rights—which has some of the characteristics of a reserve currency—was clearly not the answer, Zhou was suggesting that some sort of stable international reserve currency or basket of currencies was, at least, a direction worth considering

All the same, Zhou's remarks revealed more weakness than strength, and the reasons lie in the details of Special Drawing Rights (SDRs).[33] In quick summary, SDRs were invented by the IMF in the 1960s. A principal reason for doing this was actually to insulate debtor nations from significant fluctuations in the lending currency. If, say, Country A borrowed a sum from the IMF and the exchange rate for dollars to A's currency was liable to great flux, then the value of the debt would also fluctuate, causing financial instability, with potential debt defaults and more financial difficulties rather than fewer. SDRs were created to solve the problem by establishing a basket of currencies comprising the dollar, the pound, the yen, and the euro. This means that transactions made in SDRs are less affected by fluctuations on the foreign exchange market than a transaction conducted simply in dollars. At the same time, however, it also means that SDRs provide a point of reference for the value of a currency but are not a currency in their own right. They can't be used to pay for exports; they don't have minted coins of the realm, so to speak.[34]

Consequently, the story behind Zhou's announcement reflected growing unease about the threat of the dollar decline more than the desire to bring about its outcome.[35] Behind Zhou's speech was a technical proposal to exchange some dollar assets held by the Bank of China for SDRs at the IMF, which would reduce their immediate exposure to the vulnerabilities of the U.S. government balance sheet. This entails a circulation of American currency, not an attack on it. As Barrett Sheridan of *Newsweek* remarked, it also says something about the dynamics of financial interdependency. If you owe China a billion dollars, China owns you; but if you owe China a trillion dollars, you own China.[36]

Thus the American and Chinese economies are heavily interdependent. America has grown addicted to Chinese credit; China has grown equally addicted to American consumption. The depth of this interdependence creates a relationship that is stabilized in a kind of economic version of *mutually assured destruction*. As James Mayall of Cambridge University puts it, "The Chinese and American economies are like two drunk old men shuffling along together; if one takes a serious fall, they both go tumbling over," an oddly dependent relationship evident since the end of the Cold War.[37]

Does Beijing have important leverage in this domain? Yes. But Washington has countervailing leverage, which means that Beijing's initiatives can be balanced, and managed, if that is required. Can Beijing harm the U.S. economy and the U.S. consumer? Yes. But not irreparably, and not without harming itself. The important point here is that Beijing's ownership of American debt is manageable and balanced by China's reliance on American markets.

More serious than China's ownership of American bonds or the threat of a Chinese economic attack is how this stable system of mutual dependence has weakened America's voice in global affairs. When Hillary Clinton traveled to China shortly after taking office, she didn't just stress the need to reach a consensus with Beijing on tackling the global recession. Clinton also emphasized something else, telling an audience of journalists and Chinese Communist Party officials in Beijing that pressing China on "other issues" like Tibet and human rights "can't interfere with the global economic crisis."[38] This statement demonstrated an uncomfortable new fact in Washington's cooperative relationship with Beijing. The realities of economic interdependence blunt American influence on other issues that underpin the U.S.-led system of international liberal order, such as progress on human rights, the rule of law, and free speech in the world beyond the West.[39]

It is the relationship between economic integration and diminished American power that returns us to the main thrust of the book: China does present a serious and long-term threat to the West, but not by virtue of its military capacity in space or undersea, or the total dollar reserves in the People's Bank of China. Each of these has important caveats and qualifications that undermine its practical threat value. Instead, this book proposes that China is catalyst-in-chief for a more profound and far-reaching process; just as globalization is shrinking the world, China is shrinking the West. China is quietly helping to remake the landscape of international development, economics, community, and, by extension, politics. Crucially, it is doing so in ways that progressively limit the projection of Western influence and values beyond the NATO bloc.

NEW WEALTH AND NEW IDEAS

The roots of this problem lie in trends that began twenty years ago. Contrary to the predictions of many notable scholars after 1989, a new era of global convergence around the Western model of free-market democracy has failed to materialize. The world has evolved into a more diverse political order than had been imagined by many in the West, particularly in Washington.

This is not to deny that post-1989 capitalism had reached a new stage. All the major powers of the world today rely on free markets and free trade—though in different measures—for growth, rising standards of living, and political stability. Economic integration and advances in technology and global transport networks have duly created a new "global village" (contrary to those who dismiss Hillary Clinton's claim). We now live and work on a smaller planet, where time and distance are minimized as obstacles to commerce and where capital moves instantly around the world at the click of a mouse. Technology now goes where it finds the smartest people and the best financial incentives; manufacturing goes where it finds the cheapest labor and an undervalued currency; customers circumvent the globe instantly in a virtual world of call centers and offshore business processing.[40]

But our understanding of economic integration and its effects is also changing. Twenty years ago, it was typified by the global rise of American brands. Globalization was driven by American capitalism and its two founding ideas—that markets, not governments, drive progress, and that democracy is the optimal way to organize society.

Today, in the world beyond the West, these certainties are eroding. As Chapter 2 will explain in more detail, many Americans and their Western allies thought the great post–Cold War transition to a global market would generate a global convergence around the Western liberal order. Instead, it's brought two new developments in international relations: new sources of wealth beyond the West and new ideas about capitalism without democracy.

Since capitalism went truly global, smaller and poorer countries have gotten rich through their natural resources, cheap and abundant labor, export industries, and outsourcing. With new wealth have come new connections that increasingly circumvent the traditional architecture of Western power. Developing countries are deepening the ties within the "developing pack," trading preferentially in many cases with its leaders, namely, Brazil, Russia, India, and China—collectively christened the BRICs by Goldman Sachs in 2001.[41]

As emerging markets have become richer, they have often integrated with the global economy, but this has not necessarily meant greater integration with the West. In fact, the level of interaction among developing countries is gradually surpassing the level of interaction between many of these countries and the West. Emerging markets are increasingly turning to each other for business that would have previously been sought from the West.[42] Consider, for example, the agreement between China and ASEAN that was signed in 2005, creating a massive single market of approximately 1.8 billion people and pledging to establish a European Union–like community for ASEAN by 2020. Not only did this help China to secure vital sea lanes and access to raw materials, but it also created a major regional entity that excludes the United States and its major allies.[43]

This example is the portal to another point: New centers of economic power are giving rise to new levels of confidence among developing markets and demands for a greater say in the management of transnational issues and institutions. These sentiments were on open display in June 2009 in what has been called the first BRIC Summit, when the leaders of Russia, China, India, Brazil, Kazakhstan, Tajikistan, Kyrgyzstan, and Uzbekistan met in the Russian city of Yekaterinburg. The principal aim of the meeting was to discuss how to conduct trade and provide aid in ways that excluded the United States.[44]

Russian President Dmitry Medvedev described the meeting as an opportunity for these countries to "build an increasingly multi-polar world order," and to move beyond an "artificially maintained uni-polar system" with "one big centre of consumption, financed by a growing deficit, and thus growing debts, one formerly strong reserve currency, and one dominant system of assessing assets and risks."[45] Medvedev also called for "financial institutions of a completely new type, where particular political issues and motives, and particular countries, will not dominate."[46] When they asked to attend the meeting as observers, officials of the newly installed Obama administration received a simple *nyet*.

Antoine van Agtmael, the fund manager who coined the phrase *emerging markets,* now predicts that the twenty-five companies most likely to be the world's next great multinationals include four companies each from Brazil, Mexico, South Korea, and Taiwan; three from India; two from China; and one each from Argentina, Chile, Malaysia, and South Africa.[47] Goldman Sachs predicts that "China could overtake the United States by 2027 and the BRICs combined could overtake the G7 by 2032."[48] The trend here, note the globalization experts Naazneen Barma, Ely Ratner, and Steven Weber, is neither conflict nor assimilation with the West; instead, it is to make Western influence less relevant.[49] Underlying these new developments in non-Western wealth and connectivity is a simple "neo-Westphalian bargain." According to this bargain, sovereign states are empowered to settle the terms of existence inside their borders between the government and the governed. Internationally, they deal with each other in a strict market setting and recognize no real rights or obligations other than to fulfill agreed contracts.[50]

In tandem with these developments, meanwhile, a growing number of non-Western governments have gained wealth by spurning the Western development model of free-market democracy and the underpinning contention of the American brand—namely, that liberal economics demands liberal politics and a minimal role for the state. Many developing country leaders now admire and emulate a new kind of capitalism with two distinct components: first, a liberal economic policy that opens the economy to investment and permits the development of a private sector, albeit heavily controlled by the state; second, the persistence of authoritarian rule, which allows the ruling party to keep a firm grip on government, the courts, the military, and the flow of information.[51]

These two developments—new centers of economic autonomy beyond the West and the growing appeal of illiberal capitalism—have become dual engines for the diffusion of power away from the West. They also have a single force multiplier in the global rise of China.

Beijing has become rich enough to provide a new source of financial assistance and economic development for smaller countries, which enables these countries to sidestep the traditional sources of Western assistance. The critical distinction between Chinese and Western assistance is that China provides hard-currency loans without the conditions imposed by the West. There is no obligation to create a civil society in the Western sense, no requirement to abide by international accounting standards or accepted legal standards—and certainly no attempt to interfere in the recipient's internal affairs. China, its state-owned enterprises, and its business owners offer an alternative path to economic development. It is, in effect, an "exit option" from the often intrusive demands of global lenders like the World Bank and the IMF in areas such as good governance, human rights, transparency, and pro-Western political and market reforms.

This aspect of China's global presence poses an inherent challenge to the Enlightenment values and principles that have guided Western progress for over two centuries. As in other policy areas, China is using its $2.0 trillion of reserves as a strategic instrument. Its global commercial network is fast creating a group of grateful and compliant acolytes—but not in the Cold War sense. We are not talking about a voting bloc within the United Nations or other global institutions that accepts daily instructions from a bloc leader (though Beijing expects support on Taiwan, Tibet, sovereignty, and human rights issues). Rather, we see a growing number of developing nations that are loosely connected by an admiration for China, a desire to benefit from the power of international markets, and an equal desire to remain autonomous from Western concepts of global civic culture and liberal development economics.

Fortunately for the Robert Mugabes and Omar al-Bashirs of the world, Beijing believes sovereignty is inviolate. This view is ultimately rooted in the Chinese government's own sense of insecurity at home and the need to suppress the democracy narrative. It gains rhetorical strength from the memory of Chinese humiliation at the hands of invading European powers in the nineteenth century. The concern was propelled in the twentieth century by China's claim that the West sought to split China by recognizing Taiwan or encouraging Tibet's independence, and these themes are reflected today by China's consistent rejection of interference by outside authorities in the internal affairs of nations. Naturally, this is very attractive to autocrats, proliferators, and madcap, monarchical personality cults that have raw materials to sell or the money to buy Chinese consumer goods.

Meanwhile, China's rise also reflects a familiar historical theme—namely, that ideas travel along the arteries of commerce and power.[52] To this extent, the global marketplace has become a transition belt, via which Beijing is inadvertently promoting a most troublesome export: *the example of the China model.*

When we speak about the Chinese model, we are referring in one sense to a complex set of developments and reforms in China over the last thirty years. These reforms owe their success to the unique variables of China's own culture, demography, geography, and governing philosophies. In this sense, there is no model to speak of—no model that can be replicated or exported to places like Latin America or sub-Saharan Africa.

But in ideational terms, China is exporting something simpler, and indeed more corrosive to Western preeminence, than the individual nuts and bolts of its colossal thirty-year transformation. This is the basic idea of market authoritarianism. Beyond everything else that China sells to the world, it functions as the world's largest billboard advertisement for the new alternative of "going capitalist and staying autocratic." Beijing has provided the world's most compelling, high-speed demonstration of how to liberalize economically without surrendering to liberal politics. Officials and leaders now travel to China from seemingly every quarter of the globe beyond North America and Europe—Southeast Asia, the Middle East, Central Asia, sub-Saharan African, and Latin America—to learn from the Chinese about how to disaggregate economic and political freedom (more of this in Chapters 3 and 4).[53] Beijing, of course, does what it can to promote its model—albeit softly—through speeches, conferences, summits, and exchange programs that complement the daily fare of commercial relations.

CHINA'S PERFECT TIMING

China's premodern astronomers were pioneers in developing a sense of time and accuracy by the calendrical system.[54] The country's modern-day leaders have seemingly kept their sense of good timing. China's rise on the world stage coincides with a time when the appeal of free-market capitalism and Western democracy—as exemplified by the American brand—has, at least momentarily, been struggling to recover from in a tide of disdain across the globe. Few opinion-making circles in the developing world are exempt. Complicating matters is America's acute vulnerability to accusations of hypocrisy and incompetence and a period of historically low global approval ratings associated with the last eight years of war in Iraq and Afghanistan and a region in chaos.

Ideas have traditionally been among the West's most important exports. As Francis Fukuyama lamented in *Newsweek* shortly before the 2008 election, American power and influence used to rest on more than simply tanks and dollars. It also rested on the tendency of millions of people around the world to look up to the American form of government and to seek to shape their societies along similar lines.[55] Harvard professor Joseph Nye has famously called this "soft power," namely, the ability "to obtain the outcomes one wants through attraction rather than using the carrots and sticks of payment or coercion."[56] It is leading by example and attracting others to do what you want.

U.S. foreign policy through much of the twentieth century is the history of how American ideals supported the projection of power. The 1940s saw America rebuild much of Europe through the Marshall Plan while it created institutions that would help to stabilize the global order and solve conflicts before they led to war. These initiatives made American power highly popular in the wider world and helped American brands reach the most remote corners of the globe. Soviet collapse was an economic and political victory for the United States. It was also an ideological victory for American values and the idea of the West—seemingly irrefutable proof that the moral superiority of American democratic and capitalist values had succeeded against the promise of the "New Soviet Man."[57] Even Henry Kissinger, the iconic realist of our age, accepts that moral purpose was a key element in American foreign policy during the twentieth century.

Without question, the United States is still the unipolar power in military terms and is set to remain the single most powerful country in the world for decades to come. Yet, despite this military superiority, along other important axes, the distribution of power is shifting away from American dominance—as measured by social, cultural, and even economic terms.[58] If the American brand rests on the dual premise of market mechanisms and democratic pluralism, then both ideas have been badly bruised in the past decade.

The dramatic and bloody rejection of Coalition nation builders in Iraq and Afghanistan has stained both the moral authority of the West and the notion that democratic pluralism is universally viable. The shifting arguments used by the Bush administration to justify the invasion of Iraq caused many to conclude that "democratization" was just a code word for intervention and regime change.[59] American values were further impeached by the events at Abu Ghraib, the "extraordinary renditions" by U.S. intelligence services, and improper domestic wiretapping.

Then, in a parallel dimension, came the Wall Street crisis of 2008. The real estate downturn brought a global stock market crash; the gnomes of Zurich joined the old-line "white shoe" firms of Wall Street and Fleet Street to topple like dominoes. And at crisis hour, what did the markets do? They went cap in hand to the state—in the United States, in Britain, in Europe, and in East Asia. As one Chinese official put it, "the teachers now have some problems."[60] Insult was added to injury in May 2009, when the largest bank in the United States, Bank of America, had to sell its 9 percent stake in the Construction Bank of China, just to stay afloat. As financial correspondent Peter Goodman commented at the time, it had been purchased for $3 billion just a few years before in a wave of foreign investment in China that was supposed to be a sign of Wall Street's superior money management.[61]

Naturally, there is an obvious intellectual chasm, as *Time* magazine's Michael Elliott asserts, between Keynesian stimulus packages—or the temporary public ownership of bank stock— on one hand, and the assumption that the state can and should plan the economy on the other.[62] No one is saying that capitalism is doomed. The problem is, as *Star Trek*'s Spock would have said: "It's capitalism, Jim, but not as we know it."

Western ideas and institutions of economic management are experiencing a crisis of confidence in the global space. Chilean President Michelle Bachelet put these sentiments best. "For us, this economic crisis was no surprise," she said during the darkest days of the credit crunch. "You need strong markets,

but the market cannot do it alone; this crisis shows the necessary role that state policies must have in overseeing financial
markets and economies as a whole." President Bachelet also
underscored that beyond the West, there is a growing consensus about the "need to restructure the Bretton Woods institutions, the IMF and the World Bank," which were "created in
a different era." These institutions "need not just a new influx
of funds, but new strategies and a reform in governance, such
as giving more representation to the developing countries they
serve." Above all, she added, "We cannot repeat the errors of
the Washington Consensus."[63]

Here the Chilean president highlighted a recurring theme
in the story of China's rise. The Chinese have made their move
at a time when the doctrine of Western development economics, along with its namesake, the Washington Consensus, is tar-
nished. Chinese investment and project management, while
doing little for liberal governance, have left a succession of
infrastructure projects—roads, bridges, telecommunications
systems, and transport—across the developing world that would
not have been built without Chinese finance and know-how.

As the next chapter will explain, China's success in actually
completing large projects on time and within budget compares
well with the West's one-size-fits-all finance and development
package, whose projects have experienced notable reversals
from Argentina, Bolivia, and Mexico to Mali, Mozambique,
and Cambodia. The Chinese have subsequently walked through
an open door with an alternative philosophy that makes few
demands on the internal root and branch of client states.

All this at a time when eight years of misconceived policy
have cast a pall over the American story. A former adviser to
the U.S. Treasury Department and the Asian Development

Bank, Hilton Root, has shown that Washington follows a counterproductive pattern of backing authoritarian regimes in ways that contradict America's core values of freedom and democracy.[64] U.S. relations with energy-rich but politically oppressive regimes like Saudi Arabia and Equatorial Guinea are frequently cited as examples of the "American pot calling the Chinese kettle black."

The Bush administration—inclined to view nearly all relationships through a security lens—was also quick to forge stronger links with autocrats simply because they aided the avowed "war on terror." In the 1990s, Root explains, both Congress and the State Department sought to impose oversight through the budgetary process to ensure that American funding was not provided to human rights violators and regimes that weakened the democratic process. But then, on September 12, 2001, the Bush White House, leading from the heart and perhaps not the head, lifted all such conditions. Suddenly, countries barred from receiving American support because of violations were now eligible simply by promising to help "stamp out global terrorism."[65]

Uzbekistan is a case in point. Before 9/11, it was a country known less in Washington as a bastion of American comradeship and more as a place where political opponents had their heads boiled in large pots. Suddenly, after the September attacks, the country was the Bush administration's new best friend in Asia (more of this in Chapter 3). Pakistan was an even bolder example. U.S. aid poured into Pakistan after 9/11, but with few stipulations. Accordingly, the money was used in ways that contradicted Washington's rhetoric and, eventually, U.S. interests. The money largely helped to fund military preparations for a potential war against India or was used for luxury construction by the military brass. Sectors such as education, rural health, agriculture, and infrastructure that urgently needed support were bypassed, even though their development would have aided America's standing in the region. Today poverty in Pakistan has accelerated resistance in quarters of Pakistani society toward Islamabad's perceived anti-Taliban and pro-American policies.[66]

In fact, it is both uncomfortable and unavoidable that as the world's leading superpower, the United States must sometimes follow policies that compromise its own values. Maintaining good relations with a key energy provider like Saudi Arabia is a case in point. Yet there have been too many other occasions in the last decade when Washington's near unconditional support for autocrats in places like Uzbekistan, Equatorial Guinea, and Pakistan—or its use of "harsh interrogation techniques" and arbitrary detentions—has meant greater losses than gains. China has been quick to utilize contradictions of this kind between expressed belief and practice to advance its mantle of moral neutrality. Who are the Americans to judge, say party leaders, when they don't practice what they preach?

THE CHINA EFFECT

Beijing's global rise may be peaceful, therefore, but as its commercial relations expand around the world, so Washington and Brussels are losing ground on two vital fronts: the leverage they have traditionally enjoyed through conditional engagement with poorer countries and the market-democratic model we expected to "go global" after 1989. These developments are coalescing to produce a phenomenon I have, for lack of a better phrase, called the *China effect*. It means that simply by doing business, Beijing has facilitated a global network of economic relationships that chip away at the leverage and liberal agendas of Washington and the West just as the Washington Consensus fails to perform in the developing world (see Chapter 2 for more on this).

The record is replete with examples: In Iran's case, the China effect has helped to block attempts to control nuclear proliferation in the Middle East.[67] In Angola, Cambodia, Burma, and others, it has helped to prevent respective governments from having to make reforms that might improve governance, transparency, human rights, and economic development.[68] In places like Venezuela, it has undermined leverage over President Hugo Chavez and his efforts to agitate regional politics.[69] In Central Asia, it has served to cover up massacres, while in Africa the China effect has helped to sustain campaigns of violence that look increasingly like genocide.[70] In the multilateral setting, it has brought economic weight to influence important votes on the UN Human Rights Commission and attempts by the Directorate General for Trade (DGT) to prevent antidumping and predatory pricing violations by Chinese exporters.[71] In Africa, it has undermined Western initiatives such as the Partnership for Africa's Development (NEPAD), which seeks to link development assistance with regional peer reviews of better government and conflict resolution.[72]

CHINA: A GENERATIONAL CHALLENGE

It isn't all bad news for the American brand. Barack Obama's election in November 2008 brought a dramatic, overnight lift in American soft power and a resurgence of faith in the idea of America, with street parties from Times Square to Paris and

Nairobi. Nicholas Kristof noted that even before the final result was confirmed, the story and the personality of Barack Obama had begun to alter and soften global perceptions of the United States, redefining the American brand as being "less about Guantánamo and more about equality." These perceptions offered hope that American political capital and moral viability would be restored in the same way that the Marshall Plan had largely defined postwar America to Europeans in the 1950s or that John Kennedy's presidency did in the early 1960s.[73]

However, as Dick Martin, author of *Rebuilding Brand America*, contends, revitalizing the American position in the world is about more than undoing the mistakes of the Bush administration, and it will take more than the election of a popular U.S. president to do it. It is "the work of a generation."[74] Obama delivered a sense of immediate change to American identity. But there are larger forces changing the shape of the global order, which are harder to move.

If the magic of American leadership has faded, says French minister of foreign affairs, Bernard Kouchner, there's a very material reality to this observation: "You want modern transportation systems? Try France or Japan. New airports? Half the cities of Asia." If you were an American policy maker in 1945, laments *Time* writer Michael Elliott in similar tones, you barely needed to make the claim to global leadership. It was simpler than that. American leadership after 1945 was a material reality when much of the rest of the world was in ruins. Germany and Japan had been destroyed. Britain was exhausted; France shamed; Russia bled white. In China, war would continue for another four years. Of the industrial democracies, only the United States, Canada, and Australia had been spared destruction at home.[75] The U.S. economy accounted for nearly a half of total world output in 1945, a proportion that it has never approached since.[76]

Unless China and India suffer outbreaks of serious military conflagration or a calamitous domestic crisis, they will become the world's largest economies in the middle of this century. The potential size of their markets, their endless supply of low-cost labor, the unique combination of many highly skilled but low-paid professionals, and the investment incentives offered by their governments make for an irresistible package that attracts ever more investment away from the first world.[77]

The relocation of manufacturing centers away from the United States has begun a corresponding shift in the center of gravity for R&D as it naturally gravitates toward new hubs of progress and production. See, for example, the inside of an Apple iPhone, which is like a map of the changing geography in the modern technology industry. Apple is ostensibly an American company, but like a microcosm of the international arena, the shiny American brand name hides a different reality. None of the physical innards are American. Almost every component is from Asia. The screen is from Japan. The flash memory was developed in South Korea and assembled in China. "As goes the iPhone," says one technology report, "so goes the broader technology industry."[78]

As experts at the Organization for Economic Cooperation and Development (OECD) proclaimed in 2008, the traditional powerhouses for technological development like the United States and Japan are being overtaken in many areas by new Asian economies. The largest technology firms are still technically Western owned. But Asian companies are challenging their lead in innovation and production technology. In an arresting statistic, we find that R&D in the United States and

Europe grew by 1–2 percent between 2001 and 2006, while figures for the same period in China increased by 26 percent. Since 1996, America's overall expenditures on R&D in computers and office equipment fell by over one-third, while expenditures in China rose by 47 percent.[79]

The changing nationality of the Internet tells a similar story about the Rest catching up with the West. The Internet research firm TeleGeography has calculated this change in its report "The Internet Is Becoming Un-American." In the year the Soviet Union disappeared, 91 percent of international Internet capacity from Asia and 70 percent from Africa connected to the United States. Seventeen years later, in 2008, the share of international Internet traffic passing through the United States from Asian countries had fallen to 54 percent. Moreover, according to the Kelly Teal report, the amount of bandwidth from African countries connecting to the United States had fallen even more to just 6 percent, turning instead to Europe as the "main Internet hub."[80] Incidentally, in the same year, the United States lost its position as the biggest country on the Internet, with 300 million Chinese users overtaking the number in America for the first time.[81]

THE MYTH OF THE RESPONSIBLE STAKEHOLDER

If you're not concerned about what China represents for the shifting political and economic fortunes of the American brand, you're not alone. There's an established school of China optimists in Washington who offer a counterargument to much of what's been said here. They embrace the basic tenant of American post–Cold War wisdom: that when a country becomes more affluent, its emerging middle class will press for democratic change (see Chapters 2 and 5 for more in-depth discussion). In this context, as China embraces capitalism, the country gradually becomes "more like us"; the bigger and richer China gets, the more it relies on international markets and global trade to sustain economic growth, rising standards of living, and political stability. In turn, goes the argument, the integration of China into the global economy will gradually encourage its leaders to accept and conform to the rules and norms of the U.S.-led system.

In other words, engagement with Western powers will eventually cause China to walk and talk like a Western power. Five of the past six U.S. presidents—Reagan is the exception—have perpetuated this view, along with influential parts of the business community, a community of high-profile consultants, and many of the nation's most prestigious research organizations.[82]

As Chapter 5 argues, however, the optimists shouldn't hold their breath—and the reason lies at home. China's economic miracle has saved the ruling party from extinction, but only because the nation replaced ideology with economic growth, a rekindled sense of nationalism, and a certain amount of pragmatic flexibility. Accordingly, the legitimacy of the Chinese Communist Party hinges on its ability to deliver economic growth at an unforgiving tempo. Simultaneously, however, miracle growth has created a number of vivid side effects: endemic corruption, environmental crisis, income inequity, displaced populations, extreme poverty, an urban-rural divide, inflation, an angry nationalist youth, endemic work-related health problems, and heavy restrictions on the media.

China's leaders are therefore caught in a Faustian bargain. The more China grows, the more it generates the side effects of miracle growth. Despite regulatory and reform efforts, the only way the leaders have found to prevent these side effects from turning into widespread social unrest is continued growth at a miracle pace.

This directly affects the priorities and conduct of Chinese foreign policy. To maintain its growth at current rates, Beijing must sustain relations with regimes across the developing world, regardless of the implications of its policies for human rights, the environment, and basic freedoms for the affected local populations.

When American optimists see big enterprise, balanced budgets, market incentives, foreign direct investment (FDI), pledges of corporate social responsibility, and cooperation at the World Trade Organization (WTO), they think they're seeing signs of an inevitable acceptance of Western-style capitalism. In truth, the pressures and performance requirements of the Chinese Communist Party's position at home place a limit on the West's ability to bend China's international presence to Western standards and norms.

If China conformed to Western rules of liberal engagement in trade and politics, it would immediately lose its appeal as an alternative path to development for developing countries. And, of vital importance to party leaders, it would limit China's access to resources and markets and would downsize Chinese newfound political influence on issues like Tibet, Taiwan, and human rights.

Just in 2008, for example, autocracies were a vital source of energy for China's growing needs. In the period 2007–2008, fuel imports from Africa to China amounted to $26 billion. Africa also supplied 24.8 percent of China's imported minerals, with Angola, Sudan, the Congo, and Equatorial Guinea among the largest overall suppliers. And in the same period, Iran was China's third-largest source of fossil fuels.[83]

Neither is it in China's interest to "rehabilitate" rogue states and poor countries in line with Western standards of good governance. Beijing currently enjoys a clear advantage over the West by dealing with actors and states that have been snubbed by Western companies and governments because their ethics cannot be defended before Western publics. In Table 1.1, for example, we see the top five African sources of imports between 2004 and 2007, four of which are known for some of the worst humanitarian abuses in the world. Similarly, Table 1.2 shows major Chinese financing and aid-related economic projects, which include five card-carrying "pariahs" between 2007 and 2008.

Table 1.1 Top Five African Sources of Chinese Imports:
2004–2007 ($ millions)

	2004	2005	2006	2007	2006–2007 % Change
Africa Total	15,641	21,114	28,768	36,330	25.9
Angola	4,718	6,581	10,931	2,885	17.9
South Africa	2,955	3,444	4,095	6,608	61.4
Sudan	1,706	2,615	1,941	4,114	111.9
Congo	1,569	2,278	2,785	2,828	1.6
Equatorial Guinea	995	1,486	2,538	1,697	−33.1

SOURCE: Wayne M. Morrison, "China's Economic Conditions," Congressional Research Service, March 5, 2009, 21, http://www.fas.org/sgp/crs/row/RL33534.pdf.

Table 1.2   Major PRC Financing and Aid-Related Economic Projects, 2007–2008 for Five Pariahs

Country	Amount Pledged ($ billion)	Major Types of Project	Finance
Venezuela	16.4	oil/gas exploration and production, transportation, telecom, light industry	investment
Angola	7.4	infrastructure (railways)	loans, credit lines
Congo (DRC)	5.0	infrastructure (mining)	loans
Sudan	4.2	oil refining, infrastructure, hydro power, humanitarian	loans, grants
Burma	3.1	hydropower, nickel ore	investment, loans

SOURCE: "China's Foreign Aid Activities in Africa, Latin America and South East Asia," Congressional Research Service, February 25, 2009, 13, 15, 17, http://www.fas.org/sgp/crs/row/R40361.pdf.

Thus while the optimists are right to say that China increasingly engages with the liberal international order, they are wrong to assume that the absence of confrontation implies gradual integration with, or acceptance of, the U.S.-led system. It does not.[84] While the current regime survives in Beijing, China can go only so far in assuming the role of "responsible stakeholder." China's mercantilist foreign policy mandates that the raw materials and natural resources needed to sustain the nation's growth will be extracted from developing-world countries, regardless of whether China's activities measure up to, or fall short of, Western ethical standards and the governance that accompanies it, or deviate from global norms.

GLOBAL SHIFT

Global shifts in power are a familiar theme in history. After all, it was less than a century ago that another great shift took place over the Atlantic. The year 1919 is often marked by historians as a turning point in the distribution of power in the international system, when the United States transformed from debtor to creditor nation. This shift may have been followed by a period of isolationism and protectionism, but it signaled a new level of involvement in world affairs that eventually saw America become the world's most powerful nation. Almost a century later, China is the principal international creditor, and we see the possibility of another shift away from *Pax Americana* and toward the rising economies of Asia. The market democratic model that America has promoted as the universal endpoint of political-economic evolution has been blamed around the world—rightly or wrongly—for its unregulated excess and for bringing on a multiyear, global downturn.

While capitalism remains the lifeblood of global commerce today, there is more than one form of capitalism. Wall Street, popularly seen today as the home of fear and greed, is challenged by a new market-authoritarian model, boosted by people across the world in illiberal places like Beijing, Moscow, Singapore, and Caracas. Before the Berlin Wall came down, says Lester Thurow, the capitalist world was held together by a fear of communism. In the intervening period, capitalism has learned to stand alone; consequently, in some parts of the global economy, democracy has come to look more like its adversary.[85]

Our erstwhile ideological enemies of the last century have joined the modern market society, but not with the results we expected. Instead, they've done it in ways that demonstrate new, different, and in some cases more successful ways of *playing our game*. To analyze this process, we must first understand how the Western brand of liberal free-market fundamentalism came and went as the principle model for economic success in the developing world. This is the subject of Chapter 2.

CHAPTER 2

THE RISE AND FALL OF
THE WASHINGTON CONSENSUS

TO UNDERSTAND THE GROWING APPEAL of Chinese soft power and alternative development models, we must understand its historical context: the waning appeal of Western development economics in the global south. Like many entertaining stories, this one starts at Cambridge University.

It wasn't obvious that John Maynard Keynes would do anything of note with his life. Having graduated from Cambridge, all he wanted to do was run a railroad, on the basis that it looked "so easy." When he failed to break into the railway business, Keynes took the civil service exams and, in an often-neglected footnote to history, received his lowest mark on the economics paper.[1]

Keynes was promptly sent to the India office, from which, freighted with dusty, mundane tasks (he once said his greatest achievement was to export a pureblood bull to Bombay), he soon resigned. Back in England, he found refuge on the lighter side of English high life, writing journals in Cambridge and animating the London party circuit as a member of the

"Bloomsbury Group," a frothy social circle of novelists and essayists that included such luminaries as Virginia Woolf, Lytton Strachey, E. M. Forster, and the Granchester poet Rupert Brooke. It was only when the assassination of Austria's archduke, Francis Ferdinand, threw Europe into war, and Keynes was called to the British Treasury, that his talents as an economist were discovered.[2]

Keynes rose quickly through the civil service. By 1918, he was asked to attend the Paris Peace Conference at Versailles, where he largely kept his mouth shut. On his return, however, he published *The Economic Consequences of the Peace*, explaining that the severity of German reparations reflected a flawed policy, which would eventually destabilize Europe. The book became a best seller, and Keynes became a celebrity.[3] By the time Germany had been defeated for a second time and the Great Powers were meeting again to agree on the terms of a postbellum order, Keynes was at the heart of the discourse. He led the British delegation to the famous 1944 Bretton Woods conference, which was named after the small town in New Hampshire where the victors of World War II convened to establish an international system for postwar trade and economic development.

For the next three decades, a consensus of Western policy makers followed the general guidelines laid out in New Hampshire.[4] The underlying philosophy of the Bretton Woods conference was Keynes's idea that recessions and depressions were not necessarily self-correcting.[5] Classical economics, he argued, rested on the flawed assumption that the natural laws of supply and demand can create full employment. In reality, he noted, people and businesses often saved more and invested less during an economic slowdown. This removed large amounts of money from circulation and prevented sufficient levels of growth and, hence, employment.

Therefore, capitalism, according to Keynes, needed the state's corrective hand if the world were to avoid another economic downturn like that of the 1930s—along with the social convulsion and political extremism that came with it. The state's responsibility was to replace the missing private spending during hard times with public spending and investment. This would create jobs and increase purchasing power. Meanwhile, the government would cut back its spending during times of recovery and expansion, to avoid inflation. In other words, unemployment and inflation were alternating forces. It was the government's job to navigate the balance between the two, either by putting more money in people's pockets with public spending when the going was bad or by taking it away with more taxation when things were going well.[6]

The 1960s were the high point for Keynesian economics, as governments in Washington, London, and Europe followed its rules for macromanaging the economy. Practice seemed to confirm theory; some governments chose to have low unemployment at the cost of higher inflation, while others preferred lower inflation at the cost of higher unemployment.[7]

But then came the world recession of the 1970s. Not only did it destroy the postwar Keynesian consensus, but it also paved the way for profound changes in Western economic thought, which would transform the world and bring a new era of American-led globalization. This era brought with it a popular theory of Western development economics called the Washington Consensus.

In the context of our China story, the significance of the failed Washington Consensus cannot be overstated. The widely heralded but ultimately dysfunctional model set the table for China's feast among marginal, rogue, and autocratic states — and others as well. Western policy makers assumed from the 1980s that a carrot-and-stick approach in financial assistance could be used to lure the developing world into the direction of Western norms and institutions. Recipient countries would make pro-Western economic and political reforms in return for economic engagement. But it didn't turn out that way.

MILTON FRIEDMAN'S NEW SCHOOL

The beginning of the 1970s saw a dramatic rise in commodity prices worldwide, initially caused by a combination of high growth rates for many countries throughout the 1960s and several bad harvests. Then in 1973, the Organization of Petroleum Exporting Countries (OPEC) dropped an economic bombshell, cutting supplies of crude oil and placing an embargo on oil shipments to the West in retaliation for American support of Israel in the Yom Kippur War. The effect was to quadruple the price of oil. Businesses and governments struggled to meet rising costs, and the world plunged into recession.

This global economic crisis presented a novel problem that Keynesian theory couldn't solve, namely, that unemployment and inflation began to rise *simultaneously*. Under the Keynesian model, rising unemployment caused by the global recession suggested that spending should be increased. But at the same time, rising inflation caused by a mixture of the oil embargo and rising commodity prices suggested that it be reduced.[8] Discredited by financial crisis, the Keynesians soon found themselves on the margins of policy debate.

A new school of thinking now emerged with a compelling explanation of the crisis. Milton Friedman, a former professor and presidential adviser, appeared as the leader of a new movement called "monetary economics."[9] What began under Friedman as a response to the perceived failures of Keynesian theory would rapidly become the foundations of a new Western model for political and economic development.

Originally based at the University of Chicago, Friedman and his colleagues argued that the postwar Keynesian model couldn't carry on forever. This was because of an important "human" factor that the Keynesian school had neglected: inflationary expectations.[10] Friedman claimed that when governments tried to help the economy with increased public spending and lending, the positive effects were only temporary. As the government pumped more money into the economy, the immediate effect was to create jobs and give people more money to spend. But as people spent more money, aggregate demand increased across the economy, and vendors gained the confidence to increase prices.[11]

After a while, warned Friedman, businesses and workers began to build their expectations of rising prices and government spending into subsequent wage and price demands. Thus, the ultimate effect of state intervention was not economic growth, but a cycle of government spending and rising inflation. After an initial boost, he said, the economy ended up roughly where it started.

The global economic crisis of the 1970s seemed to confirm Friedman's theory. As Western governments moved to contain the downturn by boosting the spending cycle, the positive effects on employment and incomes lasted only as long as it took people to wise up. Approximately two years later, government

spending interventions were followed by a rapid rise in inflation that crippled many Western economies.[12]

ECONOMIC AND POLITICAL FREEDOM: A VERY WESTERN PARTNERSHIP

Not only did the monetarists diagnose the problem in the early
1970s, but they also offered a bold solution: to create a new
kind of market society. Keynes had argued that government
was the ultimate solution; Friedman now claimed the opposite,
that government was the ultimate *problem.*

Increasing demand without making markets work better,
said Friedman, would simply lead to higher inflation. Instead
of having a central body deciding what the economy needed,
went the new theory, a more effective method would be to replace the heavy hand of government with supply and demand
as the natural driving forces of the economy. Economic growth
would increase only when markets were able to operate freely
and efficiently. Thus, the way to reduce unemployment and
maximize national wealth, said the new monetarists, was to
make resources more available, more flexible, and more re-
sponsive to market forces.[13]

In practice, this meant deregulation, liberalization, and privatization for large parts of the economy. Friedman and company insisted on a number of specifics: The government had
to stop boosting the economy with public spending; loss-making
industry should not be bailed out in the attempt to protect
jobs; state ownership of service providers, from public transport to energy providers, education, and health care, should
be minimized or removed completely; competition should be
promoted wherever possible; barriers to entry in markets and
industries should be removed; and finally, the efficiency of the

job market should be increased by cutting the rate of income tax and removing legal impediments to labor market flexibility, such as maximum working hours and the terms of dismissal.[14]

The collective aim of these measures was to replace the "helping hand" of government with the "invisible hand" of the market. This approach had deep roots in the European Enlightenment. The classical eighteenth-century economist Adam Smith had coined the term *invisible hand* when he argued for free trade among nations as the basis for peace and prosperity. As Smith asserted in 1776, the individual's pursuit of personal gain in a market economy does a better job of serving society's aggregate needs than if a central organization or group of people actively sought to promote them.[15] Friedman consequently became known as one of the first neoclassical economists, with a modern application of Smith's classical notion: A society of individuals making logical decisions in pursuit of economic self-interest produces a healthy, growing economy as if guided by some "unseen hand."[16]

With this assertion, Smith and Friedman both highlighted the core idea that distinguished Western liberal political philosophy from the alternative models of communism, fascism, and absolute monarchy. The pursuit of society's greater good, they proclaimed, was upheld by the pursuit of liberty and freedom for the individual.

And so, Friedman's idea of a market society wasn't just an economic theory; it laid the basis for a comprehensive political-economic philosophy. The power of the market lay in economic freedom, but economic freedom could only exist in the context of political freedom, where the individual was free to choose how to live, what to buy, and what to produce. Thus, economic and political freedoms were two parts of the same whole.

FROM THEORY TO THE NEW "WESTERN BRAND"

What started in the 1960s as a theoretical response to Keynes expanded into a political movement in the 1970s. In the United States and Britain especially, monetarism became the focus of an intellectual renaissance for conservatism. Monetarism blended with the ideas of conservative figures like Russell Kirk and Friedrich von Hayek, who rose to prominence in the mid-twentieth century for arguing that society's function was to encourage individual activity and protect diversity. This stood in contrast to the general thrust of postwar European socialism, which countered that society should be principally concerned with moving people toward a collective, common good.[17]

From the mid-1970s, the conservative revival had become a recognized political movement under the label of the New Right, with its center of gravity in Washington and London.[18] A handful of well-funded think tanks and magazines supported the movement: the *National Interest* and the American Enterprise Institute (AEI) in the United States, and the Centre for Policy Studies in London, of which Margaret Thatcher, later to be prime minister, was the president. A new generation of talented, young activists helped to secure social conservatism at the heart of American political debate for the next three decades, typified by figures such as Paul Weyrich, who established both the Heritage Foundation and the Free Congress Foundation. Weyrich famously coined the term *moral majority* as a vanguard against what he saw as creeping left-wing secularism and moral degeneracy.[19]

With election victories for Ronald Reagan and Thatcher at the end of the 1970s, these ideas became official policy in the United States and Britain. The new conservative brand of economic philosophy now became the Western brand of free-market democracy, based on the dual premise of free markets and democratic pluralism as the optimal way to organize society. As monetarism and free-market doctrine captured the policy debate in Washington, so they came to dominate the agenda of two highly influential financial institutions that were based there—the IMF and the World Bank. Global recession throughout the 1970s had made them even more influential, leaving a number of developing countries in severe need of financial assistance. This assistance now came at a price. Governments were told they had to meet certain conditions in a process that soon became known as conditional, or policy-based, lending. This meant that if nations were to receive emergency loans and other credits from the World Bank and IMF, certain specific reforms had to be put in place. In other words, no reforms, no money.[20]

These reforms were designed to eliminate any obstacles to an efficient market, which was the presumed path to optimal growth. Loans were provided by these lending agencies when countries adopted "structural adjustment programs"—or SAPs—which were designed to follow all the rules of Friedman's new philosophy: Deregulate markets, remove controls on investment, allow interest and exchange rates to be determined by world markets, reduce the size of the public sector, and eliminate subsidies. Taken together, the various elements and mechanisms of the SAPs became known as the Washington Consensus, a term invented in 1989 by John Williamson. It was summarized by its author in ten points: (1) impose fiscal discipline; (2) reform taxation; (3) liberalize interest rates; (4) raise spending on health and education; (5) secure property rights; (6) privatize state-run subsidies; (7) deregulate markets; (8) adopt a competitive exchange rate; (9) remove barriers to trade; (10) remove barriers to foreign direct investment.[21]

THE PROBLEM WITH STRUCTURAL ADJUSTMENT PROGRAMS

In a number of cases, however, the Washington Consensus failed to have the desired effect. Though this type of lending grew significantly in the 1980s, a list of negative side effects grew along with it.

A hallmark of SAPs was how similar they were to each other, whether applied in Latin America, Africa, or the Caribbean.[22] Countries usually turned to the World Bank and IMF when their economies were in recession. In such circumstances, slashing government deficits could make matters worse in the short term, and spending cuts had the heaviest impact on the poor.[23] Nascent domestic industries were quickly overwhelmed by foreign competition. Deregulation and liberalized rules on foreign investment opened markets to speculative "hot money," causing severe inflation. Rapid privatization of state industries frequently brought fraud that fed the corruption goblin as previously owned state sectors were taken over by political cronies.[24]

This is not to say that SAPs and the Washington Consensus simply failed. There were a number of places where they saw success, such as Uruguay and El Salvador in Latin America, or Tanzania and Uganda in Africa. But as noted by Joseph Stiglitz, former chief economist at the World Bank, "the Washington Consensus policies were a mix of policies—it was a long list—and in the long list there were policies that were appropriate for some countries at some times. The problem was that the one-size-fits-all policy meant that the same recipe was pushed on all countries."[25]

Generic reform policies were often applied to developing or poor economies with little consideration of whether the conditions for success were present. Was there a robust financial system and a strong legal framework? Were there regulatory institutions and provisions for oversight? Were there available people sufficiently skilled to administer the new economy?[26] Too often these questions were left unanswered—and, sometimes, unasked. A graphic illustration of how "adjustment stress" wreaked havoc under SAP rules is the cashew nut industry in Mozambique. Mozambique's cashew industry used to be one of the largest in the world. Following independence from Portuguese rule in 1975, the new government in Maputo banned the export of raw cashew nuts, in order to stimulate the local packaging and processing industries. A ban on exporting raw materials kept their domestic price low, which effectively functioned like a subsidy for domestic packagers and processors. When Mozambique applied for international financial assistance in the wake of civil war, however, the terms of the loan stipulated that the export trade of cashew nuts had to be liberalized and the ban on raw exports removed. The U.S. National Bureau of Economic Research reports that while farmers gained income of approximately $5.30 per year from these measures, eleven thousand workers employed by the nut industry lost their jobs, and another million nut collectors lost their income.

The program did not help Mozambique, which remains today at the bottom of the league in world poverty. This example demonstrates the disconnect between theory and practice. In theory, when the market model is working properly, as inefficient industries are forced out of business, the redundant resources are relocated to sectors where the country possesses a comparative advantage. In practice, however, Mozambique was not an efficient market model. Instead, it was saddled with inefficiencies that inhibited adjustment. It had an inadequate transport system, a poor communications infrastructure, and a banking system incapable of facilitating new industries and promoting new businesses.[27]

ECONOMIC FAILURE AS POLITICAL DEFEAT FOR THE WESTERN BRAND

Between 1980 and 1995, SAPs were applied to roughly 80 percent of the world's population. Some of the more notable examples of adjustment stress include Mexico, Argentina, Bolivia, Peru, Ecuador, Venezuela, Trinidad, Jamaica, Sudan, Zaire (now Democratic Republic of the Congo), Nigeria, Zambia, Uganda, Benin, Niger, Algeria, Jordan, Russia, and Indonesia. Each of these countries saw violent protests, in many cases deadly, against specific SAP stipulations, from sharp increases in fuel prices to steep currency devaluation and subsequent price hikes, and from food-price riots to university sit-ins over the IMF-mandated doubling of the cost of bread or transport.[28]

In Argentina, for example, the IMF provided $7.2 billion on the basis of certain key fiscal and structural reforms. Within months, widespread strikes occurred in the capital and other cities, in response to both IMF-proposed labor laws that limited the power of the trade unions and to proposed cuts in the social security system. The reforms were passed a year later by the Argentinean Senate, but not without thousands of demonstrators involved in violent clashes with the police. Similarly in Bolivia, SAP reforms led to water prices climbing by 200 percent in some cities, leading to similar protests. Zambia likewise received $349 million in March 1999, on the condition that the government commit to a broad program of privatization and deregulation in public services. The subsequent crowds of protesters in Lusaka had to be dispersed with riot police and tear gas.[29]

Fareed Zakaria has described the other side of the coin, pointing out that the evolution of global markets and free trade under American and Western leadership has also seen considerable success in the last twenty years.[30] The problem of hyperinflation, for example, which used to beleaguer myriad governments from Turkey to Brazil and Indonesia, has been tamed by successful fiscal and monetary policies, largely in line with Western methodology. The share of people living on a dollar a day has fallen from 40 percent in 1981 to 18 percent in 2004, while poverty is falling in countries with 80 percent of the world's population.[31]

Similarly, Clyde Prestowitz makes the point that for the past half century, through the process of globalization, the United States has been the single most important actor in integrating national economies to create an international exchange of goods, services, money, technology, and people. These exchanges have enabled countless people to flourish. It was this process, as much as anything else, that won the Cold War by lifting billions in the free world out of poverty and creating centers of wealth and power around the planet, from Japan and South Korea to the European Union.[32]

Despite these trends, however, the development package offered to poorer countries by the Western group of industrialized nations since the early 1980s had lost both appeal and legitimacy in the eyes of many recipients by the turn of the century. Experts believe a principal reason for this was the one-size-fits-all philosophy that characterized much of the West's policy-based lending. As the economist Elisa Van Waeyenberge remarks, World Bank reports could not help but acknowledge by the late 1980s the poor economic performance of a number of countries that embraced World Bank/IMF reform programs.[33] In the last two decades of the twentieth century, Randall Peerenboom explains, fifty-seven out of eighty-three countries with a per-capita income of less than two thousand dollars stayed equally poor or became poorer. By the year 2000, fifty-four developing countries on various support plans were poorer than they were in 1990.[34]

Unsurprisingly, some of the clearest examples of disenchantment with Western economic development models are found in Africa. Ethiopian Prime Minister Meles Zenawi spoke on behalf of an emergent African bloc in 2007 when he said that the "neo-liberal reforms" advocated by the World Bank and others had failed to "generate the kind of growth they sought." The only kind of good governance that takes root, he added, is homegrown, not imposed from outside.[35] A report from the Commission for Africa in the same period described growing skepticism, at both popular and official levels, about "following an economic and political prescription . . . differing from the ones followed by the industrialized world in its own development." Developed countries, the commission argued, "did not get where they are now through the policies and the institutions that they recommend to Africa today." Most of them actively protected embryonic industries and provided export subsidies—practices that are now frowned on, if not actively banned. Mozambique, Mexico, and many others have proclaimed it unfair, therefore, that they were forbidden by the World Bank to subsidize their agriculture while Western countries spent billions on their farmers.

A DIFFERENT VIEW FROM WASHINGTON

Consequently, just as China was seeking to extend its commercial relationships with emerging markets at the end of the 1990s, it had become plain to many that the application of Western models for economic development had been imprudent and often unproductive. Before we turn to the rise of the Chinese alternative, however, it is important to understand how these events were perceived, or rather misperceived, in the political center of the West. For if the appeal of Western development models was waning in the global south by the turn of the millennium, the prevailing view in Washington was quite different.

From 1980, the application of SAPs under the aegis of the Washington Consensus coincided with a period of hyperefficiency and dynamic growth in global markets. Over the next fifteen years, a number of events overlapped to generate a new phase of openness for the flow of capital and commodities. The modern concept of next-day delivery took flight—quite literally—with the development of air express and dedicated delivery fleets that included long-range airplanes capable of flying nonstop halfway around the world. Manufacturing was revolutionized as suppliers were no longer required to be close to their assembly plants. In the same period, new satellite systems and fiber-optic cables became the nervous system for the global expansion of telecommunications and the Internet, negating time and distance on a new raceway where capital jumps the globe with a mouse click.[36] Breakthroughs in technology, freight, and communication were accompanied by the liberalization of financial transactions. Here again, the United States and Britain were global leaders. At the start of the 1980s, Washington and London relaxed financial regulations and abolished many capital controls. Investors were suddenly free to invest anywhere in the world.[37] Levels of foreign direct investment exploded as American multinational companies outsourced production to selected low-wage developing countries while accelerating global distribution.[38] The rise of the "American brand" became a literal phenomenon, as labels and industries like Coca-Cola, Nike, McDonald's, Microsoft, and CNN went truly global. By the end of the 1980s, globalization sounded in many ways like a euphemism for "Americanization"; American music, styles, clothing, films, politicians, and entrepreneurs set global fashions and dominated global markets.

Of course, in some respects, globalization was actually an odd term to describe these events during the Cold War, when half the world sat under a restrictive socialist mantle where financial markets played virtually no role. Even in the West, as economic analyst Philip Coggan recalls, free-market philosophy may have swept the board in the United States and Britain by 1985, but in other sections of the "first world," many observers still believed at this stage that the so-called Anglo-Saxon model was inferior to those developed elsewhere in Europe, Asia, and Latin America. Both Germany and Japan, for example, decided in the 1980s against allowing unfettered markets to reign. The freedom of financial markets was secondary to the priorities of social welfare and duty of care for employees. Hostile takeovers in Germany were practically unknown, while suppliers and employees were prioritized over returns to shareholders. A similar culture prevailed in Japan, where companies were protected from takeovers by mutual shareholding among friendly groups.[39]

Everything changed, however, with the demise of Soviet Communism at the beginning of the 1990s. Anglo-Saxon capitalism had seemingly lost its rival as one revolution followed another across the Eastern bloc and the socialist economic model collapsed. Almost overnight, governments the world over began shifting their priorities toward a Western economic system.

THE END OF HISTORY; THE RETURN OF HISTORY

These events gave a quantum boost to the internationalization of trade and finance, the scope of transnational corporations, and to the primacy of Western financial institutions like the IMF and the World Bank.[40] They also transformed the policy debate in the United States, which was captured by a big idea about the "end of history."

What started as an article published by Francis Fukuyama in the *National Interest* became the kernel for a broad political consensus in Washington from 1990.[41] The essence of the argument was that Soviet collapse was more than the collapse of an American enemy. It was actually the end of history in terms of the battle for preeminence among rival systems of human organization. Fukuyama contended that history's great ideological competitors — namely, absolute monarchy, fascism, and Communism — had all lost their legitimacy as political-economic models that could keep the elite in power and a sufficient majority of the people happy at the same time. The American and French revolutions had defeated monarchy as a durable theory of state. Fascism had rested on a form of ultra-nationalist expansionism and unending war that led to disastrous military defeat in 1945. And now a wave of democratic revolutions across the Soviet Union had proved that Communism was, in fact, unsustainable when the threat of force was removed. After all was said and done, went the argument, only the American experiment in liberty was left standing; it was the political-economic system that satisfied mankind's basic want for both a say in the political process and the opportunity to get rich.

Just as important as the substance of the end-of-history thesis are the reasons why it captured American political culture so broadly after the Cold War. These assumptions found acceptance in the national debate because of how they confirmed the oldest and most familiar theme of American culture. Enter the pivotal role of American exceptionalism in the U.S. public-political debate—or perhaps *reenter,* we should say. This is the nation's enduring eighteenth-century image of itself as a special people with an "exceptional" role to play in history and human progress. As Chapter 6 discusses in more detail, the rise of powerful narratives about exceptionalism is a recurring theme in U.S. foreign policy debate. It can be triggered by identifiable variables such as wars, terrorist attacks, or elections, but it remains an ongoing force just beneath the surface of political life and rises up when the nation is challenged.[42]

As pundits and politicians sought to understand the tide of world events at Cold War's end, they gravitated toward the obvious explanation: What had begun in America 250 years ago was now—in the reflection of America's global success—gradually and finally taking root everywhere else. The rest of the world was somehow destined by political physics to embrace a kind of three-point philosophy, originally born out of European Enlightenment, which asserted that (1) democratic pluralism is the optimal way to organize political life; (2) free markets are the indispensible vehicle for the creation of wealth and happiness; and (3) where you find one of these qualities — wealth or happiness — you will eventually find the other.

Consequently, the political logic following Soviet collapse seemed self-evident. Countries would have to liberalize economically if they wanted to compete and survive in the post-Soviet order. As countries approached a certain level of per-capita income, the expanding consumer culture and the emergent middle class would demand legal and political accountability, which rulers would have to grant — in either limited or comprehensive form — if they wanted their nations to prosper. In turn, market mechanisms would produce independent financial power centers and civic associations, which would become the basis for political interests and then parties that would eventually function in the public square to generate checks on central power and call for greater accountability. In other words, if economic freedom was about to fill the gap of global Communism, then political freedom was bound to follow. Soviet collapse heralded a global triumph for the *idea of the West*, as expanding global markets brought expanding liberal governance. At least, that was the theory — and we heard much of it from Bill Kristol, Richard Perle, Bob Kagan, and so on.

By this token, the most effective way to deal with autocracies such as China was to enmesh them in the global economy, letting the inherent desire for growth and stability work their magic. As Fukuyama claimed, the triumph of the Western idea was evident in the total exhaustion of viable systematic alternatives to Western liberalism. Consumerist Western culture was now seen in "such diverse contexts as the peasants' markets and color television sets now omnipresent throughout China, the cooperative restaurants and clothing stores opened in the past year in Moscow, the Beethoven piped into Japanese department stores, and the rock music enjoyed alike in Prague, Rangoon, and Tehran."[43]

The great task for the post–Cold War era was thus to build a better system for the free flow of goods and multilateral cooperation. The age-old historical trends of geopolitics had seemingly been replaced with a new age of geoeconomics and a gradual global convergence around the American brand.[44]

ILLIBERAL CAPITALISM AND ITS VARIANTS

This was all very grand, all very simple, and, as it turns out, all very wrong. Almost twenty years later, Americans are reluctantly accepting that these predictions were premature. In practice, free politics has failed to keep pace with free markets, and capitalism is learning to flourish without bringing liberalism or democracy. In fact, at least two resilient variations of illiberal capitalism have materialized to challenge the preeminence of the Western market-democratic brand as models of capitalist governance in the twenty-first century.

The first comprises various forms of resource-based illiberal capitalism run by autocratic governments. Michael Ross and others point to numerous examples—Russia, Venezuela, and the Arab and Persian Gulf states—to show how these governments have developed a set of mechanisms that can keep a balance of economic freedom on one hand and sustained one-party rule on the other.[45]

Elites in resource-rich governments can use their oil revenues, for instance, "to relieve social pressures that can otherwise lead to demands for greater accountability." Crucial to this process is what Ross calls the "taxation effect." As the historical record shows in early modern England, France, and the Americas, demand for representation in government arose in response to the sovereign's attempts to raise taxes. But when governments derive sufficient revenues from the sale of oil and gas, Ross argues, "they are likely to tax their populations less heavily or not at all, and the public in turn will be less likely to demand accountability from, and representation in, their government."[46]

Resource wealth has also provided these governments with budgets that can facilitate large spending programs and high employment rates. These programs have proved effective in many cases in reducing pressures for democracy and impeding the formation of social groups and protest movements that are necessary preconditions of democracy.[47] Political scientist Kiren Aziz Chaudhry underscores this point with the example of Gulf Arab states that have used their oil revenues to develop programs that are "explicitly designed to depoliticize the population" by essentially "keeping people happy" with sufficient job opportunities and new levels of material wealth and opportunity.[48]

The second variant to emerge as an alternative to the Western model is export-driven, state-directed capitalism, often called the East Asian model, owing to its broad application there. In the initial phase, at least, this model has employed mechanisms similar to the energy state in keeping a balance between economic freedom and political control.

The major difference is that this model generates growth by the mass production and export of products with a decisive, competitive advantage for sale on the international market. Of course, the single most successful example of this model is China. But Beijing has only refined a growth formula that was pioneered by several other Asian countries, including Hong Kong, Taiwan, Singapore, South Korea, and Japan.

These countries, often called the Asian Tigers, have consistently registered 8 to 10 percent annual growth rates. While each of these examples differs in various ways, they also share certain core characteristics: cheap labor, undervalued currency, and heavy state subsidies to achieve export competitiveness in international markets; high levels of personal and business savings to fund national investment in industries; high levels of foreign direct investment (FDI) with tax incentives; and an emphasis on improving education and highly protected domestic markets.

Randall Peerenboom notes that they also shared something else: an emphasis on economic growth rather than political rights during the initial stages of development, with a period of rapid economic growth occurring under authoritarian rule. By the 1990s, various examples of the East Asian model had liberalized politically, from postwar Japan to Taiwan and South Korea. They posed little challenge, therefore, to the rise of the American brand after the Cold War or to Washington's belief that where free markets led, so democratic pluralism would follow.

But then came China. With Deng Xiaoping's growing influence in the 1980s, a popular view formed in Washington that international engagement with China would encourage political liberalization inside the country. Some observers, including Fukuyama, believed that China had ceased to function as the revolutionary vanguard for would-be radicals, "whether they be guerrillas in some Asian jungle or middle class students in

Paris." Rather, China was now an anachronism, and mainland Chinese had been progressively drawn by the prosperity and dynamism of their overseas co-ethnics—in an ironic ultimate victory for Taiwan.[49]

This is clearly no longer the case—if, indeed, it ever were. Since those heady postwar days, the end of America's monopoly on modernity, coupled with the pride that other nations and cultures increasingly take in their own versions of it, has changed the game. The "new world order" of convergence and common global culture that President George H. W. Bush celebrated on the runway at Andrews Air Force Base at the end of the Cold War has failed to materialize. Power is now used among too many actors and states.[50]

International competition between the United States, Russia, China, Europe, India, and Iran raises new threats of regional conflict. While Communism is dead, a new contest between Western liberalism and the great eastern autocracies of Russia and China has reinjected ideology into geopolitics.[51] Some suggest that the principal characteristic of twenty-first-century international relations is turning out to be *nonpolarity*—a world dominated not by one or two or even several states, but rather by dozens of actors possessing and exercising various kinds of power. In addition to major world powers such as the United States, the European Union, Japan, Russia, India, and China, notes the Council on Foreign Relations, there are countless other power centers emerging in the wake of economic development: "Brazil and, arguably, Argentina, Chile, Mexico, and Venezuela in Latin America; Nigeria and South Africa in Africa; Egypt, Iran, Israel, and Saudi Arabia in the Middle East; Pakistan in South Asia; Australia, Indonesia, and South Korea in East Asia and Oceania. A good many organizations would also be on the list of power centres, including those that are global (the International Monetary Fund, the United Nations, the World Bank), those that are regional (the African Union, the Arab League, the Association of Southeast Asian Nations, the EU, the Organization of American States, the South Asian Association for Regional Cooperation), and those that are functional (the International Energy Agency, OPEC, the Shanghai Cooperation Organization, the World Health Organization)."[52]

Timothy Garton Ash of Oxford has invented a new name for the West—the Friends of Liberal International Order, or the FLIO—which sets it in contrast to the new forms of capitalist growth emerging in other parts. "We of the FLIO," writes Garton Ash, "must confront the prospect of a new world disorder." Countries such as Russia, China, Iran, and Venezuela "are not simply powers that challenge the West in various respects, they also represent alternative versions of capitalism. For more than half a millennium, modernity has come to the world from the West. But now in Beijing's Bird's Nest stadium and the skyscrapers of Shanghai we see a form of modernity that is both non-Western and illiberal."[53]

In the scale and speed of its developing narrative, both at home and abroad, China has become the symbolic leader of a growing world beyond the West, where elites embrace the power of market mechanisms and capitalist economic growth but continue to protect their choices from the demands of foreign interference and Western liberalism. This emergent society of states isn't structured like its Western counterpart. There is no commonly accepted theory of global civic culture, no acceptance of particular moral responsibilities, and no shared obligation to act on global questions such as human rights, good governance, or climate change. It's defined less by what it is and more by what it isn't. There is no community as such, and certainly no common narrative on universal norms. Instead, there are loose relationships that rest only on a firm respect for two things: national sovereignty and international markets.

It is the question of changing notions, changing patterns of international community, and China's central role in the process that we now address in Chapter 3.

CHAPTER 3

THE CHINA EFFECT

THE TWO FACES OF NEW CHINA

In September 2008, the World Bank revoked a large sum of financial support for the government of Chad. As World Bank officials explained, the Chadian President Idriss Deby had not kept his side of the bargain. Rather than investing in health care, education, and agriculture, the majority of government spending since 2001 had been used to arm the Chadian security services.

Weeks later, a very different image of Chad came from the other side of the world. According to senior Chinese official Zhou Yongkang, China recognized "the efforts made by the Chadian government to promote national development." In light of the World Bank's critical attitude of President Deby, Zhou extended a new commitment to intensify relations between China and Chad in the fields of trade, politics, and education.[1]

Enter the China effect. China watchers have been warning about a China threat for years, but these warnings have seldom focused on China's diplomatic skills.[2] As we've said so far,

Beijing's global rise rests on a set of aid policies and commercial practices that progressively undermine the ability of American policy makers to shape the international agenda, as well as the faltering efforts of Western financial institutions to demand better governance from the non-Western world. This chapter presents a range of country-specific examples to document the process.

It must be said at the outset of this discussion that just as the Washington Consensus's "structural adjustment loans" and one-size-fits-all approach to development failed at a critical moment, as discussed in the last chapter, Western countries do not have an unblemished historical record, nor an admirable one today when it comes to doing business with international human rights abusers and malcontents. Pick your example. Washington and Riyadh are old friends. Western oil companies such as BP, Shell, and Chevron have refused to reveal their annual payments to corrupt and violent African regimes like the Angolan government.[3] French oil companies such as Elf have used ties to African leaders in former colonies like Burkina Faso to win access to lucrative resources. When President Omar Bongo died in 2009, Gabon lost the longest-serving president in African history. For forty years, Bongo lined his own pockets while his people begged for development and democracy, both of which were stunted by his long reign. The key to his success was simply oil, which France bought by the billions of barrels. "Gabon without France," Bongo once retorted, "is like a car with no driver."[4]

It's a given law of petro-politics, therefore, that few great powers have clean hands when it comes to ensuring access to natural resources. What is documented here are the many ways that Chinese commerce has, often inadvertently, compromised the financial leverage and the political appeal of Western power.

Figure 3.1 compares recent Western and Chinese engagement with countries exhibiting serious and systemic human rights abuses. China's relationships with these regimes are far more extensive.

Figure 3.1   American and Chinese Exports to Selected Countries with Reportedly Serious Human Rights Problems, 2007–2008

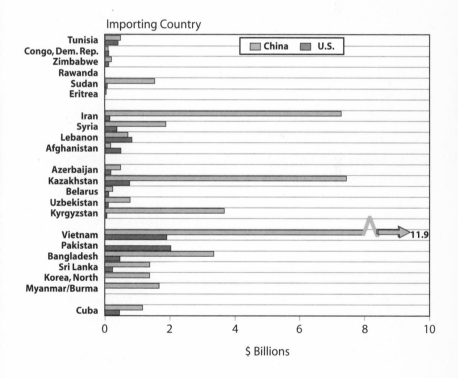

SOURCE: Thomas Lum, ed., "Comparing Global Influence: China's and U.S. Diplomacy, Foreign Aid, Trade, and Investment in the Developing World," Congressional Research Service, August 15, 2008, 57, http://www.fas.org/sgp/crs/row/RL34620.pdf.

THE CHINESE EXIT OPTION

There are numerous cases like the government of Chad. In each the syndrome is similar. Beijing no longer seeks to export communism or actively undermines the liberal international order, but it can and does offer autocrats and governments somewhere to run when they fall out with the West.[5] As James Mann wrote in 2007, pick a dictator anywhere on the globe, and you'll likely find that the Chinese are supporting him.[6] Since the end of the 1990s, Beijing has constructed a string of alliances across the globe, drawn from nations shunned by the United States and the West.[7] Examples provided below extend across the globe from Venezuela to Angola to Iran to Uzbekistan to Burma.

UZBEKISTAN

A test case for the "China effect" is Uzbekistan. After 9/11, the American and Uzbek governments reached an agreement that allowed U.S. forces to lease a military base near the border with Afghanistan in return for aid and military assistance rooting out Islamic extremists in the country. In 2005, however, prison riots in the city of Andijon developed into wider street protests. Uzbek forces responded by firing on unarmed civilians, leading to reports of a possible massacre. Washington and Brussels immediately criticized the Uzbek government and called for an international investigation. Islam Karimov, the Uzbek president, fiercely denied the allegations and took public offense at Western attempts to "interfere" with his government's internal affairs. Amid the condemnation that grew in the international press, Karimov suddenly found he had a very public ally. The Chinese government jumped to Karimov's defense, as Chinese Foreign Ministry spokesman Kong Quan announced, "We firmly support the crackdown on the three forces of separatism, terrorism and extremism by the Uzbekistan government."[8]

There was more to this rhetoric than moral Chinese support. Uzbekistan had officially joined a group of five countries in 2001 called the Shanghai Five, which originally included China, Russia, Tajikistan, Kyrgyzstan, and Kazakhstan. With Uzbekistan's arrival, it was renamed the Shanghai Cooperation Organization (SCO). Until 2005, the remit for the organization served as a forum for resolving border disputes among its members. Two months after the events in Andijon, however, Chinese leaders were instrumental in organizing a joint declaration by the SCO, which called on Washington to establish a date for full withdrawal of its military forces from the country. Tashkent then stated that it would terminate all joint counterterrorism efforts with Washington.[9] In the same period, China also announced that it was providing $600 million in loans to begin the development of a gas pipeline connecting Uzbekistan's gas resources with the Kazakhstan-China gas pipeline.[10]

This is a formulaic example of the China effect: Western governments criticized an energy-rich country on human rights grounds; it cuts ties and swaps them for a new partnership with China.

ANGOLA

Angola provides a similar story. The death of rebel leader Jonas Savimbi in 2002 brought an end to the protracted civil war that had ravished Angola since the country declared its independence from Portugal in 1975. The ceasefire also raised hopes of free elections at some point in the future. Three decades of civil war had killed some 300,000 people. But it had also left a record of pervasive corruption and bad governance among the country's proclaimed leaders. A ruling oligarchy emerged, nurtured by the profits from Angola's oil wealth—the second-largest in Africa—while the general population suffered the squalid infrastructure of a failed state. Following the ceasefire, the Angolan government began negotiations with the IMF for a development loan. The terms of the IMF loan included various measures aimed at tackling the culture of pandemic corruption in Angolan politics and ensuring that loan funds would be used for the good of the general population. These measures demanded greater transparency in economic management, especially the processing of oil revenues. Before the terms of the loan could be finalized, however, Angola suddenly broke off the negotiations. Why? Because the government had received a better offer from the Export-Import Bank of China (China-ExIm).

In contrast to the IMF package, this deal came with no conditions for economic transparency or better governance. Instead, it offered an interest rate payment of only 1.5 percent per year over seventeen years. In return, the Angolan government agreed to provide 10,000 barrels per day (bpd) of crude oil to China, with a clause mandating a rise to 40,000 bpd soon afterward.[11] The consequences speak for themselves. In the following five years, the Angolan economy lost around $4 billion in oil revenues to graft, which amounts to roughly 10 percent of the country's annual GDP.[12] In 2005, the international corruption watchdog Transparency International accused China of turning a blind eye to flagrant and large-scale corruption in

Angola. It also placed Angola as 151st out of 158 countries reviewed in its 2005 annual corruption index.[13]

CENTRAL AFRICAN REPUBLIC

As Angola prepared to jump horses from the IMF to China, a civil war was raging in the Central African Republic (CAR). UN peacekeepers had been forced to withdraw amid the escalating violence. They were replaced by a UN peace-building office, which was intended to be the first step in negotiating a political settlement for a transitional government that would include the warring factions. In 2003, however, a violent coup brought François Bozizé to power. The United Nations, the African Union, and various Western governments condemned the coup and urged General Bozizé to help international agencies restore order and political stability to the war-torn country. Weeks later, following preliminary negotiations, Beijing extended an interest-free loan and invited Bozizé for an official state visit. Shortly thereafter, Bozizé dissolved parliament and suspended the constitution ahead of "democratic elections," which he "won" in 2005.

As the UN Refugee Agency reported in 2007, the CAR's civil liberties rating has since declined, humanitarian conditions have worsened, the country's already scorched economy has further contracted, corruption has remained pervasive, and the government has practically taken over the judiciary.[14] As Bozizé announced in 2007, China had been a "reliable friend" to the Central African Republic, having stepped in and "offered the support his country needed when it faced its most difficult times" with assistance in building a new mining and telecommunications structure to stimulate the economy.[15]

CAMBODIA

Cambodia is another test case where Chinese support provides a way around the West. Since the end of the 1990s, the country's human rights climate has continued to decline while the government has resorted to ever-more-brutal methods to repress political opposition. As the prominent Cambodian intellectual Sockhem Pech explained, Western governments would hope that their assistance to the Cambodian leader Hun Sen would exert pressure on him, but because of Beijing, these efforts have had little effect. Support for Cambodia from the multilateral development banks has since declined, due to the government's failure to implement reforms that would have curbed corruption and improved governance.[16]

Again, the principal driver in this process is China. Premier Wen Jiabao announced in 2006 that China had pledged to provide over $600 million in loans and grants to Cambodia. These pledges formed part of a broader effort to strengthen China's relations in Southeast Asia, including Cambodia, Burma, and Indonesia. According to Yan Xuetong of the China Institute of Contemporary International Relations, a government-affiliated think tank, "developing good relations, especially with Southeast Asian nations, should be China's priority." Tighter relations in this region, he said, are vital to "defuse international hegemonism by the United States" with "regional alliances" that "can rival US power and cut into its influence."[17] As a result, despite numerous trips and proposed initiatives by its envoys, the World Bank has repeatedly failed to link increased aid to Cambodia with conditions for better governance. Western donors simply have little leverage now that the Phnom Penh government can turn to Beijing.[18]

SUDAN

In recent years, Sudan has provided one of the higher-profile demonstrations of the China effect. Beijing has maintained strong economic relations with Khartoum since 2002, focusing on Sudan's considerable natural resources. The terms of the relationship are a classic example of China-Africa relations. Khartoum provides drilling and exploration rights to Chinese oil companies, along with markets for cheap Chinese goods. In return, Sudan receives low-interest loans, aid, and extensive contracts with Chinese construction companies to build roads, bridges, and highways at a lower price than most Western companies would charge.

In 2003, rebels from Sudan's Darfur region began to attack government military targets, arguing that the Islamic government in Khartoum was oppressing black African communities by distributing the country's resources unequally. The government responded by mobilizing a progovernment Arab militia called the Janjaweed. This group began a program of systemic attacks against Darfur as a whole, killing civilians and raping women by the thousands. Within three years, the conflict had killed over two hundred thousand Darfurians and displaced more than 2.5 million. As the killing escalated after 2003, a steady flow of news reports and editorials appeared in the international press calling on the UN Security Council to intervene and halt the violence. From the other direction, however, China appeared as Sudan's chief diplomatic protector.[19]

From early 2004, international pressure, exerted by both the press and governments, built on the Sudanese to modify their policies. But rather than comply with the gathering outrage, Khartoum took shelter behind Chinese diplomatic protection.

Each time the UN Security Council attempted to pass a resolution to act against Khartoum, the Chinese either blocked it, diluted it, or abstained. UN Security Council Resolution 1556, for example, originally demanded that the Sudanese government disarm the Janjaweed completely and allow humanitarian assistance into the Darfur region. After China threatened to use its veto, all enforcement mechanisms in the proposal were removed, rendering the resolution essentially useless.

Over the next two years, wary of building criticism in the press, Beijing abstained from Resolution 1591, which called for sanctions against the Sudanese oil sector, and delayed a ban on offensive military flights. For the same reason, it abstained from Resolution 1593, which would indict numerous Sudanese officials before the International Criminal Court, and threatened to use its veto for a second time over a resolution proposing travel bans and financial sanctions.[20]

In the buildup to the Beijing Olympics, the Chinese government shifted its position on Sudan in response to a powerful campaign by nongovernmental organizations and celebrities to link the Olympics to events in Darfur.[21] The campaign gained important support from two Hollywood personalities. Actress and former goodwill ambassador for the United Nations, Mia Farrow, began a movement to dub the games the "Genocide Olympics," while the acclaimed film director Steven Spielberg resigned as artistic adviser for the games, claiming that China "should be doing more" to end the "continued human suffering" in the region.[22]

In 2008, adjusting to the criticism, the Chinese government softened its position and urged Sudan to cooperate in the deployment of international peacekeeping forces and to help end humanitarian abuses. This was less a change in policy, of course, and more a calculated bow to international pressure, which was timed to coincide with the final buildup to the games. The move also revealed a Chinese inclination to avoid confrontations that spur international public opinion to build against them. (As is discussed in Chapter 7, this is a vulnerability that Washington can learn to use more effectively.)

Months later, the Chinese government publically condemned the indictment of Sudanese President Omar al-Bashir by the International Criminal Court (ICC). Meanwhile, behind the wall of Chinese rhetoric, a team of investigators from the BBC News program *Panorama* released a damning report that documented persistent and recent evidence that Beijing had grossly violated the UN arms embargo against Khartoum. The *Panorama* team found Chinese army trucks in Darfur; Chinese A5 Fan-tan fighter jets being used to strafe civilians by Chinese-trained Sudanese pilots; and artillery pieces and anti-aircraft guns being used to destroy civilian houses, with up-to-date factory codes, model numbers, and registration numbers that led straight to Chinese factories. It comes as no surprise that the Chinese government declined to comment on the BBC's findings.[23]

Zimbabwe

Among the most vivid and best-known African examples of rogue dictators and Chinese "life-lines" is Zimbabwe. Robert Mugabe started his career in public life as a guerrilla hero in Mozambique, fighting in Zimbabwe-Rhodesia against the Ian Smith government. He emerged a national symbol in Zimbabwe's war of independence and became its first prime minister in 1980. Within a decade, however, Mugabe had changed the constitution to become executive leader, beginning his transition from freedom fighter to autocrat. The turning point in Zimbabwe's tragic narrative of decline came in 2000, when Mugabe sought to draw attention away from his own waning popularity and the country's incipient failure, using a campaign of black nationalism aimed at white farmers. The forced seizure of white-owned commercial farms caused an immediate decline in food production, and the country's farming-based economy, which had been known as the "bread-basket of Africa," soon collapsed. Over the next five years, Mugabe turned Zimbabwe's politics into a bizarre personality cult. There gradually emerged stories of widespread brutality, intimidation, and murder of opposition leaders, and the demolition of nearly one million homes in what Mugabe called a "cleanup" program against dissidents. Western leaders moved to condemn Mugabe. The United States declared Zimbabwe one of the world's great "outposts of tyranny." With an economy in free fall, an official inflation rate of 231 trillion percent, the U.S. dollar trading at 60 quadrillion to one in May 2009, and the international community up in arms, Mugabe faced almost total isolation.[24]

But if global conscience finally began to galvanize into calls for action, they were soon blunted by a more powerful force. China moved to use its position on the UN Security Council to block any attempt to act against the Zimbabwe regime. In July 2008, after vetoing a resolution that would have imposed UN sanctions on Mugabe and his inner circle, Chinese Ambassador Wang Guangya simply said, "To use or threaten to use sanctions lightly is not conducive to solving a problem."[25] What problem did Beijing have in mind, one asks, and what did the Chinese do to solve it?

The answer from Beijing appeared to be arms sales and related hardware that read like a worried dictator's shopping list:

water cannons to subdue protesters, bugging equipment to monitor cell phone networks, military-grade radio-jamming equipment to block non-state-controlled media, Internet surveillance equipment, small arms, munitions, fighter jets, and army trucks. The Chinese didn't stop there. Trade receipts also included a large mansion done in the Chinese architectural style, plus a helipad and an honorary degree for Mr. Mugabe.[26]

MYANMAR

A military junta has ruled Burma—today called Myanmar—since 1962, systematically impoverishing a country once recognized for its high literacy rate and abundant natural resources. Burma today is one of the poorest countries in Asia and one of the most strictly controlled dictatorships in the world. Its economy relies heavily on the transport and sale of contraband—particularly, illegal drugs. The political culture is among the most oppressive in the world, with sustained human rights abuses, forced labor, military rape of civilians, political imprisonment, torture, trafficking of people, and the use of child soldiers. It is a dark place, in other words. The last significant popular uprising in 1988 left thousands killed by the Burmese military, and the politician Aung San Suu Kyi—the leader of the National League for Democracy in Burma and Nobel Prize winner—has been under house arrest and threat of imprisonment since she won elections for a multiparty parliament in 1990—elections that were ignored by the junta. In June 2009, the regime sentenced her to five years in prison for breaching the terms of her house arrest in a bizarre incident in which an intruder, whom she didn't know, was found to have spent the night in her lakeside home. The sentence conveniently removes her from the coming 2010 national elections.

Burma has been a pariah state since 1988, when the United States began to impose a number of sanctions on financial assistance and military equipment. The United Nations initiated a series of missions to Rangoon in 2000 aimed at opening a dialogue with the junta and promoting a transition to better governance. Some ten trips have yet to yield progress.[27]

An underlying cause for the stalemate lies in Beijing. Like the leaders of Angola, Uzbekistan, Sudan, and others, the Burmese junta have little to fear from being labeled a pariah state by the West when they can get what they need in greater amounts and with less effort from China. While UN envoys were attempting, with a mixture of sanctions and promises, to exert pressure on Burmese leaders to change their behavior, Beijing became Rangoon's best friend, providing debt relief and loans, each to the tune of $30 million; FDI in excess of $280 million per year; technical assistance in oil, gas, and mining projects; and military equipment in the form of tanks, armored personnel carriers, fighter jets, attack aircraft, coastal patrol ships, small arms, and light weapons.[28]

VENEZUELA

Venezuela's flamboyant leader, Hugo Chávez, has been a particularly enthusiastic promoter of the new opportunities that China provides as a non-Western source of support in global affairs. Since assuming power in 1998, Chávez has fashioned his political persona to reflect a vivid anti-Americanism, using it to build alliances in Latin America, Russia, the Middle East, and beyond.

Domestically, the Chávez regime has overseen a gradual slide toward authoritarianism. Media outlets criticizing him have suffered heavy fines or lost their license to broadcast, as happened to Radio Caracas Television in 2007. Political dissent is increasingly suppressed through intimidation and false allegations of criminal behavior, such as those leveled at opposition leader Manuel Rosales after he lost to Chávez in the 2006 presidential vote. Rosales eventually fled the country in 2009 for political asylum in Peru. In February of the same year, Chávez won a referendum to change the constitution, ending presidential term limits and allowing him to run for reelection indefinitely.[29]

In the meantime, Venezuela's foreign relations have adhered to the overriding principle of making common cause with those who are anti-American and providing a platform for developments in the region that would assert Venezuela's independence from the United States.

Among the more notable examples is Chávez's new relationship with Moscow. In the fall of 2008, Chávez visited Russia twice, meeting with Russian President Dmitry Medvedev and Prime Minister Vladimir Putin to discuss oil sales to Russia and Chávez's proposal to switch his oil transactions from dollars to euros. Also a part of their highly publicized discussions were arrangements for joint naval exercises in the Caribbean that November led by the Russian nuclear cruiser *Peter the Great*, and Russia's extension of a $1 billion credit to purchase Russian weapons. For good measure, Chávez offered his views on the financial crisis in the United States: "The crisis is terrible. It is hard to imagine the consequences. Vladimir Putin and I discussed this situation yesterday. Thank God, Russia and Venezuela are confidently moving forward. Our cooperation is becoming stronger."[30]

In the region itself, Caracas has confronted Washington directly in attempts to change the designation of the Fuerzas

Armadas Revolucionarias de Colombia (FARC)—an organization classified as a terrorist group by the United States, Canada, and the European Union—from a "terrorist" to a "political" organization.[31] And as if to be certain he did not miss one of Washington's hot buttons, Chávez has repeatedly and publicly defended Iran's nuclear ambitions, making several high-profile trips to Tehran to do so.[32] And finally, in June 2009, Chávez endorsed the outcome of Iran's presidential elections as fair and free.

Amid all the anti-American bluster, the United States is, remarkably, Venezuela's largest oil-trading partner. This might otherwise present an opportunity for leverage by Washington, except that Venezuelan dependence on American consumers is being rapidly reduced. Once again, the path around the West goes through China, where Venezuela has found an increasingly oil-hungry alternative. As Chávez announced in 2007, China is set to rival the United States as a major oil buyer with various new agreements between Caracas and Beijing for Venezuela to expand production and ship its "heavy crude" oil to China, and for China to build a new refinery to process it.[33]

Pursuant to the Chinese strategy of peaceful development and its determination to avoid directly confronting the United States, however, China reacted with caution when Chávez threatened to stop exporting oil products to the United States, and thus drew back from a potential role in Chávez's American drama. This case demonstrates Beijing's strategic discipline: It strikes a careful balance between a willingness to circumvent American preferences on the one hand and a calibrated avoidance of undue alarm—read adverse consequences—on the other.

IRAN

China has provided a similar source of confidence for leaders in Tehran, where the former Revolutionary Guards officer Mahmoud Ahmadinejad won Iran's presidential election in 2005. After coming to power, Ahmadinejad wasted little time in clamping down on free speech and political dissent at home. He asserted Iran's right to develop nuclear energy and to administer a nuclear fuel cycle, as other nations have done, without international oversight, underscoring the issue of Iranian sovereignty. By September 2005, Iran had set the scene for an international crisis, with announcements that it had resumed the enrichment of uranium. This was coupled with a steady stream of belligerent statements from Ahmadinejad, emphasizing that Iran had the right to defend itself from Western imperialists and that Israel should be "wiped off the pages of history."[34]

Over the next twelve months, Western governments moved to isolate Tehran economically and politically. In the process, however, they found that the regime had a powerful, and by now familiar, source of diplomatic cover. As Washington and Brussels sought to mobilize an international coalition to dissuade Tehran from developing nuclear technology by threat of sanctions, Beijing moved to block them.

In September 2005, for instance, the European Union released a draft resolution to the International Atomic Energy Agency (IAEA), which threatened to bring the Iranian nuclear question to the Security Council with a view to stiff sanctions. Alongside Russia (which has extensive commercial relations with Iran), China expressed its opposition to the action and insisted the resolution be watered down if there were to be Chinese support on the Security Council floor. The resolution

was eventually abandoned. Instead, a revised version was released for vote in the IAEA, where Venezuela voted against
while China and Russia led a group of twelve abstentions, including a range of countries that Iran had courted, such as Algeria, Nigeria, Tunisia, Yemen, Vietnam, Sri Lanka, Pakistan,
South Africa, Brazil, and Mexico.[35] And then when the United
States, the United Kingdom, and France announced at a special
session of the UN Security Council on September 25, 2009,
that Iran was enriching uranium at a secret underground fa-
cility that could have only military objectives, China alone
among the "Permanent Five" refused to commit to further
sanctions barring progress by an October deadline.

Admittedly, China has since taken some limited steps to
mollify American and international concerns, such as the meeting in September 2008 between Hu Jintao and Ahmadinejad,
in which Hu iterated support for the nuclear nonproliferation
regime,[36] and China's support in November 2009 for the
IAEA's demand that inspectors have access to the "secret" site
at Qom. It is unclear, however, whether these efforts were in
essence public relations or serious policy.

In recent years, there's little doubt that supplies from China
have greatly exacerbated the most troublesome proliferation
trends in various places. These have included ambiguous technical assistance; long-range missile technology, including skins,
gyros, and warhead design; and acquiescence to "third-party"
transfers, where the ultimate recipients of sanctioned technologies are in violation of "end-user" agreements to which China
is a party. As a January 2009 congressional report concluded,
China has been a "key supplier" to all the major "serial proliferators."[37] In just the last ten years, the U.S. government has
imposed sanctions on thirty-four Chinese companies for transfers of sensitive technology and hardware to Pakistan, Iran,

North Korea, Syria, and Libya. These transfers included components for weapons of mass destruction, cruise ballistic missiles, blueprints, equipment, and chemical weapons technology.[38] (See Table 3.1 for more details.)

The all-important driver in this process? *Business, plain and simple.* In blocking international efforts to bring Tehran to account, Beijing profited from its commercial links with Iran, securing vital energy contracts. While European and American businesses removed their investments from Iran to satisfy the sanction policies of their governments, Chinese enterprise moved in to fill the gap.[39] China is the single largest buyer of Iranian oil and gas. Between 2006 and 2007, Beijing signed contracts with Tehran that guarantee annual exports of ten million tons of natural gas to China over the next twenty-five years, plus guarantees of exploration and drilling rights in Iran for China's state oil company, China National Petroleum Corporation. Chinese companies have, moreover, secured contracts for new highways in Iran alongside a billion-dollar subway system. Iran has also been a useful market for Chinese exports in arms and advanced technology, including antiship cruise missiles, antitank missiles, sophisticated naval mines, missile control and guidance systems, chemical-weapon precursors, and nuclear materials. These deals serve two functions: They help to keep the lights on and the factories running in China's high-speed industrial revolution, and they also provide a useful check on Western influence in the Middle East.[40]

AFRICA AND THE HUMAN COST OF THE CHINA EFFECT

Beijing plays the iniquitous partner—the Mr. Hyde—to the malcontents of international society, while it simultaneously plays Dr. Jekyll, an honest stakeholder in global civic culture.

Table 3.1 Chinese Entities Sanctioned for Weapons Proliferation, 2004–2008

Entity/Person	Reason: Statutes	Effective Dates
- Beijing Institute of Opto-Electronic Technology (BIOET) - NORINCO - CPMIEC - Oriental Scientific Instruments Corporation (OSIC) - Zibo Chemical Equipment Plant (aka Chemet Global Ltd, South Industries Science and Technology Trading Company)	Weapons Proliferation: §3. Iran Nonproliferation Act (unspecified transfers to Iran controlled under multilateral export control lists or having the potential to make a material contribution to WMD or cruise or ballistic missiles)	April 1, 2004 for two years
- Xinshidai (aka China Xinshidai Company, XSD, China New Era Group, or New Era Group)	Missile proliferation: Executive Order 12938 (as amended by Executive Order 13094) (material contribution to missile proliferation in publicly unnamed country)	September 20, 2004 for two years
- Beijing Institute of Aerodynamics - BIOET - China Great Wall Industry Corporation - NORINCO - LIMMT Economic and Trade Company, Ltd. - OSIC - South Industries Science and Technology Trading Co.	Weapons Proliferation: §3. Iran Nonproliferation Act (unspecified transfers to Iran controlled under multilateral export control lists or having the potential to make a material contribution to WMD or cruise or ballistic missiles)	September 23, 2004 for two years
- Liaoning Jiayi Metals and Minerals Co. - Q.C. Chen - Wha Cheong Tai Co. Ltd. - Shanghai Triple International Ltd.	Weapons Proliferation: §3. Iran Nonproliferation Act (unspecified transfers to Iran controlled under multilateral export control lists or having the potential to make a material contribution to WMD or cruise or ballistic missiles)	November 24, 2004 for two years
- Beijing Alite Technologies Company Ltd. - CATIC - China Great Wall Industry Corporation - NORINCO - Q.C. Chen - Wha Cheong Tai Company (aka Wah Cheong Tai Co., Hua Chang Tai Co.) - Zibo Chemet Equipment Corp. (aka Chemet Global Ltd)	Weapons Proliferation: §3. Iran Nonproliferation Act (unspecified transfers to Iran controlled under multilateral export control lists or having the potential to make a material contribution to WMD or cruise or ballistic missiles)	December 27, 2004 for two years

Entity/Person	Reason: Statutes	Effective Dates
-CATIC	Missile and CW Proliferation:	December 23, 2005
-NORINCO	§3, Iran Nonproliferation Act	for two years
-Hongdu Aviation Industry Group	(unspecified transfers to Iran controlled under multilateral export control lists or having the potential to make a material contribution to WMD or cruise or ballistic missiles)	
-LIMMT Metallurgy and Minerals Company Ltd.		
-Ounion (Asia) International Economic and Technical Cooperation Ltd.		
-Zibo Chemet Equipment Company		
-Beijing Alite Technologies Company Ltd. (ALCO)	Missile Proliferation:	June 13, 2006
-LIMMT Economic and Trade Company Ltd.	Executive Order 13382	On June 19, 2008, sanctions lifted against CGWIC and G.W. Aerospace
-China Great Wall Industry Corporation (CGWIC)	(transfers to Iran's military and other organizations of missile and dual-use components, including items controlled by the MTCR)	
-CPMIEC		
-G.W. Aerospace (a U.S. office of CGWIC)		
Great Wall Airlines (aka Changcheng Hangkong)	Missile Proliferation:	August 15, 2006
	Executive Order 13382	until December 12, 2006
	(unspecified transfers probably to Iran)	
-China National Electronic Import-Export Company	Weapons Proliferation:	December 28, 2006
-CATIC	§3, Iran and Syria Nonproliferation Act	for two years
-Zibo Chemet Equipment Company	(unspecified transfers to Iran controlled under multilateral export control lists or having the potential to make a material contribution to WMD or cruise or ballistic missiles)	
-CPMIEC	Weapons Proliferation:	April 17, 2007
-Shanghai Non-Ferrous Metals Pudong Development Trade Company Ltd.	§3, Iran and Syria Nonproliferation Act	for two years
-Zibo Chemet Equipment Company	(unspecified transfers to Iran controlled under multilateral export control lists or having the potential to make a material contribution to WMD or cruise or ballistic missiles)	

(continues)

(continued)

Table 3.1 Chinese Entities Sanctioned for Weapons Proliferation, 2004–2008

Entity	Reason	Date
-China Xinshidai Company	Weapons Proliferation:	October 23, 2008
-China Shipbuilding and Offshore International Corporation -Huazhong CNC	Iran, North Korea, and Syria Nonproliferation Act (unspecified transfers controlled under multilateral export control lists or having the potential to make a material contribution to WMD or cruise or ballistic missiles)	for two years
-Dalian Sunny Industries (aka LIMMT Economic and Trade Company, LIMMT (Dalian) Metallurgy and Minerals Company, and LIMMT (Dalian FTZ) Economic and Trade Organization) -Bellamax	Missile Proliferation: §73(a)(1), Arms Export Control Act §11B(b)(1), Export Administration Act	February 2, 2009 for two years Waived for PRC government activities related to missiles, electronics, space systems, and military aircraft
-Dalian Sunny Industries (aka LIMMT Economic and Trade Company, LIMMT (Dalian) Metallurgy and Minerals Company, and LIMMT (Dalian FTZ) Economic and Trade Organization) -Bellamax	Missile Proliferation: Executive Order 12938	February 2, 2009 for two years
-Fangwei LI (aka Karl LEE), c/o LIMMT Economic and Trade Company	Missile Proliferation: Executive Order 13382	April 7, 2009

Note: This table summarizes the discussion of sanctions in this CRS Report and was compiled based on publication of notices in the *Federal Register*, reports and statements of the Administration, legislation enacted by Congress, and news reports.

SOURCE: Shirley Kan, "China and Proliferation of Weapons of Mass Destruction and Missiles: Policy Issues," Congressional Research Service, July 27, 2009, 59–62, http://www.fas.org/sgp/crs/nuke/RL31555.pdf.

Nowhere is this duality clearer than in Africa. Africa is all too often the subject of broad generalizations. As one British colonialist said about the space between stereotypes and reality on the varied continent, "Africa doesn't exist. I should know—I've been there." Notwithstanding, there are certain broad themes that apply to the Chinese footprint in the region.

Chinese investment in Africa is driven as much by private companies as by state-owned enterprises, but a close relationship persists between individual corporate interests and the national government. The explosion of private and state-owned Chinese investment in Africa has been facilitated by an official "go out" policy. This has pushed investment to all four corners of the continent, using a mixture of soft loans, subsidies, business development centers, and information programs to help companies and officials match products and markets in specific countries.[41]

Chinese leaders have repeatedly said that these programs are not a form of charity, something they have little interest in. Rather, the programs are designed to establish relationships of "mutual benefit" between Beijing and African leaders who can provide what China needs in terms of natural resources, markets for Chinese goods, and business partners for Chinese companies. Chinese companies, often with government support, have brought a large number of infrastructure and industrial projects to Africa, with generally positive results. From railways and bridges to hospitals, schools, roads, electricity grids, and telephone networks, these companies have been instrumental in bringing a modern infrastructure to parts of the world that the West had chosen to overlook. The government has also been swift in canceling debts owed by African governments.

But as Senegalese journalist Adama Gaye remarks, China's sudden interest has little to do with philanthropy.[42] The

Chinese footprint in Africa is yielding negative effects, with serious human costs that often far outweigh the benefits.[43] Henning Melber, an Africanist at the Dag Hammarskjöld Foundation, argues that much of China's presence in Africa is really just "old wine in new bottles." After all, he comments, "the Chinese penetration only presents the ugly face of predatory capitalism, which for far too long has already abused the dependency of the majority on the continent."[44]

Like the West in another era, China's African presence most often benefits the elites and oligarchs in these societies, not ordinary citizens.[45] If you run an African country with natural resources, you've got a friend in the East who will write big checks with no embarrassing questions (which is different from Shell in Nigeria, for example, which is subject to the Foreign Corrupt Practices Act). This is good for leaders, but not necessarily good for their misgoverned people.[46] China's strict refusal to act in ways that would, in its view, violate a country's sovereignty has meant China has remained apart from such issues as civil liberties, rule of law, human rights, and democratic governance. For precisely this reason, relations have soured between Chinese officials and some African populations, with a widening gap in China's popularity between popular and official levels in Africa. Large Chinese corporations and state-owned enterprises are often followed by an influx of Chinese trading shops and small retailers providing a full range of services, from clothing emporiums to restaurants to bordellos. These supporting networks frequently undermine the local economy and drive out traditional suppliers with low-cost, low-quality goods. It is far from a level playing field: The Chinese businesses in Africa enjoy numerous advantages, including easy access to finance and supplies in China, and the benefit of diligent workers.

The implications of China in Africa go beyond the frustration of ordinary Africans about substandard products and the competition from Chinese small businesses. Economic history tells us that societies can only develop into "modern economies" when they begin to turn raw materials into manufactured goods. This requires industry, and it is the industrial nations that in turn become rich and powerful. Chris Alden, a leading expert in China-Africa relations, explains that if African countries wish to develop their economy and raise their populations out of poverty, as China did, they must move beyond merely being resource exporters to the outside world.[47] This cannot happen in many parts of Africa, however, so long as the countries remain trapped in their role as a primary source of raw materials and a market for substandard consumer goods from elsewhere. To this extent, the authorities in Beijing have struck a troubling deal with much of the continent. Beijing pours billions of dollars in gifts and low-interest loans into the coffers of corrupt African regimes. Meanwhile, these regimes provide access to resources and a dumping ground for poor-quality products that would be unacceptable in Western markets.

There's also a tragedy in the timing of China's rise in Africa. Renewed Chinese interest there coincides with newly discovered levels of conscience and attention from the West. From new AIDS initiatives under the Bush administration to French peacekeepers on the Ivory Coast, the first decade of the twenty-first century has seen the West's open recognition of its checkered past on the continent and institutionalized commitments to defeat poverty and disease and promote sustainable development in the region. The West still suffers, naturally, from the vestiges of European colonialism and from Cold War interventions—perceptions that have eased the Chinese presence. President Yoweri Kaguta Museveni of Uganda laid bare this dynamic in 2006: "The western ruling groups are conceited, full of themselves, ignorant of our conditions, and they make other people's business their business, while the Chinese just deal with you as one who represents your country, and for them they represent their own interests and you just do business."[48]

Despite newfound conscience and commitment from the West, Chinese commercial relations have become a more powerful countervailing force than the new Western conscience in Africa. Table 3.2, for example, shows the flow of Chinese aid and gift projects to those African states that the international watchdog Freedom House has listed as suffering from bad governance. Assistance typically includes palaces, highways, railways, power stations, stadia, and the like. Some of these provisions are highly positive in human terms—such as water supply projects and primary schools. But the trend presents an unmistakable challenge to Western preeminence. China's supportive relations with these states enable their governments to survive and develop without Western assistance and without pressure to make reforms in line with Western values and sensibilities.

Table 3.2 Chinese Assistance to Africa by Countries Deemed Totally or Partly "Unfree" by Freedom House

Country	Assistance Provided
Angola	Debt relief, US$2 billion loan
Burundi	Textile mill, hydroelectric power station, highway
Cameroon	Conference building, hydroelectric power station, hospitals
Chad*	—
Central African Republic	Agricultural technological station, radio station, training center, clinics
Congo (Brazzaville)	Stadium, hydroelectric power station, broadcasting station, hospital, factory
Democratic Republic Congo (DRC)	Stadium, trade center, people's palace, factories
Comoros	Government office building, water supply project, people's palace
Djibouti	Stadium, government office building, people's palace, housing project, Eritrea humanitarian assistance, hospital
Equatorial Guinea	Hydroelectric power station, radio station, highways
Ethiopia	Highway, veterinary center, power station, water supply project
Gabon	Health-care center, primary school, assembly building
Ghana	National theater, irrigation project, vocational training center, hospital
Guinea	People's palace, hydroelectric power station, cinema, presidential palace
Guinea Bissau	Housing project, power-generating equipment, technical cooperation
Ivory Coast	Theater, water conservation project
Liberia	Sugar mill, rice project, sports stadium, hospital renovation, office building
Malawi*	—
Mozambique	Textile mill, passenger cargo vessel, water supply project, shoe factory, parliament building, housing project
Niger	Stadium, water supply project, textile mills, housing project
Nigeria	Railway upgrade
Rwanda	Highway, cement factory, veterinary school
Seychelles	Swimming pool, housing projects, schools
Sierra Leone	Roads, bridges, stadium, sugar complex, office building, hydroelectric power station, civil housing
Sudan*	—
Tanzania	Tanzania-Zambia railway, textile mill, rice project, sugar factory, coal mine
Togo	Conference building, sugar refinery, stadium, hospital, irrigation project
Uganda	Stadium, rice projects, factories
Zambia	Tanzania-Zambia railway, roads, factories, textile mill, water supply project
Zimbabwe	Stadium, hospitals, dams, factories

* The total amount of aid is unknown

SOURCE: People's Republic of China, Ministry of Foreign Affairs, Department of Africa Affairs, "Countries in the Region" and "Regional Organizations and Issues," www.fmprc.gov .cn/eng/wjb/zzjg/fzs/default.htm; Judith van de Looy, "Africa and China: A Strategic Partnership?" working paper 67/2006, African Studies Centre, Leiden, 10–11; "Map of Freedom," Freedom House, 2008, www.freedomhouse.org/uploads/MOF2008.pdf).

CHAPTER 4

THE COMPETITIVE EDGE: "STATE-DIRECTED CAPITALISM"

SENEGAL'S PRESIDENT ABDOULAYE WADE asserted in 2008 that with fewer conditions, less bureaucracy, and a much faster timeline, "China's approach to our needs is simply better adapted than the slow and sometimes patronizing post-colonial approach of European investors, donor organizations and non-governmental organizations." As Wade recounts, "I have found that a contract that would take five years to discuss, negotiate and sign with the World Bank takes three months from inception to conclusion with Chinese authorities. I am a firm believer in good governance and the rule of law. But when bureaucracy and senseless red tape impede our ability to act—and when poverty persists while international functionaries drag their feet—African leaders have an obligation to opt for swifter solutions. I achieved more in my one hour meeting with President Hu Jintao in an executive suite at my hotel in Berlin during the recent G8 meeting in Heiligendamm than I did during the entire, orchestrated meeting of world leaders at the summit, where African leaders were told little more than that G8 nations would respect existing commitments."[1]

The terms, the conditions and arrangements, of state-directed capitalism give Beijing a distinct edge over Western competitors. State subsidies of Chinese firms provide the incentive needed to pursue overseas projects that may not be profitable, but which accomplish long-term strategic PRC investment and commodity access goals. For instance, the U.S. Congressional Research Service reports that beyond the persistent problem of bribes paid by both Chinese and Western firms, state-backed Chinese firms have paid above-market prices for shares in African state energy firms in order to guarantee access to oil supplies; these firms have also entered unprofitable bids on projects to pave the way for future contracts and closer bilateral ties.[2]

Moreover, China's political system provides a further commercial advantage over rivals in the United States, Europe, and Japan. Liberal democracies must deal with powerful domestic interest groups in business and the legislature. The absence of domestic political obstacles enables Chinese companies and government actors to forge agreements much more rapidly than their Western counterparts.[3]

Chinese success in Africa, therefore, has much to do with Western failure. Beijing's competitive edge has been equally visible in Latin America—especially during the recent global economic crisis. The *New York Times* reported in April 2009, for example, that while White House officials sought to rebuild strained relationships with Latin America, China was "stepping in" amid the gloom of the gathering downturn and offering large amounts of money to struggling and grateful economies. Deals included a $12 billion development fund for Venezuela, a $1 billion loan to Ecuador, and $10 billion each to Argentina and Brazil. These loans pointed to a deeper engagement with the region at the same moment when the new Obama administration was struggling to address the erosion of Washington's influence in the hemisphere. Reactions from the locals offered a familiar story. The Venezuelan government reiterated that Chinese aid differed from other kinds of multilateral assistance because it came without "strings attached," such as "scrutiny of internal finances." "This is China playing the long game," with financial assistance as a chip that translates into long-term political influence.[4]

To smooth this process, Beijing has approached the leaders of these smaller, poorer countries with flattery, feting them with honors and receptions they would not receive from the West. Dan Erickson, at the Washington-based think tank Inter-American Dialogue, emphasizes that smaller countries appreciate being treated as other heads of state when they come to China, so even if they come from Saint Kitts and Nevis, they get deference from Beijing, which they might not get in Washington.[5]

Though there are numerous examples of situations in which the Chinese have a commercial advantage, American national security experts like the late Peter Rodman maintained that Western companies still have an unbeatable trump card: Their technology and experience are far superior to what has been offered by most Chinese companies.[6] Rodman was correct, of course. But this argument isn't as straightforward as it sounds. Even if Chinese technology lags considerably behind its Western and Japanese counterparts, Joshua Kurlantzick retorts, a number of developing countries believe that Chinese companies are more willing to share what they have.[7]

In another dimension, China's rising influence coincides with a period of episodic and inconsistent U.S. attention. In what is bound to be a costly lesson for Washington and not easily corrected, a vacuum developed as the Bush administration appeared to abandon the active pursuit of statecraft in most areas of diplomacy except terrorism. A 2008 study for the Senate Foreign Relations Committee underscored this, concluding that since 9/11, American diplomacy had built a reputation in Africa for being interested in little more than the war on terrorism and the war in Iraq. Africa was not alone in this regard. The theme of U.S. inattentiveness was typified by then U.S. Secretary of State Condoleezza Rice's decision in 2007 to bypass the annual ASEAN Regional Forum and instead to travel to the Middle East. President Bush skipped the U.S.-ASEAN summit, which had been set for Singapore in September, and left the Asia-Pacific Economic Cooperation (APEC) summit a day early so he could turn his mind to another more pressing commitment: Iraq.[8]

COMMERCIAL RELATIONS AS DIPLOMATIC SUPPORT

Examples of the China effect enumerated in this chapter span several countries and regions. Yet, a majority of them have two elements in common: the presence of natural resources and the potential for new markets. But these are not the only benefits to China's deepening penetration of developing markets. Its affinity for questionable neighborhoods and the eager friendship of pariah regimes help to serve other important objectives. As mentioned in the preface, evidence suggests that Chinese commercial engagement in fact *does* come with conditions of a kind, albeit limited and less invasive than Western stipulations for societal change. China consistently gleans support from its trading partners on a handful of key issues: human rights, Taiwan, Tibet, and sovereignty.

Almost every time China establishes new commercial relations with a developing nation, the same formulaic communiqué is issued from Beijing. Two diplomats from their respective governments are photographed shaking hands in the Great Hall of the People. Underneath the photograph is an official description of various bilateral agreements for loans, aid, trade, and investment between China and its new commercial partner. While the statement is short, it finds space to iterate a new level of diplomatic cooperation. See China's agreement with Ethiopia in November 2005, when Chinese Vice President Zeng Qinghong "expressed appreciation for Ethiopia's adherence to the one-China policy and support for China's unification cause"; or with the leader of Guinea, who, "hailing the close coordination in international affairs, he expressed gratitude for Guinea's support on the Taiwan and Tibet issues"; or with Gabon, which "voiced support for China's reunification" and "reiterated that there is only one China in the world, with the government of the People's Republic of China being the sole legal government representing China as a whole and Taiwan being an inalienable part of China"; or with Guinea Bissau, which "will steadfastly support China's position on the issues concerning Taiwan and Tibet"; or with Mali, which "will firmly adhere to the one-China policy and support China's unification cause"; or Namibia, which promised to support China "in international affairs through close cooperation and coordination" and "to maintain close cooperation in the UN and other multilateral organizations in order to safeguard the common interests of the developing countries."[9]

China's top legislator Wu Bangguo carried out a similar handshake-and-photo performance in 2008 with the chairman of the African Union (AU), Jean Ping, who officially "reaffirmed [that] the AU Commission and most African countries will always adhere to the one-China policy and other principled positions like the Tibet issue."[10] If commercial relations buy political and diplomatic support from the African nations, then China-Africa trade statistics of the last decade provide a graphic illustration of China's increased influence (Figure 4.1).

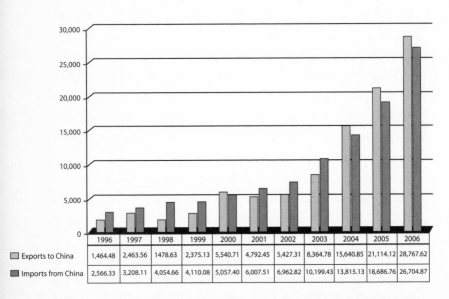

Figure 4.1   China-Africa Trade Statistics, 1995–2006 (in billions of dollars)

	1996	1997	1998	1999	2000	2001	2002	2003	2004	2005	2006
Exports to China	1,464.48	2,463.56	1478.63	2,375.13	5,540.71	4,792.45	5,427.31	8,364.78	15,640.85	21,114.12	28,767.62
Imports from China	2,566.33	3,208.11	4,054.66	4,110.08	5,057.40	6,007.51	6,962.82	10,199.43	13,815.13	18,686.76	26,704.87

SOURCE: Christopher Burke, Lucy Corkin, and Nastasya Tay, "China's Engagement of Africa: Preliminary Scoping of African Case Studies, Angola, Ethiopia, Gabon, Uganda, South Africa, Zambia," Rockefeller Foundation report, Centre for Chinese Studies, University of Stellenbosch, November 2007, 3, http://www.ccs.org.za/downloads/RF_Paper_Final.pdf.

THE DRIVE TO ISOLATE TAIWAN

An equally important element in Chinese engagement with the developing world has been its diplomatic crusade to isolate Taiwan—an ally of the United States and one that Washington has pledged to defend, as detailed in the Taiwan Relations Act passed by Congress in 1979. The map of states that have shifted diplomatic relations from Taipei to Beijing in recent years further illustrates where China's finance, trade, and investment have brought new influence. At the time of writing, the only African countries left that recognize Taiwan were Burkina Faso, Gambia, São Tomé and Príncipe, and Swaziland. This is not a new struggle. But recent years have seen a sharp decline in the number of countries that have diplomatic relations with Taiwan. The cause for the decline is simple: China's artful application of checkbook diplomacy.

In January 2008, Malawi announced it had cut diplomatic relations with Taiwan; Taipei couldn't match the Chinese offer of $6 billion in aid.[11] Malawi was the fourth country to break relations with Taiwan in three years. In a similar format, Senegal broke relations with Taiwan in October 2005, signing an agreement that reportedly included an initial $600 million in financial assistance from China.[12] Chad followed suit the following year after a series of secret meetings with Chinese officials, for which the specific amounts involved were not revealed.[13]

Thus, the Chinese government uses its growing commercial ties in Africa for diplomatic purposes. Beijing passed an anti-secession law in 2005, for instance, that legalized "nonpeaceful means" to secure Taiwan and protect Chinese sovereignty if the island declared independence. In what must be a harbinger of times to come when China's core interests are in play on the global stage, a number of African countries moved quickly to provide diplomatic support. Alongside the African Union, various governments, including Zambia, Lesotho, Egypt, Eritrea, Mali, Gabon, Ethiopia, Zimbabwe, Madagascar, Rwanda, Guinea-Bissau, Uganda, Guinea, Namibia, Burundi, Comoros, Central African Republic, and South Africa, issued formal declarations, extending their full support for the antisecession law.[14]

This kind of diplomatic support was further evident when China sought to thwart Japan's attempt to gain a permanent seat on the UN Security Council. In that instance, the Chinese mobilized various African states at the Asian-African Summit in April 2005 to stop the summit from endorsing a Japanese seat.[15] Another case in point is found on September 2007, when the UN General Assembly decided not to place the issue of Taiwan's membership on the UN agenda, blocking Taipei's fifteenth consecutive bid. An Associated Press headline at the time read, "China Thanks Africans for Defeating Taiwan's Bid to join UN."[16] According to a joint communiqué with South Africa shortly afterward, "the Chinese side noted with appreciation the position taken by South Africa and other countries, against Taiwan's bid for UN membership during the 62nd session of the UN General Assembly."[17]

Similar strategies to isolate Taiwan have worked in Latin America. (See Table 4.1 for the current status of China-Taiwan competition for recognition.) During a vote in 2007 on Taiwan's membership in the World Health Organization—something that Beijing has consistently blocked—Panama and Nicaragua both abstained, while Costa Rica voted against its membership. This is important on two levels. First, only months later, Costa Rican President Oscar Arias switched

Table 4.1   China (PRC) Versus Taiwan (ROC): Diplomatic
Recognition in Latin America and the Caribbean

Countries Recognizing China (PRC)	Countries Recognizing the Republic of China, or ROC (Taiwan)
Mexico	
Central America Costa Rica	El Salvador, Guatemala, Honduras, Nicaragua, Panama
Caribbean Antigua and Barbuda, Bahamas, Barbados, Cuba, Dominica, Grenada, Guyana, Jamaica, Suriname, Trinidad and Tobago	Belize, Dominican Republic, Haiti, St. Kitts and Nevis, St. Lucia, St. Vincent and the Grenadines
South America Argentina, Bolivia, Brazil, Chile, Colombia, Ecuador, Peru, Uruguay, Venezuela	Paraguay[a]

[a] President-elect Fernando Lugo, who took office in August 2008, announced after his election in April that his government would establish relations with China.

SOURCE: Thomas Lum, ed., "Comparing Global Influence: China's and U.S. Diplomacy, Foreign Aid, Trade, and Investment in the Developing World," Congressional Research Service, August 15, 2008, 159, http://www.fas.org/sgp/crs/row/RL34620.pdf.

diplomatic recognition to China, citing the growth of trade relations in recent years and the prospect for increased Chinese trade and investment. But secondly, Panama and Nicaragua are countries that still ostensibly recognize Taiwan. Their abstentions just happened to coincide with increased Chinese trade in both cases.

These events suggest trends more nuanced than simple bloc politics. Not only is Beijing building a string of alliances across the globe with nations overlooked and sometimes shunned by the United States, it also aims increasingly closer to America's heart by attempting, if not to win over U.S. allies, then at least to complicate the loyalties of those who continue to sit in an ostensibly Western camp.[18]

In January 2007, the *International Herald Tribune* asserted that Chinese support *does* come with conditions; it is forthcoming only for those who uphold China's position on Taiwan. This, of course, is not strictly so, for the same holds true for China's position on human rights at the United Nations. The notion that China and the developing world held common views on human rights and sovereignty was an overriding theme in 2006 at the Forum on China-Africa Cooperation (FOCAC) in Beijing.

First launched in 2000, FOCAC is often viewed as a de facto inauguration ceremony for China's twenty-first-century march into Africa. Later conferences were held in 2003 and, more recently, in 2006. In the same year, the UN General Assembly replaced the UN Commission on Human Rights with a new version called the UN Human Rights Council (UNHRC). China took the opportunity at FOCAC to release a joint Sino-African statement, which welcomed the establishment of the new UNHRC, but also emphasized that the United Nations should "make concerted efforts to ensure that the Council respects the historical, cultural and religious background of all countries and regions." Thinly veiled, the implication was clear: China and its allies believe that multilateral bodies like the UNHRC should respect the national boundaries of sovereignty, *and mind their own business.*[19] The number of countries included on the FOCAC rosters is not insubstantial:

Algeria	Eritrea	Namibia
Angola	Ethiopia	Niger
Benin	Gabon	Nigeria
Botswana	Ghana	Rwanda
Burundi	Guinea	Senegal
Cameroon	Guinea-Bissau	Seychelles
Cape Verde	Kenya	Sierra Leone
Central African	Lesotho	Somalia
Republic	Liberia	South Africa
Chad	Libya	Sudan
Comoros	Madagascar	Tanzania
Congo	Malawi	Togo
Côte d'Ivoire	Mali	Tunisia
DR Congo	Mauritania	Uganda
Djibouti	Mauritius	Zambia
Egypt	Morocco	Zimbabwe
Equatorial Guinea	Mozambique	

LET'S DO THE NUMBERS

Africa's numerical advantages and its tendency toward bloc voting have made it an important source of multilateral support for China. One-third of the votes in the UN General Assembly, and nearly half the members of the Non-Aligned Movement, are African. These votes were crucial for China in the International Olympic Committee decision to award the 2008 Olympics to Beijing.

Over the past decade, African nations provided the bulk of support for blocking eleven anti-China votes at the United Nations.[20] Some of the most recent examples of pro-China voting on human rights came in 2007. Trade relations between South Africa and China have grown rapidly since 2003, with South African minerals and iron ore going to China while appliances and textiles come the other way. South Africa caused a stir in the international press in 2007 by unexpectedly joining China in a vote to block a UN resolution censuring Myanmar for human rights abuses, bringing criticism that South Africa had "forgotten the United Nation's role in abolishing apartheid."[21] It is no surprise that Beijing forged a solid relationship with South Africa at elite and political levels. Chinese markets have also become a crucial destination for many of the largest South African companies (Figure 4.2).

Figure 4.2   Major South African Companies Operating in China

Naspers/MIH
Kumba Resources
Sasol
AngloGold Ashanti
Anglo Coal
Bateman
First National Bank
Goldfields
SAB Miller
Metspan
Old Mutual
Standard Bank
African Explosives Limited (AEL)
Spur
Freeplay
Landpac
Beijing Axis
Anglo America

SOURCE: Christopher Burke, Lucy Corkin, and Nastasya Tay, "China's Engagement of Africa: Preliminary Scoping of African Case Studies, Angola, Ethiopia, Gabon, Uganda, South Africa, Zambia," Rockefeller Foundation report, Centre for Chinese Studies, University of Stellenbosch, November 2007, 115, http://www.ccs.org.za/downloads/RF_Paper_Final.pdf.

Conforming to the new fashion, the South African government denied a visa for the Dalai Lama in 2009 to attend a peace conference of Nobel laureates in South Africa coincident with the 2010 Football World Cup. Officials indicated that they didn't wish to jeopardize bilateral relations with a major trading partner such as China. The government spokesman told Reuters that the Dalai Lama's presence "would not be in the best interests of South Africa at this time." This brought a sudden and stunning unanimous vote of protest by the conference organizers, including former Nobel Peace Prize winner Archbishop Desmond Tutu, who condemned the government's behavior as "disgraceful," saying, "we are shamelessly succumbing to Chinese pressure."[22] The Nobel laureates postponed the event indefinitely and departed South Africa.[23]

THE UN HUMAN RIGHTS COMMISSION

According to a September 2008 report on the United Nations from the European Council on Foreign Relations, the West is suffering a slow-motion crisis at the UNHRC. Support for Chinese positions on human rights—curtailing UN interventions to alleviate humanitarian catastrophes, genocides, and ethic cleansing—has jumped markedly from less than 50 percent at the beginning of this decade to 74 percent in 2008.[24] In the 1990s, the U.S./EU bloc at the United Nations enjoyed an average of 72 percent support on human rights issues in the UN General Assembly. Since then, this figure has dropped to the 48–55 percent range.

THE UN GENERAL ASSEMBLY

The figures for the United States alone were worse: A U.S. State Department annual report to Congress measuring the frequency with which the rest of the world voted with the United States in the General Assembly shows that support for U.S. positions has tumbled from more than 50 percent in 1995 to less than half that figure ten years later.[25] Forty-one nations that qualified as UN voting allies on human rights issues for the U.S./UN block ten years ago no longer do so, shifting their voting support to China and Russia. From Africa to Asia to Latin America, these include a notable list of Chinese commercial partners, such as Algeria, Angola, Botswana, Cape Verde, Central African Republic, Comoros, Egypt, Gabon, Lesotho, Malawi, Rwanda, Senegal, South Africa, Togo, Armenia, Azerbaijan, Bahrain, Bhutan, Jordan, Kazakhstan, Kuwait, Mongolia, Tajikistan, Thailand, Uzbekistan, Barbados, Bolivia, Costa Rica, Dominica, Guyana, Jamaica, and Suriname.[26] As their numbers have grown, and with success on key votes, many of these countries have joined to vigorously defend traditional sovereignty. Support for both China and Russia on this issue has exceeded 80 percent in recent years.[27]

THE WORLD TRADE ORGANIZATION

Acquiring African allies is also important to China in the World Trade Organization (WTO). There are thirty-eight African members of the WTO, again making it the largest regional bloc in that body. As China has won more friends in Africa, it has gained the power to frustrate specific rules it opposes.[28] Many of these countries, for example, have been targeted in China's pursuit of *market-economy status* (MES). This is an official WTO designation that helps to protect China from fines if it is found to violate antidumping statutes, and which the United States and the European Union currently refuse to afford to Beijing.

A bit of background is required here. Although China is considered a market economy in general terms, its two most important trading partners—the United States and the European Union—refuse to afford it official MES at the WTO on the grounds that China still exhibits significant state involvement in the economy and has an ineffective framework for dealing with critical problems such as bankruptcy and abuses of intellectual property rights.[29] MES is a valuable legal and trade designation at the WTO, especially for export-based economies such as China, because it prevents other countries from launching antidumping cases. In trade terms, dumping is a process whereby one country attempts to secure an unfair advantage in a foreign market by exporting a product to that country at a much lower price than what the product sells for or costs to make at home. If a country is accused of dumping, the complaint goes to the Directorate General for Trade (DGT) in Brussels, which determines, by comparing the price of the product abroad with the price in the exporter's own country, whether the exporter is guilty of dumping. If a serious discrepancy is found, then antidumping duties are normally imposed on the offending imports.[30]

A partly planned economy such as China can control the price of a product at home to coordinate with its price abroad. However, if the country does not have MES with the markets involved, then the DGT will compare the product price not to its home price, but to the product price in a surrogate country, such as India or Japan, to determine what the real costs of producing the goods are. Washington and Brussels are fully aware of the central interference that the Chinese government frequently exercises over the economy, and so they withhold MES. But here is where commercial ties provide the counterweight mentioned above. Russia, Egypt, Venezuela, South Africa, the ASEAN, and other countries have proven happy to extend this designation to Beijing on bilateral terms, in return for Chinese commercial engagement.[31]

Thus, in the realm of commerce and trade, unlike the military, U.S. predominance is being eroded by new connections and agreements among emerging economies and new middleweight powers that are forming their own clubs in accordance with their interests. China's growing footprint in South America is a good example. The realignment of power that flowed from the global economic crisis underscored China's new relationship with Brazil, for example, whose president, Luiz Inácio Lula da Silva, paid his second official visit to China in May 2009. The two countries have formed an easy marriage, as Brazil is rich in natural resources — such as petroleum, manganese, phosphates, bauxite, gold, iron ore, nickel, platinum, tin, uranium, timber, and hydropower — and China is hungry for the lot. Brazil is also eager to upgrade its infrastructure, and China can provide both the investment and the technical know-how to do so. It is hardly surprising, therefore, that China overtook the United States in March as the largest export market for goods from Brazil.[32] Developments of this kind have become commonplace across the region. Two months later, the China National Petroleum Corporation announced plans for Venezuela and China to build two joint refineries in China. Petrolos de Venezuela and China National Petroleum Corporation signed a framework agreement that included plans for Venezuela to export one million barrels of oil a day to China by 2011.[33]

As a Deutsche Bank study on Chinese investment in Latin America reports, between 2003 and 2006 alone, China announced a daunting raft of investments and contracts: an oil exploration deal with Ecuador; a framework agreement with Arcelor and Compania Vale do Rio Doce (CVRD) to build an integrated steel plant in Brazil, with an expected total investment volume of $1.5 billion; a deal to buy the Peruvian petroleum company PlusPetrol Norte for $200 million; a $20 billion investment in the course of 10 years in Argentina, with an $8 billion deal to expand the railway system and a $5 billion deal for oil exploration; a joint venture with Codelco, or the National Copper Company of Chile, with a projected amount of up to $2 billion; plans to invest $400 million in Venezuela's energy infrastructure, including oil and gas fields as well as railway and refinery infrastructure; plans to buy oil assets in Ecuador for $1.42 billion; a shared-production agreement for prospecting and exploiting crude oil with Cubapetroleo; and plans to invest US$500 million in Cuba's nickel industry.[34]

In 2009, U.S. Secretary of State Hillary Clinton was obliged to say that China was making "disturbing gains" in Latin America and that Washington could no longer afford to shun its various leaders, even if we don't agree with all they say. As she told an audience of Foreign Service officers at the State Department, "The prior administration tried to isolate them, tried to support opposition to them, tried to turn them into international pariahs. It didn't work."[35]

Instead, a new sense of common cause has developed among numerous constellations and associations of developing countries in opposition to Washington. The Doha Trade Round of 2008 provided the setting for China to deadlock trade talks by joining with India to insist that developing countries be allowed to impose prohibitively high tariffs on food imports from affluent countries. A majority of representatives from the global south promptly fell in line behind them. The *China Daily* described China's role as the champion of vulnerable farmers in the developing world who are threatened by the rich world. Underlying Beijing's course of action, of course, was a motive more about domestic requirements than a sense of fair trade for the global south; China's leaders needed to ensure that China's own peasant farmers could continue to produce a significant amount of the food for Chinese markets without being undercut by imports. Notwithstanding, the Doha talks had the crucial effect of helping to bring China and India together in a close partnership that stopped Western overtures in their tracks.[36]

In the multilateral arena, China is actually making progress on two fronts. The first is within international organizations that include both the United States and China, and which were previously viewed from Beijing with suspicion as U.S.-dominated institutions; these include the General Assembly, the WHO, and the WTO. The second front pertains to new multilateral organizations, where China has sought to expand its influence since the turn of the millennium with clubs that don't invite the United States to join. These include bodies like the East Asia Summit, the Forum on China-Africa Cooperation (FOCAC), and the Shanghai Cooperation Organization (SCO). In these venues, Chinese officials have not hesitated to combine soft power with a bit of muscle. African and Asian ambassadors have made off-the-record statements suggesting that China uses its aid and trade as leverage to make them tilt away from U.S. initiatives.[37] In other words, it is made plain that if the countries do not toe the line, or if they don't abstain when asked to do so, then economic projects, including foreign aid, could be put at risk.

THE POWER OF THE CHINESE EXAMPLE

The beginning of Chapter 3 suggests that Beijing has developed various ways of using its newfound financial strength to forge new relationships in the developing world and so change the complexion of international affairs. As these pages also argue, however, China's commercial expansion is equally the flagship of a second serious problem for the West. This is the growing appeal of the illiberal market model.

Across various parts of the global economy, says Eurasia Group president, Ian Bremmer, the free market is being overtaken by state capitalism, a system in which the state is the leading economic actor.[38] As the *Financial Times* reported in 2008, the topography of the world economy is being altered by the rise of state capitalism. From Asia to Russia and the Middle East, "governments are using their rising economic power in new ways. Sovereign wealth funds from the Gulf, Asia and elsewhere are buying stakes in ailing Wall Street investment banks; natural resources are falling under the control of the state; and in Russia and China, there is an emphasis on economic nationalism."[39]

What these developments really tell us is that the age of Western-style privatization and deregulation unleashed by Margaret Thatcher and Ronald Reagan in the 1980s is giving way to a world in which governments use their economic strength to buy strategic assets or exert global influence. But these events also signal the end of optimistic expectations about the transformative power of markets to globalize the principles of the European Enlightenment. The marriage of free politics and free economics is being replaced by governments determined to reassert control over their economies, enhancing both their autocratic base and their global influence. In the late eighteenth

century, laments Yale professor Jeffrey Garten, capitalism replaced feudalism, and by the end of the twentieth century, freer
markets had won the day. But now the world flirts with another major shift in the philosophy and the rules of global commerce. Unlike the changes of the past, this new trajectory does
not represent progress.[40]

If command-and-control capitalism signals a strategic rejection of the market-democratic doctrine, then it has emerged
with a handful of common characteristics. The most prominent is the development of large energy corporations and national champion companies, which are heavily in bed with
the ruling political elite. The largest thirteen oil companies
in the world are now owned and run by governments, including Brazil's Petrobas, Malaysia's Petronas, Iran's National Oil
Company, Venezuela's Petrolos de Venezuela, Saudi Arabia's
royal bureaucracy, China's China National Petroleum Corporation, and Russia's Gazprom and Rosneft.[41] Other sectors
also show a growing number of governments that are no
longer content with merely regulating the market. Instead,
they use state-owned or national champion industries to bolster their political position domestically. These industries range
from petrochemicals to power generation, mining, iron and
steel production, port management, shipping, weapons manufacturing, heavy machinery, telecommunications, and avia-
tion. Prominent examples now include uranium mining in
Brazil; nickel mining and steel production in Russia; railways,
cars, steel, and chemicals in India; telecommunications in China;
agro-industry in Algeria; phosphates production in Morocco;
diamond mining in Angola; uranium mining in Kazakhstan;
food and beverage production in the Philippines; and electricity grids in Azerbaijan.[42]

In the meantime, governments that have built up large reserves of currency through the export of natural resources or manufactured goods have often channeled this surplus into varied investment portfolios of commodities, real estate, equities, bonds, or foreign currencies on the global markets.[43] This process has seen the development of specific state-owned investment funds, or sovereign wealth funds (SWFs). As Martin Wolf observes, these are not in principle a new phenomenon. The oldest such fund actually dates back to 1953 in Kuwait.[44] In the last decade, however, SWFs have expanded dramatically in number and, of course, wealth. According to the Standard Chartered Global Research Group, the collective wealth of these funds is already valued at $2.2 trillion and could reach $13.4 trillion within a decade.[45] Notable examples include Dubai, Singapore, Kuwait, China, Russia, Singapore, Iran, Kazakhstan, Malaysia, South Korea, Brunei, Algeria, Saudi Arabia, and Qatar.[46]

Another common theme connecting these examples is the prevalence of tight links between the ruling elite and the company bosses. Commercial decisions in this context are heavily guided by political actors, and the motivation behind investment decisions are often as political as, or more political than, they are economic. The issue of domestic instability for the ruling elite holds considerable import for how businesses are managed and how markets perform.

As we've seen throughout this discussion, China is the example of this model par excellence. The country is fast becoming the most talked-about economy in the world, and yet, people still struggle to define exactly what it is—predominantly capitalistic or predominantly command-and-control? In reality, China offers the best example—a hybrid innovation—for the space that lies in between the two. Various sectors of the Chinese economy are very much private—retail, agriculture, and service industries (except for the banking industry). But then, large strategic sectors, such as steel, aluminum, energy, transport, communications, and the banking system, are owned by the government. An emphasis on domestic stability is the guiding philosophy for managing these sectors, both at home and abroad, through the application of national corporations, SWFs, and oligarchies entangled with and reliant on the ruling elite. We should also remember that economic liberalism in this context must be heavily "caveated." Periodically, the Chinese government does something to remind the rest of us that their commitment to free-market principles only goes so far. One had to laugh in May 2009, when local officials in Hubei Province were ordered to smoke a quarter of a million packs of Hubei-branded cigarettes in order to boost the local economy and stave off the downturn. Officials who failed to reach their targets or who were caught smoking non-Hubei brands faced fines. Even the teachers of local schools were issued with smoking quotas. Special task forces were unleashed on the population, barging into school staff rooms unannounced to search the ashtrays and waste baskets for evidence of "noncompliance."[47] Only in China, one might suggest, could the government propose something as inventive as banning people from *not* smoking.

On the global stage, this model of state-guided capitalism poses various problems for liberal Western agendas. In geo-economic terms, powerful companies with significant market share have become instruments of their government's foreign policy. A clear case, as we've documented with numerous examples in this chapter, is the provision of Chinese aid to repressive regimes in order to open up opportunities for companies like Sinopec and China National Petroleum Corporation.

But there's plenty of evidence that China is only the boldest node on a broadening curve. For instance, meet Gazprom, the natural-gas giant owned by the Russian government. As of December 2009, this company owned the world's largest distribution system of gas, with 97,560 miles of pipeline stretching from the Far East to Europe. It sits on 20 percent of the world's gas reserves and is the single largest gas producer in the world. Europe has become particularly reliant on Gazprom for up to 20 percent of its gas. This reliance will soon see a quantum increase, with proposals for a Nord Stream pipeline across the Baltic Sea from Russia to Germany, and a similar South Stream pipeline across the Black Sea to Bulgaria and the Balkans.

The *Wall Street Journal* described the proposed Nord Stream pipe as "Moscow's energy version of dividing and conquering Central and Eastern Europe."[48] Against the backdrop of this fast-changing energy map, Moscow can and does use Gazprom's pipes for political purposes. On New Year's Day 2009, company officials (read the Kremlin) turned off the taps to Ukraine. The ostensible reason was that Ukraine's government was overdue on payments and refused to pay market rates. Under the surface, however, was a clearly political objective to punish the largely pro-Western government for supporting Georgia in the Russo-Georgian war of August 2008 and flirting with NATO membership.[49] As the Kremlin now comfortably assumes, Europeans are trapped by their dependence on Russian natural gas—with everything this implies geopolitically in European acquiescence to Russian designs on central Asia and Eastern Europe.

Government-controlled assets are thus being channeled into global markets in ways that reaffirm the role of governments over markets.[50] Among prominent examples of late, Singapore, Kuwait, and South Korea provided much of a $21 billion lifeline to Citigroup and Merrill Lynch in 2007–2008.[51] While price details of specific funds and amounts are not disclosed, other companies known to have received major infusions from SWFs during the dark days of the credit crunch include Kaupthing, Chrysler Tower, Bear Stearns, Canadian Imperial Bank, Barclays, Morgan Stanley, and UBS.[52]

Hidden in these developing modes of economic management is a challenge to the West in cultural and political terms. Of course, the specifics of the Chinese development model cannot be easily reproduced on various counts, such as the amount of available labor, its suppressing effect on wage rates, the Confucian legacy, the high saving rates, the strong work ethic, or the fifty-year heritage of central economic planning. As discussed in Chapter 1, however, the specifics of the model are not where the power of its example lies.

What makes this model attractive is the simple, political equation behind it: the power of the market plus the stability of authoritarian rule. The government embraces certain tenets of liberal economic policy, such as opening the economy to foreign investment, allowing labor flexibility, keeping tax and regulatory burdens low, and creating a first-class infrastructure through combined private-sector and state spending. It also keeps a firm grip on government, the courts, the army, the internal security apparatus, and the flow of information.

This formula strikes a new kind of capitalist bargain between the people and the government. The state continues to improve living standards for the people; in return, the people let the state rule as an authoritarian regime. It is a bargain, says Robert Kagan, with a single, practical rule: "You can have whatever private life you want; no one's going to come in and tell you what to read or how to think as long as you keep it to yourself; you can make money, you can prosper—just keep your nose out of politics or we'll cut it off."[53] China hasn't moved to impose its own market-authoritarian model on others—but has made others aware of its approach and doesn't object if others wish to replicate it or learn from its management expertise in various areas: state control of strategic investments and a semiprivate media; macroeconomic policy on containing the inflationary pressures of large trade surpluses with sterilized foreign-exchange interventions; or boosting foreign direct investment through central regulatory mechanisms like tax holidays and other subsidies.

PIVOT POWERS

Increasingly, middle-sized regional powers are seeing an advantage of these management practices particularly at a moment when Western financial competence and the Washington Consensus are topics of derision. These include Indonesia, Vietnam, Nigeria, Turkey, Saudi Arabia, Pakistan, Venezuela, Brazil, South Africa, Ukraine, and Egypt, among others. Some are shaky "democracies"; others are inspired by China's pioneering "path around the West." They sit along a continuum— extending from those that admire the Chinese model (with some caveats), such as Vietnam, and have incorporated aspects of it into their own governance, to those such as Egypt, engaged in failed attempts to build democracy and frustrated by corruption, resource shortages, and histories untouched by the Enlightenment, but which envy China's stability and growth.

These countries may be thought of as "pivot powers." As regional leaders, they tilt toward either the Chinese or the Western models, and their actions have a ripple effect on others nearby.[54] Beijing looms large in this competition because as elites have examined the China model to see what aspects are applicable to their country's development, they see two aforementioned elements that are attractive to Second and Third World leaders across the globe: First, that China's rise demonstrates the ability of a middle-sized power to achieve high global status in a short period without regime change or ideological compromise; and second, that its model offers a path to prosperity and stability that avoids term-limited rule, raucous legislatures, critical media, and the cacophony of the public square.

As weather vanes, the choices of pivot powers provide a measure of the relative acceptance or rejection of the China model as an alternative to market democracy. Moreover, in those cases where it is accepted, shared political, cultural, and historical orientations tend to facilitate acceptance by proximate lesser countries.

CAN IT WORK FOR US?

Officials from Vietnam, Burma, and Cambodia have traveled to China in droves to examine the Chinese example for parts that might be applicable in their efforts to promote development while staving off political liberalization.[55] The governments of Syria and Iran have both publicly stated that they hope to copy a Chinese model of development that can grow the economy and control political dissent at the same time.[56]

Iran is perhaps the perfect example of the contagious appeal in Chinese ideas on hybrid governance. In 2006, its government sent a high-powered delegation of members of parliament and other officials to visit Shanghai and Shenzhen, as two booming towns that typify China's approach. The head of Iran's Parliamentary Economic Committee, Adel Azar, soon announced that he was "shocked" by the level of contrast in dynamism between China and Iran. The *Wall Street Journal* reported that Iranian officials were "looking to China for ideas on solving a riddle that has bedeviled strong-fisted governments the world over: How does a state loosen its suffocating grip on the economy without losing political control in the process?"[58] As Azar confided to the international press, "We started our debate about private business about the same time as China . . . We argued; they just got on with it." The Iranian economist Djavad Salehi-Isfahani summed it up: "The thing they like about China is that they think it shows you don't need democracy to grow."[59]

Unfortunately for the liberal internationalists, these sentiments have been spreading. The Laotian government announced in 2005: "We see that the economy of China has grown, and we think that there are lessons for Laos's economy from China—the building up of socialism while also having sustained economy growth."[60] After the president of Mongolia visited the White House in 2006 to discuss the future of U.S.-Mongolia relations, an executive assistant to the foreign minister confided that while his government publicly reiterated its commitment to democratic reform, "we really like what they are doing in China." Under that model, he explained, "you get the benefit of 10 percent annual growth, a middle class, and leaders know they have a job for more than four years . . . but without the 'side-effects' of democracy."[61]

Perhaps unsurprisingly, officials from the Cuban and Chinese governments, both communist in name at least, have undertaken various exchange trips over the years. I first spoke with the Cuban minister of economy and planning in 1992, recounting the substance of discussions held eight years earlier in China with the chairman of the Commission for Restructuring the Economy about China's early experimentation with the hybrid model. Exchanges between the two countries have been ongoing, focusing more recently on ways to help Raúl Castro maintain Cuba's frayed economy while undertaking much needed reforms. William Ratliff, a Cuba expert at Stanford University's Hoover Institution observed, "During the past 15 years, important members of the Cuban political, military, and business elite, including Fidel and Raúl Castro and two-thirds of the members of the Communist Party Politburo, have visited China and remarked with great interest on the Chinese reform experience."[62]

In Malaysia, China's model of mobilizing society for economic gain while keeping down tension had been noted as attractive for its scant emphasis on individual rights and freedoms.[63] Brazilian policy makers have made fact-finding trips to China to learn from Chinese management expertise in central economic planning.[64] Ethiopia has been following with great interest China's example of developing the economy without compromising its sovereignty to liberal international norms.[65]

Here we must return to a recurrent theme in the China narrative—Beijing's good timing. Polls of opinion outside the Western sphere and taken in 2008 suggest an increasing preference for guarantees of social order and delivery on economic promises rather than the Western liberal dream of democratization.

Between 1996 and 2000, only 27 to 37 percent of Latin Americans expressed satisfaction with democracy. Support for democracy in 2002 was lower than in the 1996–2000 period. Only 19 percent trusted political parties, 22 percent trusted parliament, and 26 percent trusted the judiciary.[66]

In a 2008 survey of world public opinion that looked at similar issues in a different way, the University of Maryland's Program on International Policy Attitudes (PIPA) asked nearly twenty thousand people in twenty countries how much confidence they had in seven key leaders "to do the right thing regarding world affairs." The two winners were Russia's Vladimir Putin and China's Hu Jintao.[67] Why?

The answer comes in three parts: First, Richard Holbrooke, the current special envoy for Afghanistan and Pakistan, makes the rather obvious point that these sentiments show "people's dissatisfaction with the way the world leadership is addressing the current crop of problems."[68] Second, the survey was conducted amid the ongoing convulsion in Iraq, the deteriorating conditions in Afghanistan, the rising instability in the South Asian region, and the continuing economic downturn broadly thought to have originated in the West. Meanwhile, both China and Russia had remained stable, with GDPs in the high single digits. In another dimension, and perhaps most importantly, the Enlightenment template of universally applicable democracy may have never penetrated quite as deeply into the psychology and politics of the non-Western world as Western, and particularly American, commentators assumed.

It's no surprise that after the debacle in Iraq, the most dramatic erosion of these ideas has been in the Middle East. Incidentally, approval of China in that region at the same time has

Table 4.2   Views of China and the United States in the Middle
East (Selected Countries), 2007

	Views of China		Views of the United States	
	% Favorable	% Unfavorable	% Favorable	% Unfavorable
Lebanon	46	48	47	52
Turkey	25	53	9	83
Jordan	46	49	20	78
Egypt	65	31	21	78
West Bank/Gaza	46	43	13	86
Israel	45	45	78	20
Morocco	26	30	15	56
Kuwait	52	17	46	46

SOURCE: Pew Research Center, "Global Unease with Major World Powers," 47-Nation
Pew Global Attitudes Survey, Pew Global Attitudes Project, Washington, DC, June 27,
2007, 3, 39, http://pewglobal.org/reports/pdf/256.pdf.

increased. In Table 4.2, the United States outranks China for
"unfavorable views" in every case but Israel.

But even beyond the Fertile Crescent, U.S.-style democracy promotion has sustained damage across the developing
world, in part because elections fix little in desperately poor
countries. More and more voters have been embracing tough
officials (like Putin or Chávez) as long as these leaders can deliver economic growth and social order in an environment
where the average condition of the average person looks
brighter from one year to the next.[69]

Latin America is a bold example. A 2003 survey found that more than 50 percent of respondents agreed with the statement "I wouldn't mind if a non-democratic government came to power if it could solve economic problems."[70]

The results of the past two decades have been particularly disappointing for countries that democratized at low levels of wealth, such as Indonesia, Cambodia, and Bangladesh. Adherents to the East Asian Model, such as China and Singapore, have seized on these examples to support a broader message that the Western template for democratic governance is not universally applicable. Former Singaporean ambassador, Chan Heng Chee, underscored the differences between the two, stressing that "developing countries may benefit from a postponement of democracy. If and when it does arrive, Asian democracy has to be expected to look different from the Western type—less permissive, more authoritarian and focusing on the common good rather than the individual rights."[71]

Singapore's former leader and founding father, Lee Kuan Yew, spoke for a consensus among regional leaders in 2008: "With few exceptions, democracy has not brought good government to new developing countries. What Asians value may not necessarily be what Americans or Europeans value. Westerners value the freedoms and liberties of the individual. As an Asian of Chinese cultural background, my values are for a government which is honest, effective and efficient."[72]

As Lee also pointed out, democratic processes can have illiberal outcomes. In parts of Africa, Asia, and Latin America, supposedly democratized nations have reverted to various forms of authoritarianism or have become mired in dysfunctional stages of democracy. Here social groups have often lacked the resources to participate effectively in the policy-making processes. Social and political cooperation have been undermined by internal disagreements and general distrust among ethnic groups, while elites from the previous regime have continued to control political power and key state resources.[73]

As we've seen in this chapter, therefore, the market-authoritarian model has leveled a powerful challenge in the realm of ideas against the preeminence of the market-democratic model. It upends what has been a cornerstone of Western thought, namely, that economic freedom needs political freedom and a minimal role for the state. A growing number of countries are starry-eyed about the new alternative development model—and its billboard in Beijing.

We've also seen how China administers a complex, multidimensional foreign policy. Beijing is determined and skillful in obtaining the necessary resources, both physical and political, while avoiding confrontation. China's challenge is oblique. It is indirect and painstakingly crafted to extract advantage from the weaknesses and discontinuities evident in the Western presentation.

When we view these issues from the political heart of the West, however, we would hardly think so. There's an established school of optimism in Washington, which says that engagement with the Western powers will eventually make China walk and talk more like a Western nation. This gradualist view of Chinese growth is popular, particularly among those living outside China. It is also mistaken, and the reason resides within China's borders. In the next chapter, we discuss the often-neglected link between Chinese strength in the world and Chinese weakness at home.

CHAPTER 5

THE MYTH OF INEVITABILITY

THE PERMANENT DUALITY OF CHINESE FOREIGN POLICY

In 2005, Robert Zoellick, then U.S. deputy secretary of state, famously called on China to become a "responsible stakeholder" in the international community.[1] Secretary Zoellick proposed this term as a standard by which to measure China's future behavior. Before long, it became a popular sound bite for those advancing the "inevitability argument." This remains a popular view in Washington. It also puts China's global rise in a reassuring light for the continued health of Western preeminence in the world.

The inevitability argument goes roughly like this: Since China's leaders have embraced a form of Western-style capitalism, they have come to rely on international markets and global trade to sustain economic growth, rising standards of living, and political stability. And so the richer and more modern China becomes, the more it relies on, and integrates with, the international community.

Over the last decade, this has become the dominant view
not only of American presidents of both parties, but also of a
raft of leading academic experts, corporate executives, think
tanks, and former policy-makers-turned-business-consultants.[2]
Bill Clinton joined the chorus before leaving office, maintaining
that unrestricted trade with China would integrate it into the
"family of nations" and "secure our interests and ideals."[3] Both
Clinton and his successor, George W. Bush, campaigned for
China's membership in the WTO with the argument that it
would encourage acceptance of global civic standards and international law.[4] "The case for trade is not just monetary but
moral," Bush declared. Examples lower down the political lad-
der are easy to find. In 2006, the State Department announced,
"China has realized, and will continue to find, that the more
it becomes a major part of the global system, the more its interests align with those of other major stakeholders, including
the U.S."[5] A paper delivered the following year at the prestigious Center for Strategic and International Studies in Washington promised, "China is becoming a more responsible
stakeholder in world affairs."[6] The Council on Foreign Relations similarly declared that U.S.-China trade and investment
weren't merely beneficial in their own right; they also contributed to the web of ties that "bind China into an orderly
world order."[7]

As we saw in Chapter 2, these notions actually have their
roots in a political philosophy that emerged in America after
the Soviet collapse. At that time, a majority of opinion writers
and politicians decided that increased prosperity under market
reform for countries like China would naturally lead to gradual
assimilation with the liberal international order and greater
pluralism at home.[8]

Except that it doesn't. There's no doubt, on the one hand, that increased trade and investment have fostered deeper levels of engagement between China and the West. There are plenty of examples to show that China's economic development has been accompanied by a deepening involvement in global affairs. China played an important role in the Asian financial crisis of 1997, and Hu Jintao called for international cooperation in the face of the global downturn that began in 2008. Beijing has also played a central role in the "Six-Party Talks" that seek to persuade North Korea to abandon its nuclear weapons program, and China's membership in the WTO has led to greater acceptance of international standards of corporate social responsibility and intellectual property law (in some areas). Moreover, as pointed out earlier in the book, China is among the largest sources of financial assistance to the developing world, and the People's Liberation Army (PLA) has contributed significant numbers of troops to various peacekeeping missions, including Lebanon in 2006, where Beijing helped to achieve a peace agreement after the Israeli intervention against Hezbollah.

A permanent "duality" between convergence and divergence with the international community, however, marks Chinese foreign policy. This duality will remain as long as the current Chinese model remains intact. This is because China's foreign policy is driven by the ruling party's efforts to handle an entrenched predicament at home, which is the Chinese growth trap.

THE CHINA TRAP

This is certainly not the first attempt to discuss the Chinese economy in terms of traps and paradoxes. The journalist and economist Will Hutton has talked about the "halfway house" of Chinese market reforms.[9] Friend and colleague Minxin Pei has argued that the Chinese economic miracle is "trapped in transition," and the lack of democratic reforms has created conditions that ultimately sap the nation's capacity to continue its impressive trajectory in growth and development.[10] Hutton and Pei both refer to "traps" in the sense of the limits they impose on further progress while the system remains authoritarian. Here we discuss the "China trap" in terms of foreign policy, and more specifically, we look at how the party is trapped into certain aspects of its global posture by the nature of political pressures it experiences at home.

Liberalizing the economy on a massive scale has kept the Chinese Communist Party (CCP) in power over the last two decades. But it has also resulted in a raft of secondary and tertiary problems: Coastal areas are growing faster than the interiors, and inner cities are ringed by poverty. Disparities of income and social stratification are deeply pronounced. Exploitation by local elites is endemic, and local authorities are infected with corruption. Moreover, the export-based economy is in a perpetual state of overheating, technological progress has brought an influx of foreign ideas, and the party has permitted the rise of a volatile nationalism to refocus the nation's identity and fill the gap left by a diminished Maoism.

These are the side effects of miracle growth. And herein lies the growth trap. The only way to prevent these problems from galvanizing into deeper unrest or from becoming a significant challenge to the central authorities is to promote continued economic growth. It is the CCP's ultimate answer for everything. China dare not stop growing at a high-octane rate.

To do so is to risk unrest, a catastrophe that Chinese leaders have avoided since June 1989.

In turn, this pressure wields a powerful influence on China's presence in the world. Were the CCP to broadly comply with the principles and standards of the liberal international order, the action would curtail China's unconditional partnerships with many states, from Sudan and Iran to large parts of sub-Saharan Africa, whose autocratic regimes meet disapproval in the West. This would reduce China's access to critical resources and markets, as well to geostrategically attractive regimes such as Cuba and Venezuela. For the same reason, it is not in Beijing's interest to rehabilitate pariah states in ways that make them more amenable to the West. Once "cleaned up," illiberal countries and malcontents would have more options, such as partnerships with Western companies and governments. Transformations of this kind would threaten China's competitive edge in the developing world, where it succeeds to no small extent by exploiting the commercial opportunities made available by an offended Western conscience.[11] It is generally uncharacteristic of great powers to surrender what they deem to be either their strategic or practical advantage. In China's case, good relations with the world's bottom-feeders provide both.

Nor can the CCP be seen by its own people to support Western liberal narratives on universal human rights and democracy; its very survival depends on containing these ideas at home. China's endorsement of liberal norms abroad could quickly blow back on the regime, giving encouragement to minorities, the Falun Gong, reformers or disaffected groups in Tibet, Xinjiang, and the hinterlands that the party might be "softening," or worse, had modified its direction.

Put simply, the legitimacy of the Chinese Communist Party hinges on its ability to deliver consistent economic growth at a rate that is unprecedented in other parts of the world.[12] This imposes great pressure on China's planners, making for a foreign policy that is indisposed, by definition, to give up the economic benefits of being morally deaf and blind.

For two administrations now, writes *New York Times* correspondent David Sanger, Washington has been engaged in a circular debate over whether Beijing is a "strategic partner" or a "strategic competitor."[13] This is a false choice. The reality is that China is *both* and *neither*. Unless the political system in Beijing experiences either collapse or radical change, China's split personality will remain a permanent fixture of the international system. As we see in the following pages, the key to understanding the inflexible parts of China's global approach lies in the dynamics that preoccupy Chinese leaders at home. Paradoxically, Chinese power and influence in the world are largely a by-product of insecurity.

THE LESSONS OF TIANANMEN AND SOVIET COLLAPSE

Two events combined in the early 1990s to transform the ruling party's attitudes toward its own survival. First, when the former secretary general of the Communist Party, Hu Yaobang, died of a heart attack on April 15, 1989, it triggered a wave of student protests across the country that led to violent suppression by government forces in Tiananmen Square three months later. These events were followed by half a year of martial law. Hu had been the de facto leader for a broad student movement that called for greater political freedom and reform to accompany the economic liberalization that had started in 1978 under

Deng Xiaoping. The nationwide scale of the protests shook the party leadership deeply. Splits had developed at the highest levels over how to handle the protests, as then General Secretary Zhao Ziyang attempted to introduce pro-reform ideas that would have lent some support to the protesters. Deng rejected this, insisting on a hard line and calling it nothing less than a matter of life and death for China.

Following a military crackdown and the house arrest of Zhao (which lasted until his death in 2005) the politburo began the urgent process of attempting to understand the causes of its near-death experience. The initial party line became a mixture of explanations with varying emphasis on a handful of key factors. The most popular was the subversive intentions of Western governments, particularly alleged American efforts to undermine the Communist Party.[14] Speeches by prominent figures like Deng and the newly appointed General Secretary Jiang Zemin also blamed the deviant thinking of young people who didn't understand what they were doing, as well as the resurgence of dangerous bourgeois liberalism.[15]

But then came Soviet collapse; Communist party-states fell one after the other across Eastern Europe. By the time Romanian President Nicolai Ceausescu's corpse had been paraded on CNN, internal party mechanisms were in overdrive. High-level, intraparty debate now centered on what went wrong in other Communist systems and how to avoid it. The early focus of discussion fell on the pernicious influence of wrongful ideologies; significant blame was directed personally at Soviet leader Mikhail Gorbachev, who was accused by senior party cadres of intentionally undermining the territorial integrity of Soviet Communism with traitorous sympathies for pro-Western, liberal ideas. After security was tightened with roadblocks and checkpoints, the tensions of early January passed without realizing the worst fears of the leadership.[16]

Over the following months and years, party analysts pored over voluminous reports and detailed assessments on the causes for Soviet collapse. Spanning a number of institutions and internal party publications, this process produced strongly divergent and often conflicting views. By the mid-1990s, however, the debate had resolved into consensus at the top of the party on the principal causes of Soviet demise. These included a dogmatic ideology, entrenched elites, dormant party organizations, and a stagnant, isolated economy.[17]

The assessment was a landmark in the evolution of the Chinese political system for other reasons. Party leaders now agreed that coercion alone was inadequate to maintain control over time, especially for an ideology whose legitimacy was receding worldwide. The speed and scope of Soviet collapse in Eastern Europe proved that even well-equipped, one-party states had to relegitimize themselves periodically.

David Shambaugh of the Woodrow Wilson Center in Washington notes that virtually all intraparty assessments were in agreement that the "totalism" of the command economy and the lack of market mechanisms had been fundamental in the Soviet system's downfall. Failure had been driven, they believed, by excessive ideological dogmatism that dismissed certain reforms as "capitalist" and therefore unsuitable, when they were actually crucial.[18]

These assessments also noted the USSR's aggressive foreign policy as a key element in collapse. CCP theorist and politburo adviser Zheng Bijia warned that the path of military hegemony under the banner of revolution was a dead end that served only to curtail access to potential sources of finance, energy, and commodities.[19] Moreover, he argued, policy makers were cut off from the outside world, which left them to take for granted that their system was the most advanced and admired in the world, when it was not (lessons Washington seemed to ignore a decade later).

Chinese officials and analysts used these ideas to develop a new slogan toward the end of the 1990s, casting China's new presence on the world stage as *heping jueqi*, or "peaceful rise." This term was meant to encompass a new Chinese approach to the world that relinquished any desire for expansionism and aggression, the pursuit of international hegemony, or the export of Communist revolution. Reflecting ongoing sensitivity about how China was being perceived, the slogan "peaceful rising," first used when Hu Jintao assumed power, was soon modified to "peaceful development" for fear that others might focus on the concept of "rising" rather than "peaceful."[20]

In a 2008 visit to the Chinese Academy of Social Science (CASS), the most prominent research institute in China and affiliated with the State Council, I was given a report that summarized the lessons learned from the shocks of Tiananmen Square and Eastern Europe. Above all else, analysts advised the government to concentrate on economic development and productivity growth. The report urged that the government seek "not only to strengthen the comprehensive power of the state but, more importantly, the material living standards of the people." It continued: Leaders must be more "ideologically flexible" and "progressive." Again, the beating heart of the policy was economic growth. The party was urged to understand better the complexity and fundamental causes of ethnic and political tensions, and to expedite economic growth as the most effective way to solve these tensions.[21]

It is this kind of flexibility and progressive transformation that has saved the CCP since the collapse of Soviet Communism. Deng first captured this when he and other reformers used the white cat/black cat metaphor to popularize the shift from ideologically driven policy to pragmatism. ("It doesn't matter whether the cat is black or white," Deng famously announced, "as long as it catches mice."[22])

The government's adopted flexibility is evident, for example, in the party's changing attitude toward the arts. Managing the visual arts is a challenge in many societies. The U.S. Constitution, through the First Amendment, protects free speech and expression, rights that have been broadly interpreted by the courts. In China during the late 1990s, provocative art, particularly renditions of party leaders or national heroes or satirical pieces depicting the Mao era, could not be displayed in public and so were restricted by the Propaganda Department. Today in Dashanzi, a vast former military complex near Beijing, satire and caricature are the cutting edge of a new Chinese art boom. Odious as it may be to the authorities for Mao to appear in lipstick and Deng to be morphed with a monkey, or for Communist symbols to adorn fake Coke or Marlboro ads, Chinese officials have determined to "give a bit" and not to stop the trend. The authorities have really taken two lines: First, they point to the satire as proof that dissent is possible in China, and second, they describe the art, which is selling well both in Asia and in the West, as a form of investment rather than social commentary and therefore not a direct challenge to party authority.

In these and other ways, the CCP has extended the *bamboo policy*—of bending in the wind rather than standing straight and eventually snapping. This was typified by the theory of the "Three Represents" promoted during the leadership of President Jiang Zemin. As Jiang announced in 2000, the party should learn to represent (1) the advanced productive forces in society, (2) advanced modern culture, and (3) the interests of the vast majority of the public. What this meant in practice was moving away from stilted socialist concepts disconnected from reality and toward creative people and practical solutions. The "Represents" policy broadened party membership, actively recruiting the "advanced, productive forces"; this included intellectuals, students, and entrepreneurs from the private sector—the very people who forty years ago would have been dispatched to labor camps in the countryside for "reeducation" and "rehabilitation."

It was a major shift in party philosophy; it recognized that without productivity and export growth, there would be no prosperity. And lest we forget, without prosperity in the form of jobs, housing, and the promise of a better future, stability for the CCP could be gravely threatened.[23] Hu then succeeded Jiang in 2003, introducing his own slogan, the "Scientific Development Concept," which added new focus on the need to meet a fast-emerging set of social problems such as the rural-urban divide and pandemic corruption.[24]

AVOIDING THE WEST'S "PEACEFUL EVOLUTION" STRATEGY

The doctrine of adaptation had its limits, however. Chinese leaders learned from their analysis of Eastern Europe and Tiananmen Square that Moscow's attempt at half-steps toward political liberalization proved ruinous. According to the former U.S. ambassador to China, J. Stapleton Roy, China's ruling elite decided after 1991 "that Gorbachev made a fundamental error by loosening the political reins faster than he was able to introduce economic reforms sufficient to cushion any changes on the political front." On this issue, the politburo concluded, there could be no compromise.[25] The Tiananmen protests had demonstrated how a limited student movement could quickly draw support from other elements and escalate beyond control. The only way forward, therefore, was three cheers for capitalism and absolutely none for democratic reform—however limited.[26]

Premier Wen Jiabao iterated the party line in 2007 with an article in the *People's Daily*. Debate had been developing in government circles about the possibilities for a concept called *within-system democracy,* which respected the party-state's monopoly on power, but allowed for freer intraparty channels of discussion and collective decision making. Wen sent an unambiguous message: Those expecting any substantial moves toward democracy would be waiting a long time. The politburo's rejection of political pluralism was justified with a powerful and effective logic: Enhancing the quality of life and extracting economic benefit from China's momentous transformation can proceed only from a stable society governed by strong central control. China, Wen wrote in classic party language, was still in the "primary stage of socialism lasting 100 years or more." The country was large and underdeveloped, he stressed, and building a modern socialist state that was rich and strong was "a long term and arduous historical task" in a big country with a population of over one billion.[27]

Perhaps the most trenchant example of the party's resistance to theories of democratic evolution came at the beginning of 2009, when top Chinese legislator, Wu Bangguo, urged the country's lawmakers to "maintain the correct political orientation" and remember the "essential differences" between China and the West. As he told the Standing Committee of the National People's Congress, "We must more fully recognize the essential differences between the system of people's congresses and Western capitalist countries' system of political power." Where the American model embraced a separation of three powers—the executive, the legislative, and the judiciary— the Chinese system was based on something else entirely: "consultation under central leadership." As Wu concluded, there would be no gradual slide in Chinese development toward a liberal pluralism or multiparty politics. While China "must draw on the achievements of all cultures" in areas such as market reforms, the Chinese system "shall never simply copy the system of Western countries or introduce a system of multiple parties holding office in rotation, a system with the separation of the three powers or a bicameral system."[28]

Chinese leaders have therefore extracted what they've needed from Western development models in terms of commercial relations, markets, private ownership, and the circulation of assets, and they've rejected what they don't, in terms of liberal norms and political pluralism.

CONFUCIUS SAY SURF THE NET

A Petri dish for this political admixture is the Internet. Among the many phenomena influencing China today, the most powerful change engine is the Internet, which continues to have a greater impact on values, norms, and aspirations—indeed, on the emerging Chinese identity—than any other. Massive additional pressures confront party planners when the gap between evolving social practice on the one hand and the rules on the other is invaded by that army of "netizens" on the "blogosphere." Beyond the hubbub of working life, there is a separate reality inhabited by China's nearly 300 million Internet users (double the previous year). According to Internet monitors in Beijing, the users of the Internet are the most active sector in society; 80 percent of them are under thirty-five. As in other countries, their exchanges cover every possible topic in several different formats: from YouTube exchanges, to tweets on Twitter, opinions, and information on everything from entertainment and rural corruption to Shanghai housing prices, office manners, and pornography. Confrontations over the spread of information are nothing new in China. What is new is the persistent presence of the "angry young online"—a semidissident community that challenges the party's "China story" and, as the economy slows, is sharply critical of the shortage of jobs, housing, health facilities, and support for education.

And yet, even this spleen venting has failed to undermine the authority of the CCP.[29] There is no question, however, that on a generalized level, the Internet has cracked open a channel for citizens to voice mass displeasure with official conduct— and even to influence official policy.

The case of Deng Yujiao demonstrates how this process can work. In 2009, Deng was a waitress at a karaoke bar in Hubei Province. Not uncommon to the area, the bar provided "special services" in a backroom spa. A local official, Huang Weide, stormed into the washing room and demanded to take a bath with Deng, who refused and ran to another room. With two accomplices, Huang forced her onto a sofa, at which point Deng took a fruit knife from her purse and stabbed Huang several times; he soon died from his wounds. Following arrest and investigation, Deng was sent to a mental ward.

But then her luck changed when a blogger, Wu Gan, discovered her case and began an "online tempest" by reporting the story. Internet discussion spread to local news reporting and then to the national level, at which point a Hubei court granted Deng an unexpected appeal and release on the basis that she had acted in self-defense. There are plenty of examples that follow this formula: an official in Guangdong who attacked a young girl and boasted that he was above the law; an official in Nanjing City who was spotted wearing a $14,500 watch, clearly beyond the terms of his government salary; a cover-up by prison officials after they beat a prisoner to death; and special killing teams who beat thousands of dogs to death as a solution to rabies. In each case, officials were sacked after eruptions on the Internet.[30]

Deng's victory therefore demonstrates the power of the Internet in raising public awareness about accountability and citizens' rights. But it's important to note what this does and doesn't say.

As the Deng story shows, public criticism and student debate is alive and well in China. But a great deal of this criticism is different from Western upheaval narratives or the flavor of protesters in Tiananmen Square twenty years ago. Chinese students today will criticize specific policies of the government or the government's behavior in particular areas. But within these terms, they are much less likely to challenge the legitimacy of the one-party system or the government's right to a monopoly on political power.[31] In fact, such public criticism actually bolsters that monopoly by presuming that the authorities will act to clean up abuses when they hear of them, providing these are "abuses" by individuals rather than symptoms of a flawed system.

By this token, Westerners like to see Internet-pressure stories as the "green shoots" of emerging liberal pluralism. But anecdotes like Deng also have a context that outsiders often ignore or don't understand. The Internet is proving to be a powerful social force multiplier in China, but it is not an engine generating a broad rebellion against one-party politics. Instead, it empowers the ordinary masses in their calls for greater accountability and their demand that the government should better serve the people. Crucially, these demands belie a very different set of cultural and political attitudes about governance from the principles laid out in Philadelphia's Independence Hall. They also raise another equally powerful reason why China shows little inclination to become more like the West, which relates to the very root and branch of Chinese society.

The CCP has learned to draw legitimacy and strength from the underlying Confucian roots of Chinese culture. Confucian precepts are based on a role-based system of ethics, in which the governed and the governors respect and protect each other's place, so long as each side fulfills its side of the bargain. Thus is the Confucian utopia for a harmonious society. The ruled are subservient to the ruler, but only because the ruler fulfils the important duties of ensuring livelihood, shelter, education, and security from foreign invasion. If the ruler fails in these regards, then Chinese peasantry have a heritage for bottom-up rebellion that is almost unrivaled in history.

This civic bargain reflects important aspects of the China model today: The ruling elites ensure quality of life; in return, the people let them retain their monopoly on political power.

It is significant, therefore, that Hu Jintao has focused party language on themes like a "harmonious society," which might sound more familiar to Chinese ears than it does to Americans.

Consequently, the Internet provides a window on the complex and changing mechanics of accountability in China. While there are cleverly coded references to events in Tibet and sometimes to Tiananmen Square, head-on challenges to the system have generally failed to gain popular momentum.[32] Admittedly, there's an ongoing cat-and-mouse game to control this environment. Beijing alone has over forty thousand Internet police assigned to police stations throughout the city, and so far, new codes directing the adventurous to dissident Web sites have been broken soon after they are created, only to be recreated and broken again.

To date, it is fair to say, victory in the contest for this now vital public space belongs to the government and its ability to maintain the delicate social bargain of political monopoly in return for stability, growth, and opportunity. The authorities are agile, continuously changing tactics to keep up, for example, learning to sprinkle the blogosphere with paid writers who are activated when needed to debunk inconvenient or embarrassing stories. The resulting cacophony often muddies the water to the degree that it is frequently hard to determine the correct facts or sequence of events and exactly what has been alleged or denied. The government also hides its censorship behind more acceptable fig leaves, such as clamping down on pornography. Large parts of the Chinese Google were shut down one Friday night in summer 2009, supposedly because the site too often linked to pornographic and erotic content. A similar argument was offered in June of that year, for the government's controversial and sweeping directive, which demanded that all personal computers sold in the country contain a preinstalled software filter called the Green Dam Youth Escort. This new software would allow the government to update all PCs in the country with an ever-changing list of banned Web sites that displayed supposedly "unhealthy information." Despite government assurances that the principal use was to block pornography, critics immediately complained across the blogosphere about the enhanced ability it would afford the censors to control other types of content. (Major manufacturers such as Dell, Lenovo, and Hewlett-Packard objected, and the government temporarily suspended implementation of the Green Dam project as of this writing.)[33]

Thus the Internet demonstrates the limits of arbitrary power for the government. But it also demonstrates the limits of the people's power and their appetite to fight for pluralism in a Western sense. Technology has given the masses greater capacity to criticize the government and demand redress for specific grievances. But this is different from challenging the nation's theory of state. These outpourings lead to demands on the government to fulfill the responsibilities and objectives of central governance, rather than reinvent them.

SOCIAL CHANGE AND THE "SOCIALIZATION OF INDIVIDUAL HAPPINESS"

Accordingly, just as the Chinese model is a hybrid system of capitalism and autocracy, so its leaders have sought to develop a hybrid form of national identity, which is able to combine the consumerism of modern China with the remnants of Chinese socialism. Meet the ruling party's big idea of material socialism. The new Chinese theory of state is a fusion narrative that strives to unify two ideas: (1) the Chinese economic miracle and (2) the big idea of "China reemerging."

As the party narratives explain, rising standards of living for the Chinese people are not only designed to support individual happiness; economic growth is part of a broader historical process—the reemergence of China on the world stage. This is a major plank in the party message that outsiders sometimes miss. China isn't emerging as a major power; it's *reemerging* after one and a half centuries of being a weak power. Against the weighty backdrop of imperial history, this seems like a brief hiatus. The Communist Party has sought to rebuild a sense of post-Mao legitimacy with a comprehensive education campaign that gives great emphasis to China's long heritage, extending to the time of Shih Huang-ti, the first emperor.

The schoolbooks emphasize a kind of Chinese exceptionalism, ironically not unlike its American counterpart in its focus on the big idea that its birth was a gift to universal human progress. Until the "interruption" of the late nineteenth century, it is noted, China boasted the largest economy in the world for some two thousand years.[34] This interruption is often referred to in party literature as China's "Century of Humiliation," which began in 1842 with the First Opium War, when Britain forced unilateral concessions on the Chinese involving foreign settlement and the right to trade with China. It continued throughout the nineteenth and early twentieth centuries. Japan claimed Taiwan in 1895 and then invaded the mainland in the 1930s. American resources and advisers were also provided to help the nationalists win the Chinese civil war that ensued with the Communists over the next twenty years—and is still not officially ended. Finally, the nationalist forces led by American ally General Chiang Kai Shek claimed Taiwan in

1949 as their new home, under the protection of the U.S. Seventh Fleet.[35]

Economic growth is thus empowering China to regain pride and international respect. As Deng proclaimed in 1978 at the beginning of China's economic reform program, "To get rich is glorious!"[36] This aphorism has been developed and nurtured by the party as reforms have deepened. Economic development subsequently became the new "mandate of the Chinese people." As you become rich, goes the political logic, so China becomes great again—and regains its rightful place at the table of great civilizations. As you exercise your right to pursue an improved quality of life, you do so in a process that belongs to the bigger "China story."

This is the "socialization of individual happiness."[37] It is the new theory of state, which seeks to bind an individual's pursuit of material wealth to a wider narrative of social cohesion and historical fate—of Chinese exceptionalism. The individual's pursuit of material wealth thus belongs to a broader social narrative of collective loyalty. China must never again be carved up and humiliated by the foreign aggressors. Disunity at home must be avoided through the protection of an ever-vigilant Communist government. The party is the engine of change and upward mobility. It is also the protective force that oversees the economic miracle as the engine of resurgent national greatness.

Hence the government's policy for social cohesion is twofold: (1) sustain growth and (2) an appeal to nationalism. These are mutually dependent. Each could lose its viability without the other. Without nationalism, market reforms might become the stimulus for social forces that challenge the party's legitimacy. Without the economic success story, meanwhile,

Chinese nationalism could turn in on itself and focus its grievance on the leadership. To this extent, the pressure of nationalism is a problem in itself for the CCP.

THE DOUBLE-EDGED SWORD OF NATIONALISM

As conversations with everyday people in Beijing confirm, few believe in Communism anymore, and so the leaders have promoted nationalist themes to bolster the legitimacy of the party. This has been implemented through a nationwide patriotic education campaign in schools and the mass media, which began in earnest in the mid-1990s. Schools added new courses to stimulate patriotic loyalty. Students won awards for reading the one hundred designated patriotic books or viewing the one hundred designated patriotic films as chosen by the party. Patriotic songs, books, and versions of history became a steady diet in the classroom. School tours descended on famous historical sites in the founding Communist story, which were renamed "patriotic education bases." These histories also focused on designated enemies, the big three being Japan, Taiwan, and the United States.[38]

But now the leaders are forced to master a delicate balance of their own making. The patriotic campaigns have done their job. A virulent form of xenophobic Chinese nationalism simmers within the popular psyche. Familiar narratives about the Century of Humiliation, or Japanese atrocities, or Taiwan's splittism and American meddling inform a flow of nationalist themes found on the Internet, in the popular press, in magazines, and on television.

But as Susan Shirk has explained, this program of nationalist mobilization has also boxed the leadership into a corner.[39]

Unplanned, faraway events such as attacks on the Olympic torch, the collision of an American and a Chinese aircraft, or the American bombing of the Chinese embassy in Kosovo can easily trigger an outpouring of nationalism. Unplanned in these circumstances are rallies, protests, and Internet chat rooms that can quickly turn their anger toward the leadership itself if they feel it has done too little or appeared too weak.

In turn, party officials risk the possibility that rival politicians will seize the moment, using the media to enlist popular support and outmaneuver them within party structures.[40] Equally, there's the fear that intense xenophobic sentiment could harm relations with vital economic partners such as Japan and the United States.

In this context, the media, at times, play a troublesome role. Since the government agreed to allow the media a certain degree of freedom, the new outlets have learned to compete with each other for market share and audience ratings. They naturally coalesce around the stories that draw the most attention. At the same time, journalists still abide for the most part by the demands of the Propaganda Department. In both cases, this usually means presenting a vigorous nationalist line on foreign events that stokes the public's anger.

Nationalism is therefore a double-edged sword for the ruling elite. It provides a crucial way to unite party members, but as a ready source of popular anger looking for a focus, it also threatens to blow back on the government or become uncontrollable. As the government knows, its political survival depends on keeping these groups unified behind the party. In turn, this means upholding the China success story and the economic miracle that is making the nation modern and great once more.

THE HOLE AT THE CENTER OF THE DONUT

American writer Gertrude Stein is famously quoted saying "there's no there, there." In this same sense, the core of contemporary China is elusive, in flux. The challenge for the authorities is to manage change in a positive way while advancing a productive sense of what it means to be Chinese. Careful and calibrated flexibility in this process seems to be the key. Except in high-profile instances when there is thought to be no alternative, as in Tibet or Xinjiang Province in 2009, or in cases where dissidents openly question the direction of the party, the authorities have learned to be flexible and subtle in managing change. Still, this mercurial quality at the center of society on China's metropolitan east coast underscores the fear of chaos and generates the need for growth, which keeps the population employed, housed, and happy.

This has been no small feat. Social dynamics in China are developing as fast as its skylines. Some say that what we're seeing is a broader cultural shift from the "we generation" to the "me generation."[41] Regardless of how they are framed, these pressures test how and why China's one-party system manages, and often limits, choice in some rather delicate areas. Chinese youth grow up today in a very different physical environment from their parents. Today's young people share less with others in terms of material possessions, a parent's attention, and living space. They have more than their parents ever did, and courtesy of the one-child policy, they often have it all to themselves. For this new generation, life is about the individual and the freedom to do what makes them happy.[42]

Many Chinese people have been empowered by unprecedented levels of choice. Asked what it means to be Chinese, most people living along the east coast are unlikely, as they would have in the 1990s, to describe themselves as good party members. Instead, they talk about where they live and perhaps how their apartment is furnished with goods from the ubiquitous Ikea stores so popular today. They talk about their employment and what's possible in the new market economy, where they shop for clothes and household goods, where their children attend school, and perhaps where the family hopes to travel in the summertime. They may mention changes in the city, joking that China's new national bird is the construction crane, and point to the ubiquitous Internet cafés, live concerts, raves, and coffee shops.[43]

Social change has also been driven by physical change. There is a popular one-liner in Shanghai and Beijing: that it's important to phone the restaurant before going to dinner, not to reserve a table, but to make sure the building hasn't been demolished.[44] Underscoring this is the worry that established ways of life and traditional forms of social organization are being swept away with the buildings. *Hutong,* for example, is the traditional term for the narrow lanes that connect rows of small one- and two-story courtyard houses in the old city neighborhoods. It describes a setting where the doors were always open, where elders sat in the front courtyards on wicker chairs, their backgammon games shaded by mulberry and ginkgo trees, while people came and went and children played together. But this has all changed in the last decade. The *hutongs* have been bulldozed to make room for new high-rise office buildings and commercial plazas, and their residents forcibly relocated—and inevitably separated—to live in new complexes of sterile, cheaply built, modern flats, now insipient slums.[45] In the new apartments, hours from their old downtown neighborhoods, when the door shuts behind them, no one visits; they are alone. This has given birth to a popular phrase in Shanghai: "better a bed in [downtown] Puxi than a house in [suburban] Pudong."[46]

Changes in Chinese living spaces and youthful expectations have also informed change in personal habits. Among them is the evolving notion of privacy. In its Western genus, this is still a new idea in China. The Chinese word for privacy, *yinsi,* traditionally suggests secrecy, conspiracy, and illicit behavior, which is quite different from the Western version of the concept, which is linked to the notion of individual rights and personal liberty. Younger employees now object to employers intercepting their e-mails. Local authorities may no longer track female menstruation in support of the one-child policy. Twelve-year-olds object to parents looking around their bedrooms, and people receiving public services now challenge the authorities on the questions they are asked in applications for water, electric, and trash removal. This is a change from a few years ago, when the public willingly gave information to a state that provided housing, employment, food rations, and travel, and women complied willingly with state procedures for monitoring their menstrual cycles to insure they did not have unwanted pregnancies. Western-style notions of privacy (parachuted into Chinese society via the Internet) have challenged the boundaries between what is rightfully in the public sphere and what the individual may keep as private.

Cambridge sinologist Anne Lonsdale refers to these developments as "little bubbles rising to the surface."[47] Still other things haven't changed at all, which underscore the halfway house of China's hybrid development. In many public toilets, people still squat elbow to elbow to defecate. Hospital patients often receive medical procedures in full view of those visiting other patients. And in conversation, China's culture of politeness imposes few barriers to casual inquiries or comments about intimate topics. It is not unusual, for example, for someone to say "You look a lot older" or "Why have you gained so much weight?" Clearly, the process of creating privacy with Chinese characteristics has a life of its own, with uneven outcomes at best.

Religious expression has also grown to fill the space left by Communist ideology. Here the ruling party is finding that it was easier when the Communist government simply condemned all religion than it is to strike a balance between what is outlawed and what is permitted.

The government is still officially atheist, but it has had to become more tolerant of religious activity since the market reforms began. In 2005, the State Council established new guidelines that afforded legal rights for state-sanctioned religious groups. Some groups are still persecuted and repressed, however, as the loyalty and the devotion of their members is deemed a social and political threat to the party. The Falun Gong, for example, appeared and grew so quickly in the 1990s that the central government called emergency meetings on how to face it. Falun Gong is a spiritual movement that combines a number of strands of traditional culture, including Buddhism, Taoism, and Qigong, a traditional form of Chinese exercise. What caused the alarm was a demonstration by Falun Gong members in 1999, in which some ten thousand members suddenly appeared near the headquarters of the CCP in a quiet and disciplined demonstration. The authorities perceived the event as a threat, and Falun Gong has been brutally suppressed ever since.

There are also somewhere between four and five million Tibetans in China practicing Buddhism. Their spiritual and political leader, the Dalai Lama, leads a government in exile located in Dharmsala, over the border in India, where he has orchestrated an international campaign calling for Tibetan autonomy. Nothing instills greater fear in the Communist leadership than the idea of "splittism." This is the official Chinese translation of the word *fen lie* that, as taken from Marxist discourse, means to "tear up." The notion of "splittism" underscores a deep-seated fear in Chinese leaders that separatists in one part of China could encourage similar sentiments elsewhere, ultimately threatening the entire sovereignty of the nation. The authorities have, for years, used this as a pejorative, such that it is now common parlance. The charge of splittism is often directed toward the Tibetans; the central government monitors the daily activities of many Tibetan monasteries through video and electronic recording devices and often arrests those who speak out against the party or the Han presence in Tibet. It has also sought to mold the next generation of religious Tibetans with "patriotic education campaigns" that teach a state-sanctioned form of Buddhism, reiterating the party narrative on unity and nationalism.[48]

A second group of potential "splittists" is found in Xinjiang Province, where a Muslim ethnic group called the Uighurs has been agitating for greater autonomy since the 1980s. The party has faced an increasing challenge from Uighurs in recent years, with bomb attacks and protests for independence. Minority Muslim populations are also found in other parts of China, where they suffered discrimination from Han Chinese and have demonstrated their desire for greater cultural and religious freedom. Meanwhile, Christianity has moved like a brushfire across China since the 1980s. The state has an endemic fear of "large congregations," meaning that the number of people who can join each church is limited. Rather than reduce the number of Christians, however, this has created a large underground Christian community. A recent report from the Pew Research Center estimated the number of underground Christians to be somewhere between fifty and seventy million.[49]

Thus, the party has been forced to allow greater space for belief and social expression as by-products of its own reform process. But it must also prevent them from becoming challenges to central authority. Groups like the Falun Gong, Buddhists, Uighurs, and Christians have forced the authorities to give priority to the challenge of fashioning and guiding a new civic culture. Only continued miracle growth powered by China's access to raw materials, energy, and compliant regimes can buy the time needed to build a revitalized civic culture in the new China.

SOCIAL STRATIFICATION

Beyond nationalism, individualism, and religion lies another potentially dangerous side effect of transformation: social stratification. The no-holds-barred development of export industries along the coast, at the expense of the interior, has also boosted income inequity to levels rarely seen outside Africa. Urban incomes, industries, and consumer markets have grown dramatically over the last decade, creating a yawning gap in wealth and employment opportunities. This difference in standard of living has created a floating underclass of migrant workers and turned Chinese cities into a two-tier caste system, divided between permanent citizens and the migrants who flock there in waves to seek higher wages and more available jobs.

Increasingly hated, yet needed by the higher social ranks they serve, this migrant class is fast acquiring the kind of social status normally associated with an ethnic minority. The rural migrants supposedly love the jobs you hate if you're an upwardly mobile urban dweller—from house cleaning and car washing to construction, demolition, table service, and street sweeping. But alongside the jobs they do, urban residents are also learning to hate the migrants themselves. The newcomers are being blamed for a number of social problems such as overcrowding and rising crime rates. Housing agencies have imposed regulations that restrict them from entering certain areas by raising the fee for temporary residence permits to prohibitively high prices. A luxury resort on the outskirts of Shanghai even produced a sign in 2005 that read, "Entrance forbidden for people in rustic-style clothes."[50] Even more, the government has quantified the social divide. When a bridge collapsed in Chongking, killing forty people, the government announced that the families of urban citizens killed in the event would receive more compensation than those relatives of migrant worker victims.

Stratification for the migrant classes is further enforced by the status and education of their children, who are usually not entitled to attend urban schools. The money allocated by the government for the education of each child is typically tied to the place where that child is registered as a permanent resident. The city schools also have vastly different standards from the provinces, which obliges rural children to repeat two or three years of education before they are considered eligible by academic standards.[51] All of these various challenges have helped to create entire, separate migrant communities in the cities, where the workers have taken the situation into their own hands, setting up their own schools and medical services. This is hardly a comprehensive solution, however, as these institutions lack any formal standards and are constantly at risk from closure by the local authorities, since they are not legally registered.[52] As BBC correspondent Duncan Hewitt wrote in 2007, these factors add together to create a growing level of social dissatisfaction: "Your kids can't go to school here, your whole family can't be together, you don't have any social welfare. We always tell you you're a worker from outside . . . and your home is in your native place."[53] Some of these groups could grow progressively bitter in the next decade.

The rural poor in general continue to inject a cautionary note. In 2005, there were 87,000 protests—many violent—over land disputes, malfeasance, alleged corruption, and extortion—up from 78,000 in 2004 and 58,000 in 2003. Construction projects like the Three Gorges Dam have required the uprooting and resettlement of millions of people (1.25 million for the Gorges Dam alone), who are forced to vacate homes where generations of the same family have lived for hundreds of years, often with short notice of weeks and even days. These mass relocations usually take place against a heavy backdrop of official corruption, kickbacks, bribes, blackmail, and state intimidation.[54]

These practices highlight an underlying source of discontent for rural and migrant Chinese. They are the most vulnerable to corruption, another by-product of development stress. As former general secretary of the CCP, Zhao Ziyang, remarked, a one-party Leninist system that subsequently attempts to liberalize its economy through a process of gradualism inevitably holds the preconditions for acute corruption. And corruption takes many forms. Partly reformed economic and political institutions provide fertile ground for a syndrome called double-dipping, where politically connected groups take advantage of both the new economic opportunities offered by the market and certain benefits still provided by the old, unreformed system, namely, immunity from scrutiny and accountability for government agents and local power brokers.[55]

Major corruption scandals have become standard and quite popular fare in the Chinese media and are guaranteed to sell newspapers. Particularly gripping was a November 2009 mass trial of gangsters in Chongqing. A veritable circus, the trial exposed a vast network of corrupt city police and Communist Party officials. The media created a vivid drama, complete with an evil "'Godmother' of the criminal underworld" with "claims . . . that she had kept 16 young lovers." With her top lieutenants, she was convicted to eighteen years in prison for extortion, loan sharking, and corrupting local officials.[56] Attempts to quantify corruption indicate that its cost ranges from 4 to 17 percent of GDP.[57] Corruption is usually worse the further one is from the coastal centers, which means that the impact is greatest on the poorest people in China. In this respect, as Minxin Pei says, China is becoming a decentralized, predatory state, where the center has a limited ability to control the behavior of local officials. [58]

THE PHYSICAL AND POLITICAL EFFECTS OF POLLUTION

Problems of corruption and religious expression pale in comparison, however, to what could be the single most problematic and intractable side effect of miracle growth: pollution.

Startlingly, the politburo has come to fear environmentalists for much the same reason it fears other groups—they have the potential to become an organized social entity directing their bile against the political center. The ruling Communist Party often seems to treat environmental advocates as a bigger threat than pollution itself . . . which is a serious mistake.

China's pollution output is greater than that of the United States and Europe put together. It has five of the world's ten most polluted cities; 120 million Chinese live in cities breathing toxic air, and over two-thirds of the country's rivers are so polluted that all the fish in them have died. Hundreds of species of plant and animal life are disappearing each year in this country. Nine out of ten Chinese cities are dependent on polluted groundwater, and China's greatest river—the Yangtze—is predicted to become over 70 percent polluted by 2015. Rural areas have seen some of the most acute effects, like the Chinese invention "cancer villages." These are villages where up to 50 percent of the residents have developed cancer in the last ten years, where the flow of water has been replaced with banks of black sludge, where dark, murky clouds shroud the surroundings, and where the soil is so contaminated that vegetation is impossible.[59]

Admittedly, in recent years, China has given greater recognition to the dangers of climate change. The government is progressively aware that pollution is hurting the national economy. The Chinese Academy of Social Sciences has calculated that pollution already costs between 8 and 12 percent of annual GDP.[60] The National People's Congress has announced ambitious plans for a 10 percent reduction in all pollutants, a 20 percent reduction in energy intensity, and a 30 percent reduction in water use.[61] We've also seen new investments in renewable energy. China has actually emerged since 2007 as a leading builder of more efficient, less polluting coal plants, gaining the edge in technological development. (In the same period, construction of low-pollution coal plants stalled in the United States.)[62]

As experts have observed, however, there are caveats behind these grand commitments to protecting the planet, which tell a different story. Most obviously, the Chinese government is unlikely to meet the targets of its hugely ambitious National Plan. The Chinese drive to improve energy efficiency has already lost pace, as the Chinese National Bureau of Statistics reported in 2008, showing that the world's top carbon dioxide emitter struggled to rein in wasteful energy use without upsetting the economy.[63] Breakthroughs in coal-firing technology also window-dress an inconvenient truth, as environmentalists like to say: Even a more climate-friendly coal plant emits twice the carbon dioxide of a natural-gas-fired plant. As long as China continues to rely heavily on coal, which supplies 80 percent of its electricity, the country guarantees that it will keep emitting record levels of carbon dioxide.[64]

Here again, a major problem is decentralization. Beijing has faced difficulties enforcing local compliance with new federal regulations. When the central government announced its ambitious campaign to decrease energy consumption, officials in regional capitals like Qingtongxia got straight to work—not to comply, according to Howard French of the *New York Times*, but rather to find creative ways to avoid the requirements.[65] In this respect, the half-reformed state of the national economy has aided the problem. Local officials now have more freedom to make their own decisions, but they still enjoy the perks of a system that has yet to establish truly effective mechanisms of accountability.

The government's predicament over diesel fuel offers another example of this conundrum. Industrial trucks are the mules of China's expanding economy. But they are also responsible for burning a particularly noxious form of diesel fuel contaminated with more than 130 times the amount of pollution-causing sulfur permitted in Europe and the United States. Meanwhile, the government subsidizes and regulates the price of fuel to maintain low diesel prices and thus prevent inflation. The subsidy, in turn, ripples through and supports China's entire export infrastructure. Price controls create a vicious cycle, however. Oil giants such as Sinopec have become private companies with the desire to make a profit. They are losing money on every gallon of diesel they refine, because of low sales cost. In turn, this means they upgrade refineries slowly—if at all—and seek out the cheapest crude oil with the highest levels of sulfur and the worst environmental effects in order to produce cost-effective diesel.[66]

While the government refuses to raise the price of fuel, the oil magnates have little incentive to foster refinery investment. But the government resists such a radical step out of fear of the cost, both to the economy and to the truckers, who often have extended families dependent on their income and have pooled savings to finance the truck. It's a perfect display of the seemingly irresolvable complexities found in a system that is part "market" and part "command" or centrally planned. If the government continues to subsidize diesel fuel, then the trucks and the oil companies poison the people. But if the government allows the prices of diesel to float freely by market terms, then truckers go out of business, threatening social unrest and commercial turbulence. The trucker community is particularly feared in government eyes as a nomadic social force, mobile by its very nature and capable of spreading bad news to the far corners of the country.

Thus, the pollution problem is a trenchant example of the development trap that Chinese leaders find themselves in, where growth has created serious side effects, but the demands of growth also restrict the party's ability to solve the problem. This predicament was manifest in efforts to limit the pollution in Beijing for the 2008 Olympics. The government closed factories around the capital city in order to clear the air for the games. At the same time, it was adding new coal-firing plants every seven to ten days in the countryside.[67] Notwithstanding the promises of Chinese officials about their commitment to the environment, the raw facts are that alternative energy sources are not sufficient to sustain China's miracle, and without the jobs that many factories provide, social stability and the ability to grow are threatened.

THE PROBLEMS AT HOME AND THEIR IMPACT ABROAD

Against the backdrop of these contradictions and tensions, the glue that holds new China together is undeniably the party's ability to maintain and improve people's standard of living. The Chinese story of economic miracle must continue to triumph over the parallel stories of repression, foreign ideas, stratification, corruption, land seizures, and environmental fallout. The record of the last fifteen years suggests that this has been the case and that these problems are not so acute as to threaten the CCP's continued rule. But this can only remain the case so long as the government continues to deliver impressively high growth rates. "Growth" is the engine that generates higher living standards and jobs for the workers leaving state-owned industries, migrating from the countryside and graduating from secondary and higher education.

The broader result is a nation boasting impressive growth—an achievement to which all aspire—but which suffers from an odd internal inertia. Though more confident in recent years (some might say assertive), China still struggles to promote its "socialization of individual happiness" fusion narrative to link communal values and individual identity to a broad theory of state. While the Chinese offer alternative ideas, finance, and the example of a successful model to the developing world, their fusion narrative is unable to offer these countries the kind of inspiration that underpinned, say, the Marshall Plan in Europe after 1945 or the socialist revolutions of Latin American in the nineteenth century. Because the question, "What does it mean to be Chinese?" remains unanswered and they are unable to convey individual purpose in their relations with locals, interaction focuses mainly on process issues.

When Chinese politicians and business leaders arrive in African capitals or address Asian trade delegations, they offer little to capture people's aspiration to better the world they inhabit. In the Chinese model of free markets and one-party politics, the only guiding ideal of society is economic growth, with everything this implies in terms of a general proclivity for poor working conditions, low wages, corruption, political oppression, environmental irresponsibility, and human rights violations. Add to this the recent and growing problems with local labor, work site disputes, and systemic animosity now evident at Chinese projects from Sudan to Papua New Guinea to Nigeria.

Much of this reflects Chinese workers' perceptions of race and culture.

Thus, China's domestic problems have far-reaching implications for the wider context. As this chapter has argued, they impose pressure on the leadership at home and subsequently limit the extent to which China can bend to Western liberal norms in the global space. Domestic growth is king, but its handmaidens are the natural resources, foreign markets, and diplomatic support that sustain China's global portfolio. While the Chinese system remains trapped in a developmental halfway house at home, these relations with the wider world also remain trapped in their current modus operandi. As we will see in the conclusion of the book, this inherent flaw in the China model is both a problem for the West and an opportunity. First, however, we meet another part of the issue, which is also a liability and an opportunity. This is the matter of how Washington views the China challenge and the role of grand scenarios and American exceptionalism in the U.S. public-policy debate.

CHAPTER 6

THE PROBLEM IN WASHINGTON

GANGS AND GRAND SCENARIOS IN THE CHINA DEBATE

When Hillary Rodham Clinton appeared before the Senate Foreign Relations Committee as Barack Obama's nominee for secretary of state, the confirmation hearing produced a transcript of over fifty-three thousand words. The hearing covered a long list of pressing issues for America's top diplomat: the global financial crisis, terrorism, nuclear proliferation, the intractable Arab-Israeli conflict, climate change, plans for withdrawing troops from Iraq and rooting out al-Qaeda in Afghanistan. In this extended congressional exchange, one major issue was barely mentioned. As a subject in itself, China used up a total of six sentences.[1]

Clinton's Senate hearing highlights another element in the China challenge, this time on the American side. Beyond Olympic games and occasional headline grabbers like violent protest in Tibet, China is often ignored or skipped over by American politicians and opinion writers, unless you belong to one of Washington's designated "China gangs." As former

Secretary of Defense James Schlesinger explained to me, the American China debate is globulated and divided into separate lobbies and single-issue groups.[2] Each of these groups is concerned with a specific part of the China question: Chinese military development, trade and labor issues, human rights, technology transfer issues, violations of intellectual property rights, or business opportunities and the benefits of commercial engagement.

While these groups proceed along largely separate lines, taken together, they create a China debate that is dominated by competing sets of grand scenarios, such as "China is coming to get us," "China is coming to buy us," or "China is coming to join us." In turn, these scenarios encourage a coalescing of positions into two broadly polarized camps of "panda huggers," who tend to preach the virtues of commercial engagement and inevitability of Western-style democracy in Asia, and "panda bashers," who warn of a menacing China threat in various guises.

The problem is that the reality of the China story defies these kinds of scenarios. The very nature of the China challenge means that no single group has the answer—or even a complete definition of the problem. The Chinese are our economic partners. But they are also our political rivals. Thirty years of successful market reforms indicate that the Chinese Communist Party is not about to crumble. But neither is it melting into liberalism. China has survived the global demise of Communism to become the world's most powerful rising power. Yet it has neither confronted the U.S.-led system nor gradually conformed to the American worldview in the two decades since Soviet collapse. Before we turn to the final chapter to discuss how to respond to these contradictions, let us identify the problem in Washington and how it has worked to suppress a proper formulation of the issue.

THE HAWKS' CLUB

Perhaps the best-known group of China watchers inside the Beltway is the hawks' club of analysts who focus on China primarily in terms of a rising military threat. A trenchant example came shortly before Barack Obama entered office. For those who thought the neocons disappeared with America's hopes of a quick and easy invasion of Iraq, there was an October surprise in the final weeks of the Bush administration, when Paul Wolfowitz authored a government report about the rising Chinese military threat. The report warned in sober tones that Beijing "seeks greatly enhanced military power and reach" in a broad policy that aims to "break out" of the Pacific. It also criticized Washington for having allowed the U.S. stockpile of nuclear weapons to "atrophy" over the last two decades.[3] Minus the details and the caveats, of course, the report became grist for the mill of military alarmists. Among the journalists who first distributed the Wolfowitz report was Bill Gertz of the *Washington Times* and *Fox News*. Gertz has argued extensively that the "most serious" challenge to America from Beijing is "China's military build-up," its emphasis on developing weapons of mass destruction and the dangers of a coming war over Taiwan.[4] Pushing these themes in books and articles with titles like "The China Threat" and "How the People's Republic Targets America," Gertz belongs to a constellation of journalists, former Cold War defense intellectuals, and think-tank members who have spent the last decade in Washington warning that China poses a serious military threat.[5] This group has been named the Blue Team by some of its own members, for the color ascribed to the American side in war games during the Cold War.[6]

Publications like the *Washington Times* and the *Weekly Standard*, along with research institutions like the Center for Security Policy, the American Enterprise Institute (AEI), and the Heritage Foundation, have duly provided a platform for what has been an important and powerful debate on these issues. When the question of U.S.-China policy arises in these forums, it is more often than not in terms of China's growing nuclear, space-based, or naval capacity and its intention to confront American power. Gary Schmitt and Dan Blumenthal of the American Enterprise Institute suggest that China "almost certainly would not be seeking these military capabilities to support a policy of mere deterrence." The bigger objective, they have warned, is a "lethal nuclear strategic capability— aimed primarily at the United States."[7]

A briefing from the Heritage Foundation makes a similar point: "China's rapid strategic forces modernization is China's 'biggest threat' to the United States."[8] Former State Department official and AEI Fellow Michael Ledeen wrote in the *Weekly Standard*, "So long as China remains a ruthless Communist dictatorship . . . the inevitability of conflict must inform all our thinking and planning."[9] The University of Pennsylvania sinologist Arthur Waldron makes this sobering point: "China is developing a formidable military force that makes no sense at all unless one assumes that a 'grab for power' of some sort is its rationale."[10] And in "How We Would Fight

China," Robert Kaplan asserted that the American military contest with China will "define the twenty-first century," as China prepares its capability to "lob missiles accurately at moving ships in the Pacific."[11]

Next to the journals and think tanks, the most powerful platform for China hawks in Washington over the last decade has been the Department of Defense (DOD). During Donald Rumsfeld's time as secretary of defense, a group of neocons and others established a consensus view at policy levels of the Pentagon, saying that China represented a serious and expanding military threat. Alongside figures such as Wolfowitz and Douglas Feith, this view was shaped and promoted, in particular, by one of Rumsfeld's key Asian advisers, Michael Pillsbury, a perceptive analyst and sinologist who sometimes translated for the then-secretary during meetings with Chinese officials. The *Wall Street Journal* called him "one of the Pentagon's most influential advisers on China." As Pillsbury told the *Journal*, most Americans misunderstood China in viewing it as a peaceful country intent on economic prosperity. America's China watchers, he said, from the lower levels of the State Department to the intelligence agencies, the business community, and the academy were, too often, "panda huggers," who failed to realize that the Chinese military nurtured ambitions far beyond the question of Taiwan and even planned to provoke small wars to secure resources for its growing energy needs. "Beijing sees the U.S. as an inevitable foe, and is planning accordingly," Pillsbury asserted, and Washington would be "remiss" not to plan likewise.[12]

Pillsbury played a key role in formulating the Pentagon's 2006 Quadrennial Defense Review (QDR), which paralleled his views closely. China's military expansion had already altered the "military balance" in the Pacific, announced the QDR, and Chinese military development now presented a major challenge to the United States in its commitments "to resist any resort to force or other forms of coercion" against Taiwan.[13]

This strong intellectual tide is, moreover, supported by institutional persuasion. As Ivan Eland at the Cato Institute suggests, beyond the coterie of defense intellectuals that settled at DOD during the Bush years, there is also an institutional tendency that influences the discussion. Threat projections from the Pentagon are naturally inclined to underscore issues such as China. The DOD is, after all, the federal bureaucracy directly responsible for meeting any military challenge from China and must have congressional support to purchase the weapons, personnel, fuel, and manpower to prevail. Thus, for the institution whose job is to spot the next threat, China draws inevitable focus as the power the United States may, one day, be compelled to confront.[14]

This forceful argument, advanced by respected policy analysts both within and outside the government, has not gone unnoticed in Beijing. Chinese policy makers have begun to complain in recent years about the prevalence of this group in the Washington debate. In March 2009, for example, Foreign Ministry spokesman Qin Gang lodged a public and official complaint against the frequent reports sponsored by the Pentagon on Chinese military development. Qin asserted that these reports "smacked of Cold War mentality" and caused "damage to the relationship between the two countries" by putting "obstacles" in the way of closer military and economic ties.[15]

CHINESE MILITARY DEVELOPMENT IN CONTEXT

There are serious reasons, certainly including its military modernization, for America and the West to be concerned about China's growing role on the world stage. China has increased its defense spending exponentially each year for over a decade. It has given priority to research and the development of space-based and undersea technologies to blunt the striking power of U.S. forces. But these developments are often depicted by the hawks' club in isolation from the wider context. The issue is more complex than China's attempting to catch up with the U.S. military in order to challenge American military supremacy. China has sought to avoid both the costly financial drain and the negative American reaction that would almost certainly accompany a serious attempt to establish force parity with the United States.

There is no doubt that Beijing has invested considerable time and money in developing a new generation of technical and military hardware, from sea-skimming missiles that can attack aircraft carriers to ballistic systems that can shoot satellites out of the sky. But this is less a policy designed to challenge, and eventually fight, the United States, and more a policy of establishing an "area of denial" around mainland China and Taiwan and an area of influence extending across the island chain to Guam. The key element for Beijing, at least for the present, is to possess a credible military threat should Taiwan choose to break the status quo and declare independence.

Central to China's evolution in recent decades has been a determination to avoid a costly arms race with the United States. Rather, China has sought a deterrent capability that targets America's reliance on high-tech equipment that provides battle-space intelligence, surveillance, target acquisition, reconnaissance, and communications. That China's military capacity remains credible is critical to the People's Liberation Army, which, in addition to the United States and Taiwan, worries about Japan and the South China Sea, and to the CCP, which remains worried about the prospect of unrest among ethnic minorities like the Tibetans and the Uighur Muslims of Xinjiang Province.

A somewhat more moderate perspective was offered by a Pentagon report published in March 2009 under the tutelage of Rumsfeld's successor, Robert Gates. This report made the point that while "China is seeking technology and weapons to disrupt the traditional advantages of American forces . . . its ability to sustain military power at a distance remains limited."[16] The Chinese military had undergone a "comprehensive transformation," said the report, from a "mass army" to one capable of fighting "short-duration, high intensity conflicts along its periphery" against "high-tech adversaries" in an approach that China calls "preparing for local wars under 'informationized' conditions."[17] The report emphasized that the secrecy surrounding the PLA, opaque practices, and inadequate military exchanges creates the potential for miscalculation. The Chinese navy, for example, refused in 2008 to enter into an incidents-at-sea protocol with the United States—a protocol that would establish procedures for avoiding potential confrontations. The international community continues to have limited knowledge of the motivations, decision making, and key capabilities supporting the modernization program. But on the basis of discernible data, the evidence suggests that the "important driver of its modernization" remains "preparing for contingencies in the Taiwan Strait, including the possibility of US intervention."[18]

Charles Freeman of the Center for Strategic and International Studies says that the real message from Beijing is less a question of "we're coming to get you," and more like "Shut up and leave us alone and let us manage our problems."[19] China's leadership has gone to great lengths over the last decade, he notes, not to supplant or challenge the American security umbrella in places like the Middle East, Southeast Asia, and Latin America. The ruling party is innately inward looking, which makes it reliably allergic to international conflict. This doesn't make conflict impossible between Washington and Beijing or Beijing and Taipei, which remains susceptible to accidental scenarios such as a collision between Chinese and Taiwanese fighter jets. But it makes the prospect of war less likely. War would be catastrophic for the CCP for economic reasons. Crucially, it would cause the party to break the social contract that binds it to the people.

THE TRADE WATCHERS, PART 1

If the China hawks have helped to fashion the notion that *China is coming to get us*, this group is closely allied with another China frame that also contorts the Washington debate: *China is coming to buy us.*

Washington has seen rising anxiety in the last half decade over Chinese foreign investment in the American economy, through state-owned entities such as China Investment Corporation (CIC), the China National Offshore Oil Corporation (CNOOC), and, of course, the People's Bank of China. The single most documented example of recent years came in 2005, when CNOOC tried to buy the U.S. oil company Unocal, trumping a competitive bid from Chevron. Before the deal could be completed, it was blocked by Congress in a tide of agitated rhetoric; Chinese investment, like a Trojan horse, was said to imperil U.S. national security.

Forty-one lawmakers from both sides of the aisle wrote an open letter condemning the deal as a threat to national security.[20] Chairman of the House Energy and Commerce Committee, Joe Barton (R-TX), wrote to the president, saying, "We urge you to protect American national security by ensuring that vital U.S. energy assets are never sold to the Chinese government."[21] Congressman Richard W. Pombo (R-CA) sponsored a resolution that declared that permitting the Chinese company to buy Unocal would "threaten to impair the national security of the United States." He underscored that Congress still retained its historical power to "regulate commerce with foreign nations," under Article I, Section 8, of the Constitution when the nation's security was directly threatened.[22] Frank Gaffney, a former deputy assistant secretary of defense, testified at a House Armed Services Committee hearing and stated that permitting the CNOOC deal was a grave mistake because it belonged to a broader Chinese strategy "to supplant the United States as the premier economic power in the world and, should it become necessary, to defeat us militarily."[23] James Woolsey, director of the Central Intelligence Agency during the Clinton administration, asserted that the deal was "naïve" and "dangerous." As he told the Armed Services Committee, "for anyone who believes that this is purely a commercial undertaking, unrelated to a national strategy of domination of energy markets and of the western Pacific, I would suggest that that view is extraordinarily naïve."[24] The American Enterprise Institute convened a panel of concerned China watchers, including Thomas Donnelly and Daniel Blumenthal, who discussed the potential risks to American military and economic security. The Heritage Foundation issued a briefing called "Say No to CNOOC's Bid for Unocal," saying that the bid threatened to provide Beijing with a powerful strategic asset should U.S.-China relations give way to military conflict.[25] Even the president of the National Foreign Trade Council, William Reinsch, claimed that the deal presented a veiled threat to national security, since "our Army, Navy and Air Force run on oil," with the implication that China might be able to curtail American access in a time of potential conflagration.[26]

Meanwhile across the Atlantic, the *Economist* magazine asked the obvious question, "Is America's energy security really at risk, as politicians claim?" The case, it suggested, was actually hard to make. Beyond the inflated rhetoric of Gaffney, Woolsey, and various lawmakers and think tanks, Unocal was in fact a puny player on the world oil and gas markets. By size, it failed to rank among the top forty oil or gas firms.[27] As a neglected report from the Congressional Research Service said at the time, Unocal accounted for only 0.8 percent of U.S. production of crude oil, condensate, and natural-gas liquids. Its production of petroleum was a minuscule 0.3 percent of U.S. consumption.[28]

While this episode did little to elevate the debate on the issues that mattered, it illustrated how quickly grand scenarios can swallow the China debate. What started as a small-scale bid in market terms grew to become a discussion about how to stop the Chinese government from threatening America's way of life.

THE GREAT GAME WATCHERS

By this token, another school that underscores the China men-
ace is the "great power historians." This time, it is history,
rather than investment, that rings the fire bell in the night. This
group pushes the China question into a heavy historical framework, which says that rising powers provoke war with established hegemons, as the former inevitably challenge the latter's
sphere of influence.

Among the most common similes for this argument is the
rise of Germany under Kaiser Wilhelm II, who infamously
oversaw the industrialization and militarization of imperial
Germany, rendering it a rising European power that threatened
the incumbent British hegemon. This view is typified by Gary
Schmitt of the American Enterprise Institute: "If it walks like
a duck and it quacks like a duck, then it must be a duck. China
quacks quite a lot like Wilhelmine Germany in keeping with
the classical rising power pattern. For this reason, it's really
bound to bump into the U.S. at some stage."[29] Robert Zoellick,
writing in the *Weekly Standard* a decade ago, was talking about
China when he warned that "failure to deal effectively with
Germany's rise led to seventy-five years of conflict."[30] Onetime
presidential candidate Pat Buchanan declared in 2005, "What
America and China must avoid is the fate of Wilhelmine Germany and the Britain of George V, when the world's rising
power and receding power stumbled into a thirty-year war that
destroyed both."[31]

According even to those who advocate greater use of "soft
power" in America's foreign relations, such as John B. Henry
of the Committee for the Republic, China raises anxiety. Mr.
Henry says, "There's bound to be conflict. I can't think of an

example of when the great power system accommodated a rising power. History says that conflicts will happen. The U.S. fits the pattern of the hegemon, and China fits the pattern of the inevitable challenger."[32]

Yet, there is a problem with this school of analysis. It rests on the outmoded, Western-centric view of the world described by Naazneen Barma, Ely Ratner, and Steven Weber in their *National Interest* piece, "The World Without the West." There they criticize a trend that too often in the United States portrays rising nations as spokes in the American hub confronted with a stark choice: Either challenge the United States for leadership (a path leading to conflict), or integrate with the U.S.-led system, which will lead to a peaceful evolution in which rising powers conform to the Western liberal order.[33]

Thus the great game watchers—making questionable assumptions and asking the wrong questions—worry about a confrontation with the hegemon, but the real world of international relations is less simple. As discussed earlier, considerable amounts of wealth now circulate, entirely beyond the reach of Western hands. The level of interaction *among* the developing-country economies is gradually beginning to rival and surpass the level of interaction between many of these countries and the West. Figures 6.1, 6.2, and 6.3, for example, show the comparative volume of international trade, in billions of dollars, between three of the BRIC countries (Brazil, Russia, India, and China, the fastest-growing developing economies) and various parts of the world. In each case, the collective share of trade with South America, Africa, the Middle East, Russia, and Asia is greater than with North America and Europe.

Emerging markets are increasingly turning to each other for business and aid. Thus, the integration of developing nations with the global economy may not presage greater integration with the West. But neither does it necessarily mean conflict. China is forging a path beyond the boundaries of traditional European history and beyond challenging the hegemon incumbent or conforming to its norms and conventions.[34]

Figure 6.1   The BRICs and International Trade:
Brazil Merchandise Exports, 2007 (US$ billion)

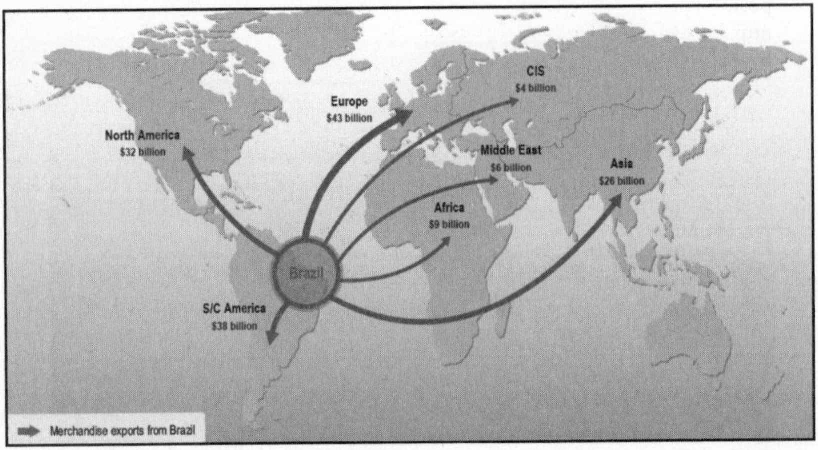

SOURCE: David Bartlett, "African Investments by the BRIC Countries," Symposium on Foreign Investment in Africa, Bartlett Ellis LLC, April 1, 2009, 5, http://sabusinesscouncil.org/wp-content/uploads/2009/04/african-investments-by-bric-countries.pdf.

Figure 6.2 The BRICs and International Trade: India Merchandise Exports, 2007 (US$ billion)

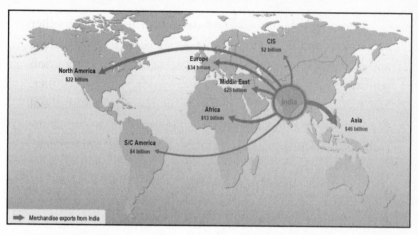

SOURCE: David Bartlett, "African Investments by the BRIC Countries," Symposium on Foreign Investment in Africa, Bartlett Ellis LLC, April 1, 2009, 5, http://sabusinesscouncil.org/wp-content/uploads/2009/04/african-investments-by-bric-countries.pdf.

Figure 6.3 The BRICs and International Trade: China Merchandise Exports, 2007 (US$ billion)

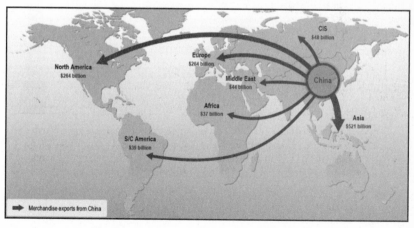

SOURCE: David Bartlett, "African Investments by the BRIC Countries," Symposium on Foreign Investment in Africa, Bartlett Ellis LLC, April 1, 2009, 5, http://sabusinesscouncil.org/wp-content/uploads/2009/04/african-investments-by-bric-countries.pdf.

THE TRADE WATCHERS, PART 2

In fashioning ominous visions of China, national security buffs and great power watchers are only part of an extensive political landscape. Beyond the majority of the public who are skeptical of China, its motives, and its practices, those specifically unhappy with current policy trends include labor and trade interests on Capitol Hill. Both groups raise legitimate concerns.

The Chinese threat to American jobs isn't new. Chinese workers first grabbed national attention in the mid-1850s, when they arrived in significant numbers on the West Coast seeking work in California's gold mines. As the gold rush abated and mines ceased to produce, Chinese workers migrated to construction jobs—some local, some on the continental railway—and service jobs in restaurants, laundries, and private homes. Migrant communities soon formed their own "Chinatowns," some of which continue to thrive in San Francisco and Los Angeles today. By the 1870s, however, American workers and labor activists coalesced in groups that drew upon the prejudices of the time to form anti-Chinese movements throughout the West, spreading fear of "the Yellow Peril." Signs reading "No Chinese or dogs" were found on saloon doors. Chinese workers taking American jobs pushed down wage rates because they were willing to take almost any job for less money.

By a long evolution, similar fears and grievances are reflected by labor groups and trade watchers today. As they point out, Americans are losing jobs because U.S. companies are moving their production facilities to China, where Chinese workers are prepared to work longer hours for less money. American small businesses have been pushed out of the market, undercut by the influx of bottom-dollar Chinese imports. As American manufacturers protest, China's currency is undervalued, which affords a heavy advantage to Chinese exporters, whose products are sold at artificially low prices. By the same token, the undervalued currency causes the prices of U.S. exports in China to be artificially inflated.[35]

All of these issues present legitimate concerns. But as they become part of the domestic political debate, they are used and abused by politicians in ways that present oversimplified answers. New Mexico Governor Bill Richardson, former presidential candidate, U.S. trade representative, and ambassador to the United Nations, proclaimed in 2008 that "China is a strategic competitor . . . and we've got to say to China, you've got to stop fooling around with currency."[36] Senators Charles Schumer (D-NY) and Lindsey Graham (R-SC) accused China of breaking the rules of free trade by "years of currency manipulation." The answer, they proposed, was to impose tariffs of 27.5 percent on all Chinese imports "unless China agreed to play by the rules."[37] During the darker days of the recent global recession, congressional representatives rallied to calls for a return to protectionism. When the Obama administration moved swiftly after taking office to enact a $789 billion economic stimulus package, Congress attempted to add a "Buy American" clause to the bill, under the leadership of Schumer, Lindsey, and other like minds such as Representative Pete Visclosky, who chairs the Congressional Steel Caucus. The added clause required the many public works and building projects funded by the stimulus package to use only U.S.-made goods in industries such as iron and steel, cutting out market share for major Chinese exporters as well as others from India, Brazil, and Russia.[38]

These arguments are broadly popular. But in practical terms, they contribute little. First of all, they are only half the picture. Chinese industry may have depressed American economic health in some areas. But it doubtless boosted the U.S. economy in others. As Burton Malkiel, professor of economics at Princeton University, put it, when Chinese exporters sell Americans their lawn mowers, microwave ovens, skis, and designer purses, the Chinese don't bury their earnings in coffee cans in the ground. The profits are turned into cash savings, which are then used by the Central Bank of China to lend money to the U.S. government, as well as investing in corporate bonds and shares in U.S. companies. This has kept interest rates low, made credit easier to obtain, and enabled American businesses to expand. Easier credit has kept mortgage rates lower, allowing more people to buy houses. It has allowed the government to keep taxes lower and create jobs. Malkiel adds that free trade is often a tough sell, especially during times of hardship, because it doesn't affect every individual in equal fashion. A textile worker, for example, whose job was lost because Chinese imports shuttered his or her factory, will feel the economic pain far more acutely than consumers will feel the positive effects of Chinese economics, such as cheap clothing, more credit cards, and low-rate mortgages. This kind of economic pain is often localized, whereas the benefits are spread more broadly.[39]

Second, American politicians have used the big idea of a China threat to present primitive and impractical solutions to a problem that goes far beyond China. As former Chairman of the Federal Reserve Alan Greenspan explains, stiffer duties on Chinese imports would simply shift the source of U.S. imports to other low-cost suppliers.[40] As demonstrated in reports submitted to the U.S.-China Economic and Security Review Commission, recent years have seen an accelerated shift of production away from the United States. The data reflect an ongoing global corporate restructuring and an increased capital mobility now evident throughout the world. U.S.- and foreign-owned multinationals are shifting production from high-wage countries to multiple low-wage destinations, both nearshore and offshore.[41] China, one example, certainly has the highest political profile in the American public space. But it belongs to a bigger picture, which cannot be changed by protectionist legislation aimed specifically at Beijing. In the last five years, we've seen a major increase in production shifts out of the United States, not only to China, but also to Mexico, India, Southeast Asia, Latin America, the Caribbean, Eastern Europe, and even Canada. In a single three-month test case, for example, 23 percent of production shifts from the United States went to China, but 27 percent went to Mexico, 12 percent went to India, 14 percent went to other Latin American and Caribbean countries, 15 percent to other Asian countries, and even 7 percent to a mixture of Belgium, Canada, France, Ireland, Israel, New Zealand, Sweden, and the United Kingdom![42]

Accordingly, a sharp increase in the value of the yuan relative to the U.S. dollar is not the magic bullet that Congress suggests it is. It would only suppress the Chinese credit stream that feeds the American growth cycle. The effect would certainly not bring the manufacturing and job growth so often described. U.S. textile imports, for example, alongside computers, toys, and similar products would simply shift from China as the final assembler to other emerging-market economies in Asia and perhaps in Latin America. "Few, if any, American jobs," said Greenspan, "would be protected."[43]

As James Fallows remarks, American politicians like to talk up the Chinese threat to American jobs and business, calling for China to reduce its trade surplus and somehow play a fairer game. In the same breath, however, they ask China's financiers to continue buying U.S. Treasury bonds and stocks in U.S. companies with the dollars they get from that very trade surplus. "We can't have it both ways," Fallows stresses, "the Chinese can give us money, or they can give us back some jobs, but not both."[44]

Powerful as the trade caucus is, however, it is simply a part, even a small part, of the extensive and often visceral community making up the panda bashers' camp. Beyond the groups mentioned above are the human rights organizations, including the pro-Tibet lobby (which seems to grow stronger each time it confronts Beijing), consumer groups highlighting food and drug safety issues, the construction lobby (most recently concerned about asbestos in Chinese-made drywall), the cyberwatchers who warn that Chinese hackers are breaking into American computers to steal technology and national secrets, communities watching foreclosed homes auctioned off to Chinese vulture funds, and even pet owners worried about what the Chinese have put in their dog food. While these groups work to fashion the image of China as America's greatest adversary, or worse, they also face a countervailing set of voices in Washington, who are doing all they can to reverse this image and promote the opposite idea—China as America's *greatest partner*.

THE COMMERCIAL ENGAGERS

Meet the panda huggers, usually so called by their opposite numbers. There are various groups that populate this category, from politicians to the business councils and the academy. At heart, they propose varying forms of the same popular notion that we saw in Chapter 5. As Western companies invest in the Chinese economy, goes the argument, Beijing increasingly conforms to the norms of Western liberal behavior, both abroad and at home.

A major platform for this message has been the U.S.-China Business Council, based in Washington. By its own admission, the council has two roles. The first is providing business advisory services to its roughly 250 client companies that operate in Chinese markets. The second is equally important—providing a form of "advocacy and lobbying" in the American debate. As two officials from the council explained, a significant part of their job is to "actively promote a specific message," which is that "trade and unimpeded commercial engagement is good for the U.S., and it's also good for China." Accordingly, the council produces literature and mobilizes supporters on Capitol Hill to "encourage engagement" and "take a stance against harmful legislation that would affect our member companies." In the process, the officials noted, the council is "constantly butting heads with lawmakers on the Hill—who are hostile to our approach and seek to curtail our freedom to act." An important part of this message, they contend, is the social and political benefit of what the council seeks to do. "From the perspective of political and social development," they argue, "we're helping China to go forward. The PRC is making progress, and we're driving the process—we're helping to open up the debate in China. We feel strongly that we're contributing to improving the situation in China. Our work and China's WTO status have helped to enforce better transparency from Chinese companies, and we've been a source of increased pressure on Intellectual Property Law (IPR). So we actually see ourselves as helping China to develop towards a freer and more ordered society."[45]

The U.S.-China Business Council is by no means the only source of optimism in Washington on the transformative magic of economic engagement. Before leaving office, Bill Clinton promised that economic liberalization in China would "increase the spirit of liberty over time . . . just as inevitably as the Berlin Wall fell."[46] In making the case for free trade with China during the 2000 election, George W. Bush asserted, "Economic freedom creates habits of liberty, and habits of liberty create expectations of democracy."[47] In 2005, he added there was "a whiff of freedom" in the Chinese marketplace, which would "cause there to be more demand for democracy."[48] More recently in the 2008 election, Republican presidential candidate Mike Huckabee typified the optimism, saying that China was a "good news" story, as it was "becoming much more a part of the mainstream, in its economic development and even in giving greater liberties to its people."[49] A policy paper from the American Enterprise Institute offered a comparable thesis: "The means for achieving democratic change in China" had apparently "increased" through "external economic engagement." Even though "the resulting prosperity has lent legitimacy to the Chinese Communist Party," it had "also unleashed forces that will push toward political pluralism."[50]

While this idea could be forgiven as legitimate optimism twenty years ago, prudence now suggests that China's hybrid system of economic liberalism and political autocracy is here to stay, for a generation at least. China's authoritarian political system is proving a durable status quo, with powerful forces at work that preserve its balance and legitimacy and inhibit any far-reaching change.[51] As Fallows wrote from Beijing in March 2009 after a two-year sabbatical in China, "when people complain, it is usually about those crooked bosses, reporters, mayors, or bureaucrats—not about the system or its rulers."[52]

CHINA: THE MICROCOSM OF BAD HABITS INSIDE THE BELTWAY

What we find in Washington, therefore, is a pattern in which single-issue interest groups fixate on one aspect of the China challenge, magnifying and distorting it to the exclusion of most other variables. Familiar as the story is, one cannot help but return to the metaphor of the blind men and the elephant in describing Washington's appreciation of the China challenge. For the few who haven't heard the story, a group of blind men find themselves in a room with an elephant. Each man touches a different part of the animal and compiles a starkly different picture from the next. For the person touching the tusk, the creature is smooth and small. For the man who handles the belly, an elephant is broad and daunting. For the man holding the ears, the animal is leathery and irritable.

The story demonstrates the obvious problems in a policy debate as variegated and vast as the China question. What it doesn't explain, however, is the deeper cultural problem underlying it, which helps to anchor the debate in reductive dichotomies. Like so many other questions of American foreign policy, the China debate belies a recurrent condition, in which the nation habitually reacts to a challenge through the thick lens of *American exceptionalism.*

American exceptionalism is the nation's founding eighteenth-century idea that the United States was born out of exceptional circumstances that gave it a special role to play in history and human progress. Of course, the question of *what makes America different* has captivated American—and Western—intellectuals for over two hundred years. Charles Dickens rather harshly asserted that nothing existed equivalent to America's money-mad materialism. James Bryce marveled at the apparent distinctiveness of its federal system. Wyndham Lewis proposed that ethnic-demographic patterns in American living held the seeds of "cosmic man." Herbert Croly wrote of a new "promise" unique to the American way of life. Waldo Frank believed in a juxtaposition of power and childishness in the young American political mind. Sir Dennis Brogan suggested there were unique contradictions between the federal system and a new rugged-individualist culture. André Siegfried asserted that American society was a new type of civilization created by the mixture of immigrant streams and Anglo-Saxon tradition. Thorstein Veblen reckoned that American enterprise had fashioned a new type of society with new opportunities for upward mobility.[53]

The whole discussion was started, to some extent, by a Frenchman; Alexis De Tocqueville arrived in the United States during the 1830s, hoping to understand how the American Revolution had succeeded where its French counterpart had failed. The answer, he decided, lay in the Americans' lack of a feudal past, a situation that made them more individualistic, more socially egalitarian, and more libertarian than their European counterparts.[54]

Whether or not the United States is truly exceptional, the nation's undying belief in this idea certainly is. As foreigners who live or travel in the United States often note, there's a distinctive American penchant for overt patriotism, which seems to inform everyday life in ways that are pronounced when

compared with many other countries. The rhetorical frames
of American exceptionalism persist in the daily language of
politicians, teachers, religious orators, and salespeople. The
symbols of this rhetoric line the shelves of Wal-Mart, Costco,
and Target in a merchandise industry that thrives on them
(Wal-Mart alone sold over half a million flags, trinkets, and
other patriotic items in the first twenty-four hours after 9/11.)
They also help political messaging as it is crafted in Washington
to retain its impact, from K Street and Sunset Boulevard to the
white picket fences and megachurches of Midwestern towns.

Accordingly, beneath the surface of single-issue groups and
China-watching clubs lies an ingrained tendency to reduce issues of foreign policy to two basic framing concepts. Both have
their roots in founding American narratives, and both provide
popular traction for prevailing China themes. The first is the
enduring notion of a zero-sum, win-or-lose struggle between
American liberty and foreign tyranny, which helps to give traction to the idea of an historic, inevitable showdown between
Beijing and America, the leader of the free world. If you need
a reading list, start with titles like *Showdown: Why China
Wants War with the United States, War Footing: 10 Steps America Must Take to Prevail in the War for the Free World, The
Coming Conflict with China,* and *Hegemon: China's Plan to
Dominate Asia and the World,* which will likely leave you con-
vinced that Beijing is hell-bent on nothing less than displacing
the United States as the world's sole superpower.[55]

The second framing concept is the idea of America as the
leading proponent in a universal system of liberty, freedom,
and human progress, which feeds popular notions about the universal destiny of the American Revolution and the "inevitability
argument" of the panda huggers. For a classic rendition of

this frame, try *Good Capitalism, Bad Capitalism*, by William Baumol and others, who say, "the odds are with the optimists" that economic growth will "democratize China." As they assure, "one reason for being optimistic is to look at America's early history and especially the experiences of many of the country's founding fathers, which demonstrate that business skills can hone the talents needed to achieve and maintain self-governance."[56]

It would be unusual in political cultures such as London or Paris to root the analysis of current China policy in stories about the Glorious Revolution in 1688 or the beheading of Louis XVI in 1793. But somehow in the United States, the terms of reference on most current issues of foreign policy, including political progress in China, fit naturally into the framework of a time when Americans wore knee-high breeches and powdered wigs.[57]

These broad and popular assumptions, rooted as they are in the familiar and comforting themes of American national mythology, help to force the China issue into the framework of false choices and grand oversimplifications. Will China be a strategic partner *or* a strategic rival? Will China integrate with the U.S.-led system *or* challenge it? Is China an opportunity *or* a threat?" Will China embrace free-market democracy *or* remain authoritarian? The reality, of course, is more complex and less emotionally satisfying than all of these formulations. China is increasingly a land of opportunity and economic freedom, but it doesn't permit free speech. The Chinese government espouses a form of "consultative democracy" between party factions that compete in debate and consultation over the direction of policies. But it refuses to embrace pluralism or allow political parties. China refuses to conform to the liberal codes and values of international good governance, but it also strives to avoid intimidating the West as a "rising power" or a great power competitor.

Aided by these complexities, the China debate is like a microcosm of the larger systemic weaknesses that afflict the public-political process in Washington. Across the matrix of news outlets, think tanks, policy groups, and political camps of government, the China discussion has an element of the Tower of Babel, with competing lobbies and zealots making a collective noise that suppresses effective discourse. Unlike the foreign policy discussion in China, which is usually focused and integrates strategic and other concerns, the American debate is too often a noisy dirge in which each of the special interests has a part. As we've seen in this chapter, think tanks like AEI, the Heritage Foundation, and the Center for Security Policy are weighted heavy with preconditioned responses, as are organizations like the U.S.-China Business Council and the consulting firms, albeit for different reasons.

Unfortunately, the electronic media offer little relief and tend to focus on China in ways that reflect their structural limitations. It's little secret these days that news and political debate are presented, at least in part, as entertainment in order to maximize market share, ratings, and advertising revenue. As a result, editors are guided by what sells, which is, too often, a combination of sensation and patriotism. The subject of China suffers accordingly. As a former Beijing correspondent for the *Los Angeles Times* has noticed, after two-minute segments on Olympics games and health scares, media debate usually leaves the issue as fast as possible, along with all the complexity that might be involved. American corporate media outlets are loyal to the same handful of frames on China that dominate the Beltway, be it China the Cold War–style rival, China the threat to our jobs or dog food, or the bright new "shiny China" that makes everyone rich and happy.[58]

The very format of this environment is unsuitable to the most important themes. We will wait a long time before the foreign news leads with stories like "China: The Contradictions of a Partly Reformed State," or "China: Protagonist in a Global Battle of Ideas." These frames are neither simple nor entertaining enough.

THE GREAT CYCLE OF AMERICAN FOREIGN POLICY DEBATE

The ever-present footprint of the nation's history is present in today's policy debate and points to a cycle that could affect the China question.

The last sixty years reflect a pattern in which U.S. foreign policy debate oscillates between the clarion call of providential mission on one hand, and withdrawal and healing on the other. Following World War II and Europe's initial reluctance to stand up to Hitler at the infamous Munich conference, mainstream political debate clutched the Munich analogy, hearing the "tap, tap, tap of Neville Chamberlain's umbrella on the cobblestones of Munich" whenever and wherever freedom was under attack. After this had drawn the United States into Vietnam and the United States was severely wounded by the outcome, there developed in the early 1990s a culture of reluctance in the Balkans. This experience, in turn, fashioned an overzealous and highly activist approach from the neoconservatives, which found voice in the U.S. national security strategy of 2002. For decades, says the *Atlantic Monthly*, two analogies have competed for supremacy in American foreign policy circles: the analogy of Munich and that of Vietnam. The former often thrives after a lengthy and prosperous peace, when the traumas and costs of war are far enough removed to appear abstract. The latter usually thrives following national trauma.[59]

A major question for U.S. policy makers in meeting the China challenge is identifying where the issue sits between the ideology of universal mission and the sanctuary of withdrawal. Both have their supporters inside the Beltway, and neither is an option.

Bush-era rhetoric that projects the ideas and norms of the Western liberal order now goes unheard among world audiences that have stopped listening to American lectures. At the same time, the United States can hardly afford to withdraw to its other default setting, a strictly conservative and narrow definition of the national interest. Washington is already losing the battle for hearts and minds, for leverage and liberal agendas, in the global south and various quarters of the developing world. Now is precisely the time that American power has to expand and reapply itself throughout the world, albeit in notably different ways. As earlier parts of the book have explained, the Chinese are trumping America and the West in the application of soft power throughout the emerging markets and the global south.

The next chapter, the conclusion, argues in more detail that Washington must reinvigorate American ideas and involvement across the international context, but through a new kind of post-neoconservative approach. This is easier said than done, of course, not least of all because America's underlying weakness is also one of its greatest strengths: *the primacy of ideas in American political discourse.* While the American preoccupation with its own exceptionalism has at times been its undoing, this trait has also been one of America's most powerful gifts to the world.

On more than one occasion, the nation's leaders have called upon an inherent sense of mission and providence to rally the American people behind a cause that goes far beyond their own borders. In a political culture that has sometimes relished its separation from the international realm, the paradigm of exceptionalism has endowed the United States with the capacity to fashion public support at crucial moments, such as Franklin Roosevelt's notion of an arsenal of democracy in 1940, and Harry Truman's declaration of aid to Europe seven years later.

There's no better evidence of the power of American ideas to inspire and captivate the rest of the world than the election of Barack Obama. And here we focus on what *Obama's election* meant to the world community; we are setting aside, for the moment, the philosophical questions his administration poses on the role of government in contemporary America and the immense economic, budgetary, and programmatic problems that now accompany his domestic programs and that have led to an inevitable decline in his approval ratings.

With the nation beleaguered at home and abroad, Obama's election bore witness to the country's awesome powers of reinvention and self-renewal. When he entered the White House in January 2009, Obama didn't just carry the expectations of America. With a global economic crisis, fresh wars in the Middle East, old ones in Africa, nuclear proliferation in Iran and North Korea, a failing Western mission in Afghanistan, the kernel of optimism in war-torn Iraq, a newly resurgent Russia, a rising China, and a planet in environmental crisis, Obama also carried with him the hopes of the entire attentive world.[60]

Few could seriously argue that any of these problems could be solved without the full faith and power of the U.S. government.

As American interventions in Afghanistan and Iraq remain, at great cost, unresolved, America has been in a period of reflection. With American credibility in play abroad while the economy struggles at home, America can sermonize from the international podium or retreat to circumspection and disengagement. But if Washington is to revitalize the American brand, it will have to get this delicate balance just right. While the global community might have tired of American interventionism, an America that withdraws to heal its domestic wounds will serve neither itself nor others.[61] The final chapter now summarizes the nature of the China challenge and looks in more detail at the choices confronting the United States.

CHAPTER 7

CONCLUSION

PART OF THE DIFFICULTY IN FORMULATING an effective policy debate on China was made clear to me by Winston Lord, a former ambassador to China, who had accompanied Henry Kissinger on the famous "secret trip" to reopen U.S. relations with Beijing in 1972. Lord explained that the country presents a set of contradictory images that can all be true at once: "You want to argue that China is an economic juggernaut, that's true, but if you want to argue that China is wrought with serious economic weaknesses and the ruling party feels constantly vulnerable, that's also true. You want to argue that the military is growing at a colossal rate that causes concern, that's true. But if you want to argue that China's military is a joke, that can also be true. You can argue that the Communist Party has total political mastery over the Chinese people, and you can just as easily argue that another Tiananmen Square is potentially waiting right around the corner."[1] After two years of living in Beijing, the veteran reporter James Fallows made a similar point in 2008. "The most important fact" about analyzing China, he wrote, is that "no one can sensibly try to present the 'real story' or the 'overall picture' of this country. It is simply too big and too contradictory."[2]

Former U.S. ambassador to China, James Lilley, sees these contradictions translating to "a certain schizophrenia in dealing with the U.S.—which explains a lot of what seems inexplicable or counterproductive."[3]

Understanding modern China, therefore, can be an elusive quest. China has seen as much change in the last decade as Europe saw in half a century after 1945. Playing catch-up with the pace, the people and the politics of new China brought the realization that while China may consist of *many Chinas*, and while these many Chinas might be pulling in myriad directions at once, contrary to my earlier belief, the Chinese Communist Party has mastered the art of keeping them all together.

Just about. It is often a far from happy union: keeping the conservative old guard in line with the younger, reform-minded entrepreneurs; laying claim to the mantle of a "harmonious society" while brutally suppressing ethnic groups in Tibet and Xinjiang, or religious groups nationwide; keeping the military brass loyal to a government that affords them ever less emphasis in the national mythology; embracing information technology while maintaining information censorship; enforcing contract law and the legal framework for doing good business, while staving off calls for legal accountability; decentralizing party control while clamping down on corruption; and, perhaps most of all, placating the 650 million rural Chinese, or the migrant urban underclass, many of whom have yet to see the rising quality of life they have helped to create for the new middle classes of the eastern seaboard and river cities.

Modern China, then, is an index of contradictions. Notwithstanding this, it is also governed by a ruling elite that has proved its metal in the last twenty years at bending rather than breaking, at adapting to change and constantly adjusting its strategy to maintain the seemingly impossible balance of governing a fragmented and colossal polity.

CHINA'S FEAR OF CHAOS

A realization of the many paradoxes within China, in turn, led to a further discovery: The erosion of central control, which I initially set out to find, might not be clear and present. But the leadership's fear of it certainly is. If there's an underlying verity for the many Chinas that compete for our attention, if there's a constant in the fast-changing substance of modern China, it's the underlying role of the ruling party's fears. More specifically, it is the fear of chaos, of losing political and social control, that runs like an iron spine through the entire Chinese body politic.

Historically, this kind of fear is as old as the Yangtze River flooding its banks every spring. The nation's leaders are harassed by the ghosts of their own dynastic past. China's long, imperial history presents a recurrent cycle of economic turmoil, peasant revolt, and dynastic change, which saw the end of at least five dynasties, including Qin, Han, Sui, Yuan, and Ming.[4] China has a history of bottom-up rebellion almost unrivaled anywhere else in the world.[5]

That this fear runs through China's global posture presents a difficult problem for Western policy makers. At its core, we have pointed to a curiosity captured by Robert Louis Stevenson. Dr. Jekyll and Mr. Hyde are alive and well in Beijing—and present a perplexing duality on the global stage. As this book has mentioned at various stages, the world is growing increasingly familiar with the emergent identity of China "the good neighbor." Dr. Jekyll's Beijing provides troops for peacekeeping operations and aid for disaster relief; it hosts the Six-Party Talks and helps to lift the global economy out of recession.

Behind China the good neighbor, however, lies a second, entirely different creature. Mr. Hyde's China writes the checks that sustain the most brutal and backward regimes in the world. It sells technical expertise and hardware for making weapons of mass destruction to the worst proliferators we know about, and it frequently makes a mockery of diplomatic attempts to sanction rogue states. These two Chinas coexist in the international system: the good neighbor and the rogue state. As I began to realize, this duality in China's global posture cannot be gradually transformed by the will of Western engagement or the leverage of Western coercion. This is because China's growing presence in the world at large is a function of the ruling party's drive to maintain control at home—and its immovable, historical fear of chaos.

When we look at China through the Washington lens, we are impressed by the breadth of analysis. But as we saw in Chapter 6, this discussion is "globulated" into a collection of single issue groups and lobbies, which approach China predominantly as a military issue, or as a trade issue, or a human rights issue, or a hegemonic-power issue. While these groups proceed along separate lines, taken together they obscure a larger problem.

HOW CHINA CHALLENGES THE WEST

China presents a growing challenge to America and the West. But when it comes to understanding the nature of this challenge, the core of the issue is not military or humanitarian or even economic per se. The real China challenge is political and cultural.[6]

Beijing is the catalyst in chief for two parallel trends that are coalescing to compromise the reach and influence of the Western liberal order. Developing countries and emerging markets no longer have to abide by the Western conditions of financial engagement. Nor must they choose between emulating the Western model and rejecting capitalism. In consequence, the U.S.-led system is losing leverage as a politicoeconomic bloc and losing appeal as a politicoeconomic model. Both of these developments have a life of their own. But they also share the same cheerleader in China. The process works as follows.

As explained in Chapter 5, by embracing liberal market reforms in the last three decades, the Chinese Communist Party has succeeded where the Soviet Union failed. China delivered sufficient economic opportunities, and higher living standards, to persuade the populace that the future held a better quality of life. In a country the size of China, this policy has only been made possible through private businesses and economies of scale, which can guarantee a sufficient number of jobs for the millions leaving state-owned enterprises and Communist social safety nets. Stability at home, therefore, depends on feeding the beast of high-rate economic growth, year upon year. In turn, this means ready access to foreign resources and markets— sufficient to keep the factory belts moving and their produce flying off the shelves. This means Africa for access to oil, iron ore, copper, zinc, lead, tin, and uranium. It means Latin America for access to soybeans, steel, and more oil. It means contracts to sustain the global turnover for fast-growing Chinese telecommunications and construction giants. It means access to consumer markets from Europe to South Asia for the endless flow of Chinese textiles, shoes, clothing, electrical appliances, household wares, and office equipment. And as the record shows, it also means seeking out every possible business partner the world has to offer, no matter where they sit on the spectrum between dictator and democrat.

In the substance of these relations lies the real China challenge for America and the West. China does business with the good, the bad, and the ugly—as long as they pay. As Chapter 3 documented, Beijing has worked hard in the last decade to become an alternative source of aid, trade, loans, and investment to any state that falls below Western standards of good governance. Not only are Western observers offended by the deeds and dictatorships that this policy helps to sustain, but we are also apparently powerless to do anything about it.

THE FLAWS OF THE WASHINGTON CONSENSUS

Here in a single policy decision, the Chinese have delivered a mortal blow to the entire theology of Western development economics. For at least twenty years, the First World winners of the Cold War have assumed that we hold within our means the power to shape the future of the international system, and guide it gradually toward the norms and values that we imbue with a sense of universal destiny. But we also assumed that these qualities would flow from the application of development packages like the Washington Consensus, in which poorer countries would turn to us for financial help because they had to. In so doing, they would also have to swallow a sizable pill of conditions and structural reforms in economic and political governance—transparency, rule of law, anticorruption measures, social investment, and more effective budgeting. These were the carrots and sticks with which the West expected to bring developing nations to a more pluralist and democratic persuasion.

As we saw, however, it hasn't worked out like that. Joseph Stiglitz, former chief economist of the World Bank, has explained that the Washington Consensus proved to be "neither necessary nor sufficient" for economic development in a number of cases. Various countries in East Asia and Latin America experienced what Stiglitz called "a lost decade" from the late 1980s to the end of the twentieth century, in which the application of structural economic reforms brought a fall in annual growth rates, sometimes from levels above 6 percent down to 2 percent and below.[7] Income rates often declined, while poverty and unemployment rates increased.

The essence of Western development packages in this period was based on a formulaic commitment to free-market fundamentalism, which emphasized privatization, liberalization, and price stability. In the process, it placed significant emphasis on template measurements of GDP as the calculus of success, which could increase even as many parts of a country grew poorer. It also ignored key local factors, such as land reform, the health of the financial sector, education levels, and bad-governance issues in both the public and the private sectors. While many of the reforms served the interests of technocrats and special interests, they showed little regard for areas such as distribution of income and social justice. In consequence, a generation of politicians and economists across the developing world were ready for an alternative to Western theories of development economics, even before the Chinese went global at the turn of the millennium.[8]

THE G20 AND THE NEW GEOPOLITICAL MAP

Now, a decade later, China's growing love affair with the developing world is having various effects. The most serious human rights abusers in the world have a new sugar daddy, as do the proliferators, the "genociders," and just about every other category of state malcontent. And not only does China's global posture impede the course of values and freedoms dear to Western hearts, but it also has a growing impact on debates in global forums that the West founded and presumed to dominate, such as the United Nations, the IMF, the World Bank, and the WHO. The newcomers in these institutions are increasingly forming clubs and other associations that outnumber the old-timers in a process that threatens to leave Western governments feeling like strangers in their own houses. Merely the size of the meeting table at the London G20 meeting in early 2009 highlighted an important new reality: that the answers to the world's problems no longer lie primarily in Washington and Brussels. They also lie increasingly in new centers of economic power and new forms of global cooperation beyond the member list of NATO.

Then we come to the shrinking of Western appeal as a politicoeconomic brand. Important parts of the global economy are seeing a strategic rejection of Western free-market doctrine. China is again the flagship of the process. As we further saw in Chapter 4, the levers of economic power and influence belong increasingly to the authority of the state in various parts of the world. A long line of countries, from Russia, Brazil, Venezuela, and Saudi Arabia to Iran, Morocco, Algeria, Libya, Angola, Dubai, Azerbaijan, Kazakhstan, Malaysia, Vietnam, and others, now provides prominent examples of governments—rather than private interests—directing the major economic sectors.[9] And on lower political rungs at the popular level, it's also possible to see a decline in the appeal of American ideas. Toward the end of the Bush administration, the Pew Research Center conducted an extensive polling survey of global opinion across forty-seven countries, with some startling results. In almost all countries polled, people said they liked American ideas about democracy *less* in 2007 than they had in 2002. In many countries, the declines were steep, including a 27 percent drop in Venezuela, a 25 percent drop in Turkey, and a 23 percent decline in Indonesia (Table 7.1).[10]

Table 7.1   **Where American Ideas About Democracy Have Lost Favor**

Greatest declines	2002 %	2007 %	Change
Venezuela	67	40	-27
Turkey	33	8	-25
Indonesia	51	28	-23
France	42	23	-19
Czech Rep.	64	46	-18
Slovakia	54	36	-18

SOURCE: Pew Research Center, "Global Unease with Major World Powers," 47-Nation Pew Global Attitudes Survey, Pew Global Attitudes Project, Washington, DC, June 27, 2007, 25, http://pewglobal.org/reports/pdf/256.pdf.

Roger Cohen of the *International Herald Tribune* reminds us that the global rise of the Chinese example coincides with the very moment in history when the power of Western ideas and free markets—the American mantra of recent decades—is in retreat before state intervention. This retreat has even been led, in certain respects, "by a chastened United States," which has all of a sudden "discovered some merit in the oft-mocked European model."[11] Ian Bremmer adds that a new wave of capitalism has now arrived, "hastened by the recent global economic slowdown. But this time, the governments of the world's wealthiest countries, and not just those of emerging-market countries, are the ones intervening in their economies."[12]

The most prominent demonstration of the last decade, of course, has come from Beijing. The decision makers of many developing countries are not only looking to China as a convenient source of non-Western finance, but also seeing Beijing as a bright, shining demonstration for the increasingly popular doctrine of state capitalism. Joshua Cooper Ramo, a onetime consulting partner at Kissinger Associates, proclaims that China is marking a path for smaller and poorer governments, which are trying to figure out not simply how to develop their economies, but also how to fit into the global economy in a way that allows them to remain independent in their political choices.[13]

The growth in new centers of wealth and new models of capitalism is a hydra-headed animal. But they come together in a powerful singular force with the new global China. It's important to remember, however, that *China hasn't deliberately set out to diminish the power of the Western bloc or the appeal of its brand.* These realities, though sobering, are rooted, ultimately, in the ruling party's determination to stay in power at home. Moreover, as long as the political system remains intact within China, they are unlikely to change. As Chapter 5 makes plain, China's leaders have caught themselves in a kind of growth trap, which in turn affects how much leverage the West has with them in the international space. Liberalizing the economy may have kept the CCP in power, but it has also come with a high cost in environmental and social terms, from income disparity to endemic corruption, "cancer villages," and arbitrary land seizures. In these side effects lies the kernel of potential unrest, which worries the leadership. The only method the leadership has found, however, to keep a lid on the forces of political dissatisfaction is ever-more economic growth at breakneck rates. China's problems at home thus place an immovable limit on the degree to which China can bend to Western liberal norms in the global space. Political stability inside China relies on a global commercial portfolio forged on the principles of moral blindness and noninterference.

This is why Washington is wasting its time in endless debates about whether China is a partner or a rival. These are not useful terms; nor is this a useful way to frame the China challenge. China is both, neither, and everything in between, depending on which aspect of its global posture you focus on. China will duly continue to rely on and support the structures of global governance for its benefit while it simultaneously subverts them for the sake of commercial advantage and political stability at home.

Against this backdrop, the China question must be framed within terms that go beyond Washington's penchant for formulations of Scenario A versus Scenario B, or questions of "Is China this, is it that?" For at least half a century, Beltway policy wonks have liked to think in terms of grand slogans. A major challenge is usually accompanied with a rush to coin the next policy catchphrase, which can somehow encapsulate both the problem at hand and an entire formula for dealing with it. In China's case, the challenge is too complex to accept a solution that can fit around its many and varied angles like a stretchy sock. There is no grand strategy, in other words, that works on China. The devil in any solution here is in the multifarious details. Pundits have suggested terms like *containment* or *engagement*—and even "congagement"—as the magic-bullet answer. At best, these are vacuous notions that achieve little. At worst, they risk obscuring the various levels that exist within the "China challenge."

NO G2

The first of these levels, naturally, is managing the relationship between Washington and Beijing. Accordingly, this book makes a clear and simple proposal for how to think about U.S.-China relations: Let's not pretend anymore that the West can gradually housebreak China to abide by liberal international norms. Stop the wishful thinking; China's growing participation in the international system is not the same as a growing willingness to play by U.S. rules.[14] This flawed expectation fails to take into account that China's domestic needs for resources drive its foreign policy.

Of course, America must remain dedicated to engagement with China on wide-ranging areas of common interest, such as coordination in rebuilding the global financial system and pressuring North Korea to compromise on its nuclear weapons program. Beneath the surface of these initiatives, however, is an immovable verity: *We are not partners.*

The credit crunch and the arrival of a new administration in Washington in 2009 brought a wave of high-level calls in the city about taking U.S.-China relations to "a new level," including the likes of Zbigniew Brzezinski and Secretary Clinton herself. And Washington doesn't suffer alone in this regard. The seduction moves easily across the Atlantic, where it equally infects policy circles in Europe. In May 2009, for example, British Foreign Secretary David Miliband proclaimed that China was the new "indispensable power," the same phrase that former U.S. Secretary of State Madeleine Albright famously used to describe the United States a decade before. Washington and Beijing were a new kind of G2, Miliband intimated, with the potential for a G3 if Europe could fashion an effective collective voice.[15]

This book offers caution. Elevating U.S.-China relations to the bilateral status of a special G2 relationship is not the answer. Washington and Beijing have fundamentally different interests, different values, and different priorities. As Elizabeth Economy and Adam Segal have suggested, the good news is that the United States and China share some basic goals, like kick-starting economic growth, maintaining an open global economy, maintaining peace and stability in East Asia, and halting climate change. But the bad news is that even after three decades of engagement, Washington and Beijing disagree fundamentally about how the world should work, with dramatically different views on questions of sovereignty, sanctions, and conditions for the use of force. Washington sees politics and economics as deeply entwined and guided by broadly accepted communal values; Beijing believes that politics and economics should remain separate. American companies investing in Asia need to protect their patents; Beijing lacks the legal infrastructure to enforce intellectual property rights. U.S. policy makers have developed a newfound sense of conscience in Africa, with AIDS relief programs and sustainable development assistance. China has commercial relations with every dictator on the continent. Washington has called for UN-sponsored condemnations of governments in Myanmar, Iran, and Sudan; China has blocked these calls for disapproval. The White House has urged transparency in bilateral military relations; Beijing consistently balks. The point here is that Chinese leaders are highly focused on their domestic position and determined to survive. In the end, our objectives and theirs are not the same, and it's unwise to enshrine the status of U.S.-China relations in rhetoric that pretends such compatibility. The results will lead to recriminations and disappointment more than they will to successful partnership.[16]

So here's another idea: Washington may no longer have the ability to define the terms of international engagement with Beijing. But it *does* have the unique power to leverage large parts of the international system. By the same token, Beijing may no longer feel that it has to listen to edicts and cajoling from Washington. But it *does* care a great deal about its position in a wider global context, as this is the lifeblood of stability at home. Amid these observations lies a more productive path for Washington in managing its relationship with Beijing.

BETWEEN DECLINE AND UNIPOLARITY

Before we proceed to the details, it is important to underscore that America remains the world's most powerful nation. Popular literature is riddled with absurdities and false extremes on the state of American power. A common dichotomy emerging in this debate lies between the new "declinists" and a stubborn core of "unipolarists." At one end of the spectrum, for example, are arguments such as "Empire Falls," written for the *National Interest* by Robert Pape in early 2009. The United States has fallen into a state of decline, Pape announced, a condition as familiar to history as "Rome, Imperial China, Venice, Spain, France, Great Britain and the Soviet Union." Even worse, according to Pape, the United States is somehow suffering "a far greater loss of relative power in a shorter time than any power shift among European great powers from roughly the end of the Napoleonic Wars to World War II."[17]

At the spectrum's other end, meet George Friedman, a new pundit on the U.S. talk-show circuit and the founder of Stratfor.com, a popular online think tank for foreign affairs. I read Friedman's book *The Next Hundred Years: A Forecast for the 21st Century*, in response to several recommendations, only to find that it suffers from a classic case of "Beltway-itis." Friedman, reflecting a syndrome common to the populist commentariat, remains fixated on the supremacy of America's position in hard-power terms. Forget South Asia, East Asia, or the Pacific; North America has apparently "replaced Europe as the center of gravity in the world, and whoever dominates North America is virtually assured of being the dominant global power." For the twenty-first century, says Friedman, "that will be the United States." The principal reason, he explains, is that control of the world's trading system belongs to "whatever country controlled both the North Atlantic and the Pacific."[18]

Clearly, the conditions of American power sit between the extremes of decline and the dominant global power. Yet, the first ignores the durable characteristics of American power, and the second has been long superseded by the complexity and diffusion of international power since the 1990s.

THE WORLD ISN'T FLAT; IT'S A PYRAMID

Among the most sensible analyses of recent years is that of Leslie Gelb, former president of the Council on Foreign Relations and onetime official in both State and Defense Departments. As Gelb explains, "We are not in, nor are we entering, a post-American era."[19] But nor can we dominate as we used to. The United States remains by far and away the single most powerful nation on earth. But no longer does this kind of raw and indexed power give the United States the capacity to dominate. America has the largest economy in the world, with a per-capita GDP of $48,000. It remains the most technologically advanced country, and its military budget is frequently more than the combined military spending of the next fifteen to twenty competitors.[20] But there are too many other expressions and centers of power now growing around the world.[21]

Gelb envisions the power structures of today's international system as looking like a pyramid of different levels. At the top sits the United States. Underneath are *the major eight*—Britain, France, Germany, Japan, Brazil, Russia, India, and China—which share the lion's share of power with Washington as managing directors of the global realm. Next are the *oil and gas states*—Saudi Arabia, Venezuela, Iran, Nigeria (and Russia again)—which derive considerable power simply from natural resources. Below these are the midlevel *regionals*, such as Mexico, Pakistan, South Africa, South Korea, and Taiwan, which have a prominent voice in international affairs only when a problem erupts in their stomping ground. Next are the *state-responsibles*, which generally take care of themselves and cause little trouble to anyone else; state-responsibles include Switzerland, Singapore, Norway, Botswana, and Chile. These are followed by the *bottom-feeders* — the rogues and failed states — where civil wars, genocide, and brutal dictators provide many of the major challenges to those on the levels above. Last, there is the fast-emerging nexus of *nonstate actors*, such as media groups, terrorist groups, and business groups, which are intertwined with government and society at a global level and share in the distribution of power.[22]

The shape of international power is not "flat," therefore, as the columnist Thomas Friedman famously argued in 2005. It is "decidedly pyramidal," says Gelb. But international power is also becoming diffused to unprecedented and complicating degrees. This diffusion has been characterized by three startling historical developments: First, military conflicts between great powers, the kind that dominated power politics in Europe from the seventeenth century to World War I, have become too destructive and dangerous to be in anyone's interest. Second, the weak have established the capacity to resist the strong through a combination of nationalism and insurgency and by playing off great-power benefactors against one another — a capacity that has come to rival the power of the strong to command. Third, the waning value of raw military power has coincided with the development of international economic power.[23] Since war has receded as the principal vehicle for the accumulation and safeguard of power, the national interest today finds its most common expression in commercial transactions and a state's economic power.[24]

THE PARADOX OF SO MUCH AMERICAN POWER

These trends of economic globalization have also created a paradox for American power, as this book has contended. The historical shift in focus from warfare and military expansion to capitalism and international markets has helped to vouchsafe the centrality of America in the international system as the largest capitalist economy on earth with the most consumers, the currency of global reserve, and, until recently, the strongest financial system—an epithet that will likely regain its status when regulation and recovery have replaced the recent recession. At the same time, economic globalization is bringing serious challenges to American power on what Joseph Nye calls "little cat's feet in the night."[25] As capitalism deepens around the globe, so is the raw and relative preeminence of America diminishing.

Thus, for all the power centered in American hands, it is not enough to safeguard American interests in the world. As Nye wrote shortly before the United States invaded Iraq, American power might be daunting, but it isn't sufficient to meet challenges such as terrorism, climate change, and nuclear proliferation, without involving other nations.[26] The only way to manage these problems is with international partnerships, coalitions of key states, and the quid pro quo of horse-trading compromises in the international political marketplace.

But then here's the flip side of America's new position: Washington might not have the unipolar power it claimed after 9/11, but what it *does* have is the power—and indeed the expectations of others—to lead. There may be plenty of problems that America cannot face alone, but they are also problems the other great powers can't face without the United States. And many of them know it. As the previous chapter asserted, few could argue that any of the serious transnational problems can be solved without American application and leadership. It's also important to remember what the history wonks of "American decline" have ignored; there is no Roman competitor waiting on the periphery of the American Carthage. Washington may be losing its sense of monopoly on power, but in the twenty-first century, no other great power actually covets America's role as head boy of the financial system or regional balancer in places like Pacific Asia, where the American security umbrella keeps regional powers from starting a nineteenth century arms race with Beijing. Neither do the powers want to see the United States recede from its position as a global economic driver; what they want is stability in the system, so that everybody can get on with the business of doing business and creating wealth—the modern-day index of power.

GETTING HELP

These dynamics are crucial in the approach to Beijing. In dealing with China, the United States needs to solicit the help of the rest of the world.[27] Take this as step two of formulating a China strategy. If step one is recognition that we can't cause China to grow into the global civic culture, the next step is to take the myth of a special G2 diplomatic love-hug and replace it with something else. As the beginning of this chapter described, fear is the iron spine that runs through the Chinese body politic. It shapes every major decision by the ruling elite, in a society that is constantly grappling politically with its economic success.[28] Accordingly, fear is an area where Washington still retains a measure of leverage over Beijing. More specifically, this leverage pertains to the CCP's fear of two separate international scenarios: isolation and criticism. Let us deal with each in turn.

China's aversion to any sense of isolation or exclusion may offer an opportunity to reposition relations in a more productive context. Washington needs to route U.S.-China relations through the integrated circuitry of larger partnerships. Here lies an alternative path between the hopeless notion of building alliances *around China* and the overworked notion of bilateral engagement *with China.* The days of being able to insist upon allegiance to an "American way" in the wider international context are over. The most effective model for encouraging China to cooperate with American objectives is to build larger multilateral initiatives based on power coalitions and associations of states, which are both important to China and friendly to American objectives. The onus is then on China to join the party of responsible major powers—a status it longs for—or be left out.

TEST CASES FOR PARTNERSHIP: CLIMATE CHANGE AND ENERGY

Take climate change as a hypothetical example. China, along with the United States, is one of the largest sources of CO_2 (carbon dioxide) emissions. In the last decade, as the issue has become a front burner, so to speak, the United States has become a marginal player in the debate. Meanwhile, China has established limited initiatives with other countries on a bilateral basis, such as technical cooperation with Japan in carbon storage, while it uses American inaction as an excuse to do little itself. In this context, Washington could lecture or prod Beijing endlessly on the need to combine forces and face the problems of climate change, likely to little effect.

Another approach would be to consult with powerful allies, such as France, Germany, Canada, Japan, and, more recently, India, with a view to coordinating a single environmental initiative, with a common charter of principles for making a healthier environment. In the process, this charter could involve issues that really matter to Beijing, such as infrastructure development projects and technical resources.[29] As David Sanger of the *New York Times* has hypothesized about this sort of initiative, "my guess is that the Chinese would say nothing at first—other than 'very interesting,'" but in time, it would have "a clear appeal." It would also likely unnerve Chinese leaders if serious transnational cooperation in infrastructure, technology, and engineering left them out of the geopolitical loop.[30]

A similar sort of model could work in the area of energy security. As General Brent Scowcroft (USAF, ret.) asked me, "Why don't we open an energy dialogue that involves the Chinese?" There's so much global demand, he said, "Washington could say, 'Let's share in the shortage of resources and cooperate to get results,' but we haven't done that yet. And so the Chinese are saying, 'We gotta grab ours fast, because the U.S. is out there with all these giant oil companies.'"[31]

Again, if Washington simply calls for more U.S.-China cooperation on energy resources, we'll be likely to see little meaningful reaction from Beijing. Alternatively, we could take a leaf from the Chinese playbook of the last decade: Talk less and do more. A 2008 commission on American soft power, chaired by Joseph Nye and Richard Armitage, called for the next administration to set up and help to fund a Joint Technology Development Center. Its aim could be to coordinate international collaboration on energy security policies across a broad coalition of advanced and developing nations. Again, the basis of a charter could emerge, including provisions on issues that directly concern China, such as protection of sea lanes and critical energy infrastructure.[32]

China, of course, could simply say no. But Washington has less to lose and more to gain by trying this sort of model of "get the party started and wait for China to join." Beijing or no Beijing, this model would benefit America's reputation and the American brand, especially among developing countries.[33] It would also have the added advantage of actually getting American policy makers, bureaucrats, and diplomats back out into the hub of international talking-shops after a long hiatus focused on military unilateralism in the Middle East. In recent years, China has certainly shown the step-by-step potential of expanding quietly across the international sphere, one communiqué or photo shoot at a time. It has also shown the enormous political capital gleaned from this process of showing smaller powers that you're listening and you care. The secret of any success in this kind of effort is exploiting China's intense desire to be included in the top-table discourse of major powers, whether it's on financial stability, energy security, nonproliferation, climate change, or pandemic disease.

CHINESE "FACE" AND FEAR OF CRITICISM

Meanwhile, if Beijing is determined to avoid isolation and confrontation, then it has an equally strong aversion to international criticism of Chinese behavior.[34] Like so much of the Chinese posture abroad, this has its roots at home. Here again, Washington has some measure of leverage, and again it depends on the capacity to garner support across broader coalitions.

As the American psychoanalyst Gregory Mavrides has explained through his work in China, the Chinese concept of "face," or *mianzi*, is hard to understand from a Western perspective. A survey by the *China Youth Daily* put it best, where 75 percent of respondents acknowledged that making a mistake was by far the most humiliating experience they could imagine. In Western politics, the act of apologizing can be a political winner, depending on the context. Barack Obama famously left a voice mail for a female journalist during his presidential campaign to apologize for calling her "sweety." "I am duly chastened," he said, in a message that gained broadly positive coverage in national media for showing humility and respect.

Not so in China. Lying to avoid admitting a mistake in China is not viewed as an ignoble lie in the same manner as it is in Western cultures. It is often considered more respectable and rational than the humiliation of losing face.[35] These dynamics play an important role in the day-to-day interactions of Chinese culture and on the national level, where the solemn dynamics of dictatorship add to the mixture.

As we saw in Chapter 5, the Chinese government's policy for social cohesion has actually been twofold. Beyond sustaining growth, there has been an appeal to nationalism. In the wake of the Tiananmen protests, the Communist Party implemented a nationwide patriotic education campaign for both schools and the media, which has proved its effectiveness. A *New York Times* study of Chinese students on the twentieth anniversary of Tiananmen underscored the point. Students today show a general lack of idealism on campus, said the report. Instead, they are clearly utilitarian. Everything is based on "whether or not it is useful to me." Students may not like all the policies of their government, but nowadays, they often share a huge sense of pride in the government because it has moved so many people to a better life.[36]

Accordingly, there are many private Chinese media outlets now competing for sensational stories that appeal to the national pride of their listeners and viewers. In the process, Beijing has created what Susan Shirk calls an echo chamber of nationalism. In this environment, Chinese officials feel intense public pressure to take tough stands against international criticism.[37] The Chinese Olympic Torch relay of 2008 is a notable recent example, in which Chinese media outlets and blogging sites erupted in fury at the attempts of foreign protesters to disrupt the torch's global procession.

There are various fears that torment Chinese officials in these circumstances. First is the fear that they might look weak in front of the people. Second, because of this perception, officials fear that political rivals might outmaneuver them in the murky bureaucracy of high-party politics, where no one's ascension is guaranteed and falling foul of political superiors can have unpleasant results. Third is the fear that public anger could turn to public protests, which can potentially transmute into general unrest directed against government forces. Last, and perhaps most important, Chinese officials fear that losing face and looking weak might embolden the government's internal enemies, or the "splittists," such as Tibetans, Uighurs, and anti-Chinese politicians across the Straits in Taiwan.

WASHINGTON STILL HAS LEVERAGE

These circumstances also present Washington with opportunities. We can take advantage of the party's aversion to international criticism—more so than we have done in recent years.

American criticism leveled from the White House to the For-bidden City is usually of limited political value, as it only con-firms negative stereotypes in the public Chinese space about American arrogance. As the recent historical record suggests, however, Chinese officials have been unnerved by the broad and unified critique of international public opinion. In various cases, such as Chinese tactics in Tibet, Chinese support of Sudan, and arms shipments to Zimbabwe, coordinated global indignation has brought a reluctant and calculated bow to in-ternational pressure and a shift, at least marginally, in the policy. In Zimbabwe, the Chinese turned the arms shipment around; in Tibet, the government agreed to meet with the Dalai Lama; in Sudan, the Chinese accepted some proposals to condemn Khartoum.

What these events tell us is that Washington does have a limited element of leverage in China's fear of international criticism, but only if we can effectively — and perhaps subtly — encourage multiple voices of international opinion to pressure Chinese officials. This is another example of initiatives that only work if the United States doesn't go it alone. To this ex-tent, the CCP is fearful of the Tibetans for the wrong reason. The real power held by Tibetans and their advocates lies not in their ability to challenge the government security forces, but in their capacity to make front-page news above the crease in the global press. Each time they do, China suffers a public de-feat in the dimension of ethics, ideas, and governance. China aspires to a seat at the table of great powers, and here in its own backyard, the government is forced to resort to state vi-olence and cultural genocide in order to force-draft Tibetan acceptance of the Chinese hand. This is more than a question of sovereignty and splittism. It's a question of governance models and their legitimacy. Party leaders have a dead hand where official rhetoric is concerned on Tibet—and they know it.

Powerless as they may seem, the Tibetan people actually enjoy what many others would like to have—namely, the ability to confront and defeat the Chinese in an important strategic realm. Tibetans might be dragged through the streets of Lhasa, but China is simultaneously dragged around the global stage like a "field hand" who hasn't learned how to behave in the "big house on the hill."

THE BALANCE SHEET FOR BUSH: AMERICA PURSUED BY ITS OWN DEMONS

If the United States has leverage in the China relationship, therefore, it must rely on its ability to fashion consensus elsewhere. In this regard, U.S. foreign policy needs urgent repair. China has done well in the last decade by allowing the United States to be pursued and distracted by its own demons in Iraq and Afghanistan. Beijing even maintains a section in its defense establishment that focuses on applying the theories of military strategists, including Sun Tzu, to the modern context, most notably how to extract advantage when an enemy deceives himself and how best to capitalize on an enemy's mistakes.[38] What George W. Bush did over two terms has suited China's investment in this small staff perfectly.

The Center for Strategic and International Studies (CSIS) in Washington lists a number of factors that have undermined the American ability to deploy soft power and thus to fashion consensus support. At a basic level, America's status as the only superpower after the Soviet collapse generated distrust and resentment toward what was seen as unbound dominance. Meanwhile, globalization brought painful domestic adjustments in many economies, which invited many to blame America as the principal promoter and beneficiary of economic integration. Then, from the turn of the century, Washington remained apart from, or found it necessary to abrogate, treaties that had broad international support—the Kyoto Protocol on climate change, the International Criminal Court, the Mine Ban Treaty, the Missile Test Ban Treaty, and the Convention on the Rights of the Child—compounding the perception of go-it-alone arrogance and unfettered power. Conversely, these sentiments were soon entwined with scolding perceptions of American impotence on the streets of Iraq and among the debris of Hurricane Katrina.

George Joffe of Cambridge University observes that Washington "securitised" its relations after 9/11, across economic, political, and diplomatic spheres. All issues were seemingly pushed through a security lens. The effect was to shut down alternative forms of interpretation and to crowd out suggestions of risk management.[39] It also prioritized emotional language about American power over narrower or more limited definitions of the national interest and alienated traditional allies in Europe with much evangelizing about America's global mission.

The White House also managed to offend its friends across the water with concepts of old and new Europe. Then it attempted to bully a resurgent Russia, while largely neglecting Latin America and slighting Southeast Asia. As the CSIS report concluded, "with Washington preoccupied in the Middle East, China has deftly stepped into the vacuum left by the United States, primarily to pursue its own economic interests, but possibly also to pursue its long-term strategic goals of becoming a global power rather than simply a regional one."[40]

Machiavelli famously said it was safer to be feared than to be loved. Today, in the global information age, America must get better at being both.[41] The roots of effective leverage and cooperation in the China challenge rely on our reserves of soft power. Which brings us to the great zone of competition between Washington and Beijing. There is no greater test of American soft power than its condition in the developing world.

This is where China has established the most serious threat to Western interests. Hilton Root of George Mason University observes that more than half of global economic growth now occurs in the developing world. American security is therefore closely linked to establishing a better relationship with emerging economies.[42] As Africa expert Jennifer Cooke reminds us, however, competition for African commodities has increased not only from China, but also from India, Brazil, Russia, and even South Africa. The continent, therefore, has options, and U.S. influence is diminished.[43] China has strengthened its hand to no small extent in the last eight years by moving into areas that American policy makers neglected.

Southeast Asia is an example, where China has become energetically involved in numerous Asian security and political arrangements, including the ASEAN Regional Forum, the ASEAN + 3 process, and the East Asia Summit. Seemingly everywhere, from the equator south, China has been breaking into new markets, scoffing up natural resources, forging big energy deals, and forgiving debt, filling the gap left by perceived U.S. disinterest while the United States has been mired in the Middle East.

COMPETITION IN THE DEVELOPING WORLD: WHO'S THE VICEROY NOW?

It's frustrating that in pure dollar terms, the United States still spends the most in donorship to poor countries.[44] And yet China is seemingly making all the breakthroughs in soft power with developing countries. According to the Pew study mentioned earlier, the publics of many advanced nations are increasingly concerned about the negative impact of China's economic power on their own countries. In the developing world, however, the story is very different. China is seen as having a large and growing influence in both Africa and Latin America, where it is viewed in widely positive terms. Across Africa, favorable views of China outnumber critical views by two to one, or more, in every country except South Africa, where opinion is divided (Table 7.2). The data are similar, though less constant, in large areas of Latin America, where 73 percent in Chile and 67 percent in Venezuela say that China's rising influence in their economy improves their lives. These trends continue on around the world. China is generally viewed in favorable terms across Asia, with large majorities of 83 percent in Malaysia, 79 percent in Pakistan, 74 percent in Bangladesh, and 65 percent in Indonesia. Even in South Korea, where the locals have traditionally viewed China with suspicion or fear, 52 percent feel favorably toward China overall. The gap in perceptions of the American and Chinese presence in the global south comes down to a simple point. The Chinese are better at sending the right signal and giving poorer states what *they* want.

Jon Alterman has observed these dynamics in the Middle East: "It was confidence in the sincerity of U.S. anticolonialism that paved the way for U.S. influence in the Middle East. The

Table 7.2 China's Influence More Positive Than America's

	China's Influence		America's Influence		
	good thing %	bad thing %	good thing %	bad thing %	"Good" Difference
Africa					
Kenya	91	6	74	16	+17
Ivory Coast	90	6	80	12	+10
Ghana	90	5	79	13	+11
Senegal	86	6	56	23	+30
Mali	84	7	63	25	+21
Nigeria	79	12	58	27	+21
Tanzania	78	13	36	52	+42
Uganda	75	13	65	24	+10
Ethiopia	61	33	34	54	+27
South Africa	49	32	55	24	-6
Latin America					
Venezuela	58	28	36	47	+22
Chile	55	20	28	46	+27
Bolivia	42	34	14	64	+28
Peru	36	29	22	46	+14
Brazil	26	54	20	60	+6
Argentina	21	51	5	80	+16
Mexico	20	63	22	60	-2

Based on respondents who say China/U.S. has at least a fair amount of influence on the way things are going in their countries. Question asked only in Sub-Saharan Africa and Latin America.

SOURCE: Pew Research Center, "Global Unease with Major World Powers," 47-Nation Pew Global Attitudes Survey, Pew Global Attitudes Project, Washington, DC, June 27, 2007, 45, http://pewglobal.org/reports/pdf/256.pdf.

United States was in the practice of sending businesspeople, not viceroys, and was welcomed in the region because of it." While they lacked both scholarship and administrative experience in the Middle East, Americans won affection for exercising a light hand in Arab lands. "One hears echoes of these views," adds Alterman, "in early Twenty-first Century perceptions of China."[45]

We can never compete, of course, with the level of influence that Beijing enjoys with the worst regimes in places like Khartoum, Rangoon, Harare, Caracas, or Tehran. But this leaves much of the former Third World unaccounted for, where Washington can develop better means to compete with Beijing. Notably, soft power in many parts of the developing world is not a zero-sum game. Washington and Beijing can compete in many of the same developing markets.

Consequently, this chapter makes a bold suggestion: We must learn from China's success. Classical pragmatists as the Chinese are, they've been copying us for years in matters of finance and microeconomic management—and now we confront new realities in business and trade. As John Maynard Keynes once told a reporter who accused him of inconsistency, "When the facts change, I change my mind. What do you do, sir?"[46] The facts have changed in the developing world, and the Chinese have adjusted more quickly than we have.

There are lessons to be learned about the provision of concessionary loans, debt relief, generational investment, infrastructure programs, humanitarian and medical aid, increased cultural and academic exchange programs, and more engagement with local priorities. Here we can learn from others how to work with developing countries toward their objectives, as much as ours. What is most important to U.S. policy makers in Africa, for example, is energy and security, namely, oil contracts and terrorism. What is most important to Africans is transport and power infrastructure, technical resources, training, employment, GDP growth, schools, and national sports facilities. It is a region where games like soccer play a social role, both in the national pride of governments and in the upward mobility of aspirant underprivileged youth, who see football as a route out of poverty. Chinese officials have understood this for some time, in case some wonder why so many stadia are built with Chinese cranes.

In this respect, Chinese actions simply speak louder than Western words. Look at the initiatives President Hu Jintao announced at a recent summit for the Forum on China-Africa Cooperation. These are not overly expensive or burdensome initiatives. We need to learn from this approach, replicate it, and improve on it:

- Deploy one hundred top Chinese agricultural experts to Africa by 2009.
- Establish ten agricultural technology centers.
- Build thirty new hospitals.
- Provide $40 million in grants for anti-malaria drugs, prevention, and model treatment centers.
- Deploy three hundred Peace Corps–like volunteers.
- Build one hundred rural schools in Africa.
- Train fifteen thousand African professionals.
- Double the number of Chinese government scholarships for African students from two thousand to four thousand per year.[47]

THE SPECIFICS OF RESPONSE

There is reason to be optimistic. It's as well to remember that the rising popularity of China in the developing world is dramatic, but the nation's reputation isn't unblemished. Like a microcosm of China's global posture, as we saw in Chapter 3, the Chinese presence in Africa is double-edged. Economist Ben Simpfendorfer makes the point that China's exports to the developing world have "surged from $190 billion to $570 billion in the past five years." Chinese market share in the emerging markets has brought "factory closures and job losses from India to Syria," and "export subsidies . . . pegged to the [declining] dollar have only aided Chinese exporters."[48] While Chinese firms provide some local employment, training and technical expertise, and numerous public goods—often in the form of major infrastructure projects—they tend to use their own imported workforce, leave negative environmental footprints, and bring secondary waves of merchants that put locals out of business. The Chinese presence has already incurred a popular backlash in areas such as South Africa, Zambia, Nigeria, Angola, and Gabon, where many believe the China relationship has benefited the elites, marginalized merchants, and disadvantaged ordinary working people. These trends beg the question of how long and under what conditions the Chinese can rely on a ready flow of natural resources from Africa.

Although China has forged strong new links with ASEAN, for instance, the region remains ripe for an American charm offensive. Washington's failure to help the region in a time of need during the 1997–1998 Asian financial crisis remains a source of local uncertainty about American commitment when the region's interests are at stake. But the United States still enjoys high popularity ratings in Southeast Asia, where it is viewed as a guarantor of regional stability and a source of economic assets.[49]

These are all factors that limit China's soft power. They also open a window for the United States to restore its own. A number of specific initiatives should be taken in this regard:

1. First could be the creation of an American version of the Forum on China-Africa Cooperation (FOCAC). Let's invite African leaders to Washington; provide a red-carpet welcome, a tour of the Capitol, stops at the Lincoln and Jefferson memorials for a moment of thought about America's founders and our principles of governance, and a visit to the White House, with photos and brief, private meetings with the president. Set dates for the next meeting; conclude contracts, agreements, and pledges.

2. It's popular in Washington, particularly in Republican circles, to assume that if the answer is more government, then you're asking the wrong question. However, in consultation with a group of regional experts and former policy makers, Nye and Armitage have spearheaded a group who have called for a high-level, soft-power agency. The purpose would be to develop and manage a strategic framework for development policies, and it would work with the relevant congressional committees to secure funding for broad strategic purposes. It would produce a publication that would help to focus the policy debate—something like a *Quadrennial Soft Power Review,* to parallel the Defense Department's *Quadrennial Defense Review.*[50] The point here is that we need a single, powerful institutional channel, similar to what the Chinese have,

that brings together the different arms of development assistance, humanitarian relief, diplomatic presence, medical aid, and educational exchanges, so that they can be integrated and guided into broad strategies that promote the national interest.

3. In the discourse of development, Americans must recover a level of initiative that can exorcise the didactic tones of the Washington Consensus. This discourse must embrace a new idea: that there is no single set of policies to foster sustained growth, and that governments enjoying success in this respect have done so in the face of different obstacles, with varying policies on regulation, export, and technological innovation. Countries should be free to experiment with policies designed to address their specific circumstances; Washington should lead the global lending organizations and aid agencies in encouraging this experimentation.[51]

4. We should bolster this discourse with compromise on certain types of agricultural subsidies. The current stalemate at the Doha trade talks is all to China's political advantage. The United States remains unprepared at the time of writing to address its subsidies on cotton and other commodities until it secures enhanced market access for its farm products in developing countries. Oxfam, one of the largest development pressure groups in the world, has warned African countries not to rush into imbalanced agreements that could fast put local producers out of business.[52] China has thus been able to position itself as an outspoken defender of the developing world, teaming up with India and voting against American proposals, with the argument that the farmers of developing

countries have too often suffered unfair competition from advanced nations. Washington's political capital in the Doha debates would increase significantly if it could lead initiatives that cut certain subsidies and provided smaller and poorer developing countries with greater access to consumers in the United States, Europe, and Japan. Policy makers will have a hard fight at home in this regard, with stiff congressional resistance from politicians loathe to confront the farm lobby in their own constituencies. But in larger strategic terms, America needs to give some ground in order to gain more.

MEETING THE CHINA CHALLENGE AT HOME

Accordingly, Americans must also look inward to meet the challenges of staying competitive abroad. Just as this book has sought to illustrate the links between Chinese politics at home and its posture on the world stage, we must similarly understand how America's international power is affected by the policies it pursues at home. Alongside military advantage, the bases of American international power for half a century have been our economic competitiveness and our levels of education, productivity, and ingenuity.[53] As the economist Clyde Prestowitz commented at a recent reunion for his high school class of 1959, "we graduated at the peak of the post-World War II golden age, when the huge economies of scale of history's first mass market made American companies and American labor by far the most productive in the world." It was truly a time when American workers could compete, Prestowitz recalled, "with any on the planet."[54]

Exactly forty years later, Gelb paints a different picture. We must go beyond the faltering parts here and there to a frontal stare at the deteriorating whole. The federal budget deficit is skyrocketing toward $2 trillion, with Medicare and Social Security pushing it ever higher. The United States has become the largest debtor nation in history; its heavy industry has largely disappeared, moving to foreign competitors in a shift that compromises our sense of independence. Across the board, public school students trail their peers in math and science in a system that looks increasingly ill equipped to prepare them for competition in a globalized economy. It's shocking, Gelb adds, that generations of adult Americans read at a grade-school level and know almost no history, not to mention geography. "They are simply not being educated" and are unsuited to be the guardians of the most powerful democracy on earth.[55]

The recent rise of China, India, Brazil, Russia, and numerous smaller economies should signify to Americans that our competitive edge in the globalized economy is not a given; it is not to be taken for granted. Prestowitz correctly points out that while China has an effective industrial policy, this is less significant than America's lack of a strategy and its inability to maintain a highly trained workforce, or to interest and educate our students in the sciences and engineering, or to increase R&D efforts. For years, he says, U.S. strategy has been not to have a strategy, on the false assumption that market forces will always somehow work to our advantage.[56] Accordingly, there are numerous ways we can make important changes. Here, various specific initiatives might be considered:[57]

1. Beyond stimulus packages and bank bailouts, for example, we need policies that better balance the federal budget

by stimulating more savings in the U.S. economy. Here
we should draw on the Japanese and South Korean development models after 1945, which established intricate
systems of incentives that engendered high national savings rates.

2. We need more funding and larger development programs
   for domestic infrastructure, R&D, skilled workforces,
   and the education of students in key areas of high-tech
   and engineering sectors. We could kill two birds with one
   stone and transfer some of the money used to subsidize
   agriculture into subsidizing education.

3. Energy independence is of equal import in reducing both
   the trade deficit and our vulnerability to events elsewhere.
   In the wake of the recent collapse of several major U.S.
   automobile companies, Congress has the perfect opportunity to require automotive manufactures to build cars
   that use less gas. As both a large guzzler and the largest
   single source of R&D, the Defense Department is
   uniquely placed to develop and deliver new fuel solutions.

4. Obviously, we can never compete with the level of government subsidies, tax rebates, and loans at little or no
   interest that Chinese companies enjoy. But we can learn
   from our competitors by encouraging more overseas investment in America by using incentives and tax breaks
   similar to those used by China and other countries.

ON THE GLOBAL CHESSBOARD

Beyond the granular level of specific initiatives, we must also
formulate our response to China on the grand, global chessboard. After two terms of an administration that allowed the

streets of Iraq to consume the corridors of Washington, there is no time to lose. Almost without announcement, globalization has inaugurated a power shift from the Atlantic to the Pacific. According to Bill Emmott, former editor in chief of the *Economist*, Asian powers are being pushed together, and economic integration is knitting Asia into a single, vibrant market for goods, services, and capital, stretching all the way from Tokyo to Tehran. Naturally, there is no absence of tension within this vast global strip—between Pakistan and India, India and China, China and Japan—but it will also constitute the single largest economic development of this century.[58] A good number of the protagonists certainly seem to think so.

While he was still president of Pakistan in 2003, Pervez Musharraf traveled to China to consolidate bilateral relations with Beijing. As he told an audience of Chinese business leaders hoping to invest in his country, "The past belongs to Europe, the present belongs to the United States and the future belongs to Asia." And there was no doubt, he added, about the cheerleader of this trend: "China's economic miracle of the last 20 years is a beacon for all developing countries like Pakistan."[59]

INDIA AND JAPAN

The first move on the global chessboard should be to encourage a deeper U.S.-India relationship while remaining sensitive to India's reluctance to enter a formal alliance with the United States.[60] As discussed in Chapter 1, while China remains India's largest trading partner after the European Union, in recent years the growing rivalry between India and China has encouraged Delhi to be more receptive to Washington's overtures. China and India are rivals in space, where a month after Chinese astronauts walked in space in September 2008, India sent an unmanned mission into orbit. The two countries are competing to invest in Afghanistan; India pledged $1.2 billion in August 2009 just as China invested $3.5 billion in an oilfield project. In the Indian Ocean, a face-off between Chinese warships and an Indian submarine nearly erupted in violence in February 2009. Meanwhile, China has developed deepwater facilities for its nuclear submarine fleet in Gwadar, Pakistan, Sri Lanka, and Bangladesh. India has responded to China's string-of-pearls strategy by establishing naval facilities in the Maldives and enhancing bases in the Andaman Islands. And in Africa, China's two-way trade has increased by a factor of ten since 2000, reaching $107 billion in 2008 while India's trade with Africa reached $30 billion that same year.

In the fall of 2009, China-Indian tensions reached a high point with Chinese claims to the northeast Indian state of Arunachal Pradesh on the basis that China does not recognize the McMahon line agreed by Britain and Tibet at the 1913–1914 Simla Accords. In March 2009, Beijing attempted to block a $2.9 billion Asian Development Bank infrastructure loan, part of which was earmarked for Arunachal Pradesh, insisted that Indian Prime Minister Singh not campaign in Arunachal Pradesh during the 2009 state elections (which he did), and issued a formal demarche objecting to the Dalai Lama's visit to the region in November of that year (both the Indian government and the Dalai Lama ignored the demarche).

Just for once, the Obama administration is able to build on positive groundwork laid down by the previous administration. In 2008, the Bush White House finalized a nuclear deal with New Delhi that marked a new chapter in the two countries' relations, which had remained tense for much of the Cold War. The new agreement removed a thirty-year American freeze on nuclear trading with India, providing nuclear fuel and technology for India's civilian nuclear energy program. It was the beginning of something that should be continued to confirm a vital strategic shift in America's favor. It could serve to allay concerns across the subcontinent about Chinese power; it could also provide the cornerstone for a cross-regional contact group that included the Japanese, in ways that unleashed countervailing pressures on Beijing.[61]

RUSSIA

By a similar logic, Washington must also meet the China challenge by looking toward Moscow. Russian expert and president of the Nixon Center, Dimitri Simes, explains that Washington has, up until now, pursued the error of treating post-Soviet Russia as a defeated enemy. Victory for one side, he warns, does not necessarily mean defeat for the other. U.S.-Russia relations have subsequently deteriorated, to no small extent because of arrogant American posturing linked to expectations that post-Soviet leaders join the U.S. side in the post-Soviet order.[62] This expectation ignores a basic problem: Just like Washington and Beijing, Washington and Moscow have different interests on various fundamental issues, such as sovereignty and spheres of influence not only in Europe but also in Central Asia. These differences were clear for all to see as the United States antagonized Russia in the second Bush term by formally recognizing Kosovo as "a sovereign and independent state" in a traditional Slavic sphere of Russian influence, alongside designs to extend NATO borders east and locating antimissile systems in Poland and the Czech Republic.

As the sinologist David Shambaugh contends, the United States must learn to find ways of breaking the Beijing-Moscow duopoly that often splits the UN Security Council and other groupings against American preferences.[63] This requires a new approach. The Obama administration famously pledged to press the reset button with Moscow immediately after taking office. But simply offering a return to the kind of convivial dialogue that typified U.S.-Russia relations in the 1990s is already outdated. Moscow's current leaders view the supposedly warm decade of relations with Washington after 1990 as a shameful period of Russian weakness and Western exploitation.[64] E. Wayne Merry, a former State Department official, explains that we need a whole "change of operating system," more than merely pressing reset.

We must learn to minimize deliberate challenges to Russian interests and recognize that where we push—as with NATO expansion and sponsoring Georgian sovereignty over the disputed regions of Abkhazia and South Ossetia—they will almost certainly push back. We must also accept the end of the neoliberal dream for post-Soviet Russia; it's gone. Just as we won't be housebreaking China, nor will we be doing anything similar in Russia. Last, we must recognize that it's quid pro quo or nothing on issues like cooperation in Afghanistan and Russian hegemony in Central Asia.[65]

U.S.-Russian relations cannot exist on two parallel tracks, says Simes, "one in which we demand the Kremlin's cooperation on such things as non-proliferation and terrorism, and another in which Russian perspectives are contemptuously dismissed."[66] It's obvious which track must be followed for American interests. Then and only then, we might reasonably hope to gain more traction in Moscow vis-à-vis our policies toward Beijing.

System Reform

Another priority at the structural level of international relations, say Emmott and other experts like Fareed Zakaria and Minxin Pei, is institutional reform and the need for Washington to lead the process.

Washington must urgently take the lead in reforming the architecture of the international community as it once did in 1945, except this time, the priority lies in remaking what is woefully out of date. The Security Council is dominated, as Zakaria points out, by the victors of a war that ended sixty years ago; the G8 excludes the three fastest-growing large economies in the world; the IMF is always run by a European; the World Bank is always run by an American.[67]

Washington must make the case that India, Brazil, Japan, and Russia are all very important to the United States—just as important as China. Several organizations, inter alia the G8, the UN Development Program, and the Conference on Trade and Development, should be "scrapped or reformed."[68] This would help to remove some of the bile among non-Western governments that view Washington as the stubborn incumbent in chief of an outmoded Western superiority complex. Rather than responding to calls for reform, American politicians should lead them. The G8 can simply go. *The permanent seats at the UN Security Council should be expanded to reflect the changing status of emerging global power. India and Brazil should be included, along with Japan, Germany, and, perhaps, South Africa.* In these initiatives, Washington has an opportunity to articulate empathy with developing markets and to be seen to lead the discourse on structural reform, rather than responding to it.

Americans authored the first chapter on globalization. In the next, they will have to work to uphold their status as an indispensible part of the story. As Nye reminds us, the very nature of power has changed in the information age; success is not merely about whose army wins, but also about whose story wins.[69]

CHINA'S GREATEST FEAR: AMERICAN IDEAS

The issue of competing stories in an information age delivers us back to the anecdote that started this book, and the contention of China's public information chief, Li Chang-Chun, that the global information space of the twenty-first century has become a crucial strategic battleground for ideas and influence. As I have argued throughout, this is the area where China poses its most serious strategic challenge to *Pax Americana*. But it is also the area where America poses the greatest challenge to China.

On June 4, 2009, President Obama delivered an important speech in Cairo, satisfying a promise made during his campaign to deliver a major address to the Muslim world. His address would reintroduce America to the one-fifth of humankind that are now deeply alienated from the United States and from the rest of the West. It was also a distillation, lightly tempered with some post-Bush circumspection, of the basic principles that underlie the civic bargain and secular beliefs of the Western model for society.

America does not presume to know what is best for everyone . . . but I do have an unyielding belief that all people yearn for certain things: the ability to speak your mind and have a say in how you are governed; confidence in the rule of law and the equal administration of justice; government that is transparent and doesn't steal from the people; the freedom to live as you choose. . . . There is no straight line to realize this promise. But this much is clear: governments that protect these rights are ultimately more stable, successful and secure. Suppressing ideas never succeeds in making them go away.[70]

In these brief words, Obama codified the principles that have largely guided America's global rise over the past century. They represent a basic agreement, resting on the consent of the governed and committing government to ensure the rights of speech, belief, assembly, and political expression, provided it is peaceful, tolerant, and guided by compromise. They also represent a kind of political hammer, which is America's to use and China's to fear in equal measure.

The violence that followed Iran's presidential election was an example of both. The initial unrest saw a week of deliberation in the Obama White House before the president departed from more measured tones to use the word *justice* in a quotation from Martin Luther King, Jr.: "The arc of the moral universe," he retorted, "is long but it bends toward justice."[71] While protesters on the streets of Tehran drew inspiration, the leaders in Beijing drew sharp breath and cringed. President Mahmoud Ahmadinejad, they announced, should be supported as the "choice of the Iranian people."[72] Beyond economic shocks, which they have learned to handle, and bellicose rhetoric over the Taiwan Straits, which they are learning to retire in partnership with their counterparts in Taipei, these ideas are what

Chinese leaders fear the most. They are also America's product. What remains is to make it attractive to those nations transitioning from the "Third World."

CONFUCIUS VERSUS JEFFERSON: A FINAL THOUGHT

Building on the Asian model pioneered by the Japanese in Manchuko in the 1930s and refined in Korea, Japan, and Singapore, China embraces principles of governance that challenge the social contract found at the center of these ideas. The CCP has also embraced a format that is deeply rooted in China's own Confucian culture and has been thought, over the generations, to reflect the natural order of society. This often escapes Western analysts. Many in Washington have sought a platform in Chinese thought to introduce the Western notions of civil rights, "the loyal opposition," and the freedoms of belief, expression, and assembly. I believe identifying such a point of entry will be difficult.

Whereas the Western ruler has a responsibility to insure the people have the right of political expression, assembly, and debate in the public square and the people have a duty to exercise those rights, the exact opposite is true in Confucian societies. There the ruler has a responsibility to protect and support while the people have a duty to obey.[73]

We see two modern political systems, therefore, that are enormously influential in global affairs, together providing the foundation for global economic growth, but with profoundly different values and priorities, each projecting its values into the various domains of world affairs—the UN, the IMF, the developing world—and each attempting to "make its story win," as Nye would say. The popular caricature of eventual military conflagration or a dramatic economic showdown between two clashing systems is not the longer-term danger; rather, the structures and ideas that have characterized Western preeminence since 1945 face the less spectacular threat of simply and quietly losing their relevance. Perhaps even worse, the principle weapons of America's enemies in this regard are of its own making—capitalism and the global marketplace.

There's been a new joke in London since the recent crisis on Wall Street: *Capitalism saved China in 1989; China saved capitalism in 2009*. As these pages have argued, the intervening period has seen China grow to pose a serious challenge to the United States, not by virtue of its military power or its accumulation of U.S. dollar reserves, but as the catalyst for a global shift in development economics, away from the market-democratic model and toward a new type of capitalism, which can flourish without the values and norms of Western liberalism. There is no grand strategy for responding to this kind of predicament. Washington must disaggregate the challenges. At one level, only through power coalitions and associations of key states can we hope to influence China's behavior. Our leverage with the CCP comes in our collective ability to exploit its fear of criticism and its ingrained aversion to exclusion from international clubs. Both depend on our ability to build multilateral partnerships.

The United States continues to be number one by traditional measurements of comparative military and economic size, but from here on, as Joseph Nye says, being number one just "ain't gonna be what it used to be."[74]

This is particularly true if we accept the *conventional wisdom that the China relationship is on track. It is not.* With global developments pitting democratic pluralism against various forms of authoritarian government, one asks why the Obama administration seems blind to the appeal and strategic implications of the China model. Managing a commercial and military balance with China in the near term has simply obscured the oncoming battle of ideas in the middle term. The expanding appeal of China's governing model is shrinking the West—making our notions of society and government less relevant—and will do more to alter the quality of life for Americans and the West in the twenty-first century than any other development. When Brent Scowcroft says the world may no longer be susceptible to Washington's domination, but without its leadership, "nothing much is achieved," this is not a palliative. It must be seen as a clarion call to this administration and those that follow, that America is engaged in a global struggle to assert and sustain the primacy of Western values.

NOTES

PREFACE TO THE PAPERBACK EDITION

1. Harvard University professor Joseph Nye is credited with the phrase "It's not whose army wins, it's whose story wins."

2. François Jullien, *The Propensity of Things* (New York: Zone Books, 1999), 25.

3. "The Chinese in Africa: Trying to Pull Together," *The Economist*, 23 April 2011, 74.

4. China's navy would use assault ships, such as the *Kunlunshan*, with a displacement of 18,000 tons and deck space to accommodate four helicopters. While the invasion was under way, the main units of the North China Sea Fleet and the East China Sea Fleet would take up positions to block U.S. aircraft carriers from approaching the island. (One wonders why such explicit—and destabilizing—plans have been made public by the Chinese navy.)

5. Data from the Bank for International Settlements, "Triennial Central Bank Survey Report on global foreign exchange market activity in 2010," Monetary and Economic Department, 1 December 2010, http://www.bis.org/press/p101201.htm.

6. Beijing's current strategic focus on the global information space reflects a theme prominent in Chinese strategic thinking since the fourth century BCE. It holds that when a confrontation lapses into kinetic warfare, it indicates a failure to properly plan and calculate the political, physical, and psychological variables bearing upon the situation. Great generals expend most of their effort well in advance of a physical clash and don't enter the battle space until it is clear the circumstances are heavily weighted in their favor. Domination of the global information space would allow Beijing to frame unfolding news events and influence the news flow in a China-friendly way—thus winning the battle for world opinion.

7. http://news.xinhuanet.com/english2010/china/2010-07/01/c_13378575.htm.

8. BBC, "China's Xinhua Launches Global English TV Channel," *BBC News Asia Pacific*, 1 July 2010, http://www.bbc.co.uk/news/10473645.

9. "Use Modern Media to Enhance Our National Image," *People's Daily*, 10 March 2011.

INTRODUCTION

1. Jane Macartney, "World Agenda: Tentative Steps Towards a New Beginning for US-China Relations," *Times* (London), February 19, 2009.

2. "Clinton Urges Stronger China Ties," *BBC News*, February 21, 2009.

3. "China, US Pledge Cooperation to Tackle Global Challenges," *China Radio 86*, January 14, 2009.

4. These ideas were developed in conjunction with Joel Rogers.

5. Edmund Conway, "WEF 2009: China Warns over Protectionism," *Daily Telegraph*, January 29, 2009.

6. David Charter, Rory Watson, and Philip Webster, "President Obama to Water Down 'Buy American' Plan After EU Trade War Threat," *Times* (London), February 4, 2009.

7. Reuters, "Global Crisis Brings Threat of Protectionism," March 27, 2009.

8. Keith Bradsher, "As China Stirs Economy, Some See Protectionism," *International Herald Tribune*, June 23, 2009.

9. Guy Dinmore and Marco Pasqua, "G20 Communiqué Steers Clear of Protectionism," *Financial Times*, March 29, 2009.

10. Charlemagne, "The Left's Resignation Note," *Economist*, December 11, 2008; Anthony Faiola and Ariana Eunjung Cha, "Downturn Choking Global Commerce; Chinese Exports Fall Furthest in 7 Years," *Washington Post*, December 11, 2008.

11. Willy Lam, "Beijing's Glorification of the China Model Could Blunt Its Enthusiasm for Reforms," *China Brief* (published by Jamestown Foundation, Washington, DC), July 11, 2008.

12. Ibid.

13. David Frum, "The Coming Chinese Slowdown," *National Post* (Toronto), August 9, 2008; Reuters, "End of the Chinese Miracle?" July 23, 2008.

14. "China Tops World with 80% Foreign Trade Dependence: Expert," *People's Daily Online*, September 12, 2005.

15. "Economist: China to Post 8% GDP Growth This Year," *China Daily*, February 22, 2009.

16. "Chinese Imports to Get Forex Fund Boost," *China Daily*, February 19, 2009.

17. Jason Subler, "China Protests Shift with Economic Growth," Reuters, June 4, 2009.

18. "Suspended Animation: The New Middle Classes in Emerging Markets," *Economist*, February 12, 2009.

19. Simon Romero and Alexei Barrionuevo, "Deals Help China Expand Sway in Latin America," *New York Times*, April 15, 2009.

20. Kishore Mahbubani, "Lessons for the West from Asian Capitalism," *Financial Times*, March 18, 2009.

CHAPTER 1

1. The 45 billion yuan amounted to roughly $6.8 billion at the time of announcement. "Beijing in 45B Yuan Global Media Drive," *South China Morning Post*, January 12, 2009.

2. "Big Offers for English Speakers in Media Jobs," *South China Morning Post*, January 11, 2009.

3. Willy Lam, "Chinese State Media Goes Global: A Great Leap Outward for Chinese Soft Power?" *China Brief* (Jamestown Foundation) 9, no. 2 (January 22, 2009). See also Willy Lam, "Beijing's Glorification of the China Model Could Blunt Its Enthusiasm for Reforms," *China Brief* (Jamestown Foundation) 8, no. 21 (November 18, 2008) (wherein the Chinese newspaper articles from *People's Daily*, October 17, 2008; *Xinhua*, September 8, 2008; and *Xinhua*, December 28, 2008, are cited).

4. Lam, "Chinese State Media Goes Global"; Lam, "Beijing's Glorification"; *People's Daily*, October 17, 2008; *Xinhua*, September 8, 2008; *Xinhua*, December 28, 2008; Timothy Garton Ash, "China, Russia and the New World Disorder: Is Authoritarian Capitalism a Stable, Durable Model? That Is Among the Greatest Questions of Our Time," *Los Angeles Times*, September 11, 2008.

5. Li Chang-Chun, interview by author, Cambridge University, December 2008; see also Peter Ford, "Beijing Launching a 'Chinese CNN' to Burnish Image Abroad," *Christian Science Monitor*, February 5, 2009.

6. U.S. Department of Defense, "Annual Report to Congress: Military Power of the People's Republic of China, 2009," Office of the Secretary of Defense, March 2009, 1, www.defenselink.mil/pubs/pdfs/China_Military_Power_Report_2009.pdf.

7. Ibid., vii, 1, 31, 35.

8. Andrew Ericson and Michael Chase, "Information Technology and China's Naval Modernization," *Joint Force Quarterly* (3rd quarter 2008): 25.

9. U.S. Department of Defense, "Annual Report to Congress," vii, 33.

10. "Tracking GhostNet: Investigating a Cyber Espionage Network," *Information Warfare Monitor*, March 29, 2009, 5–6, 47.

11. Ibid., 11.

12. The Science Applications International Corporation (SAIC) of McLean, Virginia, a prominent defense, intelligence, and aerospace contractor, experienced 3,500 cyberattacks per day against its computers in 2008. The attacks originated in China (former senior SAIC executive, interview by author, July 2009 [name withheld]).

13. "Tracking GhostNet," 11–12.

14. U.S. Department of Defense, "The Budget for Fiscal Year 2009," U.S. Department of Defense, 45, www.gpoaccess.gov/usbudget/fy09/pdf/budget/defense.pdf.

15. Yang Yi, interview by author, National Defense University, Beijing, 2008. Rear Admiral Yang is president of NDU.

16. Shirk, *China: Fragile Superpower* (New York: Oxford University Press, 2008), 194.

17. David Sanger, *The Inheritance: The World Obama Confronts and the Challenges to American Power* (New York: Harmony, 2009), 379.

18. "U.S., Chinese Military Officials to Meet Next Week," Reuters, June 19, 2009.

19. Robert Kaplan, "Indian Ocean Rivalry," *Foreign Affairs Quarterly*, March–April 2009.

20. See numerous articles in *The Hindu* and *Deccan Chronicle* from October 14 through October 25, 2009, regarding the tensions in Arunachal Pradesh and in Jammu and Kashmir, and on the Dalai Lama's visit. See also Edward Wong, "China and India Dispute Enclave on Edge of Tibet," *New York Times*, September 4, 2009.

21. "Mainland Endures Position as Taiwan's Largest Trading Partner," *People's Daily Online*, March 3, 2008.

22. Brent Scowcroft, interview by author, Washington, DC, April 11, 2008.

23. Shirk, *China: Fragile Superpower*, 211.

24. People's Republic of China Embassy in the United States of America, "Joint Communique of the People's Republic of China and the United States of America," August 17, 1982, www.china-embassy.org/eng/zmgx/zywj/t36258.htm.

25. Shih-chung Liu, "U.S. Inauguration Inspires, Worries Taiwan," report, Brookings Institution, Washington, DC, February 24, 2009.

26. People's Republic of China Information Office of the State Council, "China's National Defense in 2008," January 2009, Beijing, quoted in "White Lies: Defence White Paper in China," *Economist,* January 22, 2009.

27. Will Hutton, *The Writing on the Wall: China and the West in the 21st Century* (New York: Little Brown, 2007), 22; John Wiedemer, Robert Wiedemer, Cindy Spitzer, and Eric Janszen, *America's Bubble Economy: Profit When It Pops* (New York: Wiley, 2006), 48–49.

28. Shirk, *China: Fragile Superpower*, 27.

29. Owen F. Humpage and Michael Shenk, "Chinese Inflation and the Renminbi," *Journal of the Federal Reserve Bank of Cleveland*, February 7, 2008.

30. Ibid.

31. Peter Foster, "Chinese Premier Wen Jiabao Worried About US Debt," *Daily Telegraph*, March 13, 2009.

32. Zhou Xiaochuan, "Reform the International Monetary System," March 23, 2009, People's Bank of China, Speeches Web page, www.pbc.gov.cn/english/detail.asp?col=6500&id=178.

33. Brad Setser, "The PBoC's Call for a New Global Currency, the SDR, the US and the IMF," editorial blog, March 29, 2009, Council on Foreign Relations

blog archive, http://blogs.cfr.org/setser/2009/03/29/the-pbocs-call-for-a-new-global-currency-the-sdr-the-us-and-the-imf/.

34. Barrett Sheridan, "The Short, Wondrous Life of the International Reserve Currency," *Newsweek*, March 30, 2009.

35. Arvind Subramanian, "Is China Having It Both Ways?" *Wall Street Journal*, March 25, 2009.

36. Sheridan, "The Short, Wondrous Life."

37. James Mayall, interview by author and Joel Rogers, Sydney Sussex College, Cambridge, April 23, 2008.

38. Richard Spencer, "Hillary Clinton: Chinese Human Rights Secondary to Economic Survival," *Daily Telegraph*, February 21, 2009.

39. Jayshree Bajoria, "Cooperating with China," Council on Foreign Relations, *Daily Analysis*, February 20, 2009.

40. U.S. Congress, "Testimony of Clyde Prestowitz Before the 2005 Report to Congress of the U.S.-China Economic and Security Review Commission," 109th Congress, 1st sess., November 2005, Law Library Archives, U.S. Library of Congress, Washington, DC.

41. Naazneen Barma, Ely Ratner, and Steven Weber, "A World Without the West," *The National Interest* 90 (July–August 2007).

42. Kishore Mahbubani, "Lessons for the West from Asian Capitalism," *Financial Times*, March 18 , 2009; see also Barma, Ratner, and Weber, "A World Without the West."

43. U.S. Congress, "Testimony of Clyde Prestowitz," 229; Zakki P. Hakim, "China, ASEAN to Begin FTA Despite Business Anxieties," *Jakarta Post*, July 18, 2005.

44. Michael Hudson, "Washington Is Unable to Call All the Shots," *Financial Times*, June 15, 2009.

45. Dmitry Medvedev, address to St. Petersburg International Economic Forum's Plenary Session, St. Petersburg, June 5, 2009, www.cdi.org/russia/johnson/2009-106-8.cfm.

46. Ibid.

47. Fareed Zakaria, "The Rise of the Rest," *Newsweek*, May 12, 2008.

48. Goldman Sachs Economic Research Group, "BRICs and Beyond," July 2007, 153, available at www2.goldmansachs.com/ideas/brics/BRICs-and-Beyond.html.

49. Barma, Ratner and Weber, "A World Without the West."

50. Ely Ratner, "A World Without the West," *TPM Café*, June 25, 2007.

51. Rowan Callick, "The China Model," *The American*, November/December 2007.

52. Peter Rogers, unpublished typescript in correspondence with Joel Rogers, Cambridge, September 2008.

53. Daniel Altman, "With Interest: 'China Model' Is Tough to Copy," *International Herald Tribune*, July 30, 2005

54. Chun-chieh Huang and John B. Henderson, eds., *Notions of Time in Chinese Historical Thinking* (Hong Kong: Hong Kong Chinese University Press, 2006), 223.

55. Francis Fukuyama, "The Fall of America, Inc.; Along with Some of Wall Street's Most Storied Firms, a Certain Vision of Capitalism Has Collapsed. How We Restore Faith in Our Brand," *Newsweek*, October 4, 2008.

56. Joseph Nye, "Barack Obama and Soft Power," *Huffington Post*, June 12, 2008; Joseph Nye, *Soft Power: The Means to Success in World Politics* (New York: Public Affairs, 2004), 5–6.

57. Yoosum Koh, "The Sources and Character of American Power in the American System," paper delivered at the Centre of International Studies, Cambridge, 2008.

58. Zakaria, "The Rise of the Rest."

59. Fukuyama, "The Fall of America, Inc."

60. "When Fortune Frowned," *Economist*, October 9, 2008.

61. Peter Goodman, "Lessons the Teacher Forgot," *New York Times*, May 16, 2009.

62. Michael Elliott, "Shifting on Its Pivot," *Time*, June 17, 2009.

63. Michelle Bachelet, "Ending the Washington Consensus," *Newsweek*, April 25, 2009.

64. Hilton Root, *The Alliance Curse: How America Lost the Third World* (Washington, DC: Brookings Institution Press, 2008).

65. Ibid., 10–11.

66. Ibid., 8–9.

67. "Ahmadinejad: 9/11 Suspect Event," *BBC News*, April 16, 2008; Anna Langenbach, Lars Olberg, and Jean DuPreez, "The New IAEA Resolution: A Milestone in the Iran-IAEA Saga," editorial, Center for Nonproliferation Studies, November 2005; Matthew Lee, "China Blocks New Iran Sanctions Talks," Associated Press, October 16, 2008; Shirley Kan, "China and Proliferation of Weapons of Mass Destruction and Missiles: Policy Issues," Congressional Research Service, January 7, 2009; Joshua Gleis, "Chinese, Russian Stall Tactics on Iran," *Boston Globe*, August 9, 2008; James Phillips and Peter Brookes, "Iran's Friends Fend Off Action at the U.N. Security Council: Here's Why," *Heritage Foundation Lectures* 1071 (May 11, 2006).

68. For the China effect in Angola, see Indira Campos and Alex Vines, "Angola and China: A Pragmatic Partnership," paper presented at the conference for the Center for Strategic and International Studies (CSIS), Prospects for Improving U.S.-China-Africa Cooperation, Chatham House, London, March 2008; "All the Presidents' Men," *Global Witness Report*, March 2002; Ian Taylor, "China and Africa: The Real Barriers to Win-Win," *Foreign Policy in Focus*, March 9, 2007; UN Office for the Coordination of Humanitarian Affairs, "Angola: China Entrenches Position in Booming Economy," report, April 17, 2006, www.irinnews.org/report.aspx?reportid=58756. For Cambodia, see Yan Xuetong, quoted in Paul Marks, "China's Cambodia Strategy," *Parameters Journal* 30 (2000): 94. For Burma, see "No Progress in Burma, Says Group," *BBC News*, September 26, 2008; Mathea Falco, *Burma: Time for Change* (Washington, DC: Brookings Institution, 2004), 11; "China Grants Loan, Debt Relief to Burma," *VOA News*, November 24, 2006; Daniel Byman and Roger Cliff, *China's Arms Sales: Motivations and Implications* (Santa Monica, CA: Rand

Corporation, 1999), 19–21; Myanmar Central Statistics Organization, Ministry of National Planning and Economic Development, "Foreign Investment of Permitted Enterprises by Country of Origin," www.csostat.gov.mm/S25MA0202.asp.

69. Charlene Barshefsky and James T. Hill, chairs, "US-Latin America Relations a New Direction for a New Reality," Task Force report no. 60, Council on Foreign Relations, May 2008, 9; Richard Lapper, "U.S.-Venezuelan Relations: Preparing for Another Term with Chavez," editorial, Council on Foreign Relations, December 1, 2006; "Chavez: China to Become Top Oil Client," *South Atlantic News Agency*, March 26, 2006.

70. C. J. Chivers, "China Backs Uzbek, Splitting with U.S. on Crackdown," *New York Times*, May 25, 2005; Lionel Beehner, "Severing of U.S.-Uzbek Ties Over Counterterrorism," editorial, Council on Foreign Relations, September 30, 2005; Ariel Cohen, "The Dragon Looks West: China and the Shanghai Cooperation Organization," *Heritage Foundation Lectures* 961 (August 3, 2006).

71. "China Still Striving for 'Market Economy' Status from EU," *Electric Commerce News*, May 22, 2009; "China Still Striving for Market Economy Status from EU," *China View*, May 21, 2009.

72. Chris Alden, Dan Large, and Ricardo Soares de Oliveira, "China Returns to Africa: Anatomy of an Expansive Engagement," *Real Instituto Elcano*, December 11, 2008.

73. Nicholas D. Kristof, "Rebranding the U.S. with Obama," *New York Times*, October 22, 2008.

74. "Obama Poised to Rebrand America, Experts Say," *CNN.com*, November 20, 2008.

75. Australia did suffer some minor bombing and naval bombardment during World War II.

76. Bernard Kouchner, quoted in Michael Elliott, "America: The Lost Leader," *Time*, October 23, 2008.

77. U.S. National Intelligence Council, "Global Trends 2025: A Transformed World," United States National Intelligence Council, November 2008, vi–xii, www.dni.gov/nic/NIC_2025_project.html; Clyde Prestowitz, *Three Billion New Capitalists: The Great Shift of Wealth and Power to the East* (New York: Basic Books, 2005), 20–21.

78. "Rising in the East," *Economist*, December 30, 2008.

79. Ibid.; Organisation for Economic Cooperation and Development, "Science, Technology and Industry Outlook 2008," executive summary, Organisation for Economic Cooperation and Development, Paris, 2008, 1–5.

80. Kelly M. Teal, "Report: Internet Traffic Flows Beyond U.S. Shores: Change Part of Web's Natural Evolution, Analysts Say," *VON.com*, December 12, 2008.

81. Bobbie Johnson, "US Role as Internet Hub Starts to Slip: An Internet Traffic Boom in Africa and Asia Has Reduced US Dominance over Web Capacity," *Guardian*, December 8, 2008.

82. James Mann, *The China Fantasy: How Our Leaders Explain Away Chinese Repression* (New York: Viking, 2007), 24.

83. Wayne M. Morrison, "China's Economic Conditions," Congressional Research Service, March 5, 2009, 2.

84. Naazneen Barma, Ely Ratner, and Steven Weber, "Chinese Ways," *Foreign Affairs*, May–June 2008.

85. Lester C. Thurow, *The Future of Capitalism: How Today's Economic Forces Shape Tomorrow's World* (New York: Penguin, 1997), 1–10.

CHAPTER 2

1. Todd G. Buchholz, *New Ideas from Dead Economists: An Introduction to Modern Economic Thought* (New York: Plume, 1999), 207; Robert Reich, "John Maynard Keynes," *Time*, March 29, 1999.

2. Donald Edward Moggridge, *An Economist's Biography* (New York: Routledge, 1995), 214.

3. John Maynard Keynes, *The Economic Consequences of the Peace* (Whitefish, MT: Kessinger, 2005).

4. Under American and British leadership, the "Bretton Woods system" saw the establishment of two international financial institutions. The first was the International Bank of Reconstruction and Development (later the World Bank), whose job was to make loans for national economic development. The second was the International Monetary Fund (IMF), created to eliminate the competitive currency devaluations of the 1930s that had halted trade and exacerbated international tensions. In their place, the IMF offered a more stable monetary system, where the value of each country's currency was pegged to the U.S. dollar, which in turn was pegged to a fixed amount of gold.

5. Roger Backhouse, *A History of Economics* (New York: Penguin, 2002), 302.

6. Dudley Dillard, *The Economics of John Maynard Keynes: The Theory of a Monetary Economy* (Whitefish, MT: Kessinger, 2005), 310–312.

7. Backhouse, *History of Economics*, 294–295.

8. Robert A. Solo, *Opportunity Knocks: American Economic Policy After Gorbachev* (Armonk, NY: M. E. Sharpe, 1991), 15–16; Backhouse, *History of Economics*, 295.

9. Edward Nelson and Anna J. Schwartz, "The Impact of Milton Friedman on Modern Monetary Economics: Setting the Record Straight on Paul Krugman's 'Who Was Milton Friedman?'" working paper W13546, National Bureau of Economic Research, St. Louis, January 9, 2008.

10. Milton Friedman, "Nobel Lecture: Inflation and Unemployment," *Journal of Political Economy* 85, no. 3 (June 1977): 451–472.

11. Milton Friedman, "Government Revenue from Inflation," *Journal of Political Economy* 79, no. 4 (July–August 1971): 846–856.

12. Milton Friedman, *Price Theory* (New Brunswick, NJ: Transaction Publishing, 2007), 227; Angus Maddison, *The World Economy: A Millennial Perspective* (Paris: OECD Publishing, 2001), 130–131.

13. Jim Granato, *The Role of Policymakers in Business Cycle Fluctuations* (New York: Cambridge University Press, 2006), 92–93; Niall Fergusson, "Fried-

man Is Dead, Monetarism Is Dead, but What About Inflation?" *Daily Telegraph*, November 19, 2006.

14. Jamie Peck and Henry Wai-Chung Yeung, *Remaking the Global Economy: Economic-geographical Perspectives* (Thousand Oaks, CA: SAGE, 2003), 170–173.

15. Adam Smith, *The Wealth of Nations,* book 4, (1937), 423.

16. Ibid.

17. Wesley McDonald and Russell Kirk, *The Age of Ideology* (Columbia: University of Missouri Press, 2004), 23–24.

18. Alfred Regnery, *Upstream: The Ascendance of American Conservatism* (New York: Threshold Editions, 2008), 56–84.

19. "Obituary: Paul Weyrich," *Daily Telegraph*, January 6, 2009.

20. Niall Fergusson, *The Ascent of Money*: *A Financial History of the World* (London: Allen Lane, 2008), 308.

21. Ibid., 308–309.

22. Soren Ambrose, "The Roots of Corporate Globalization in IMF/World Bank Structural Adjustment Policies," *Public Eye* 18, no. 2 (summer 2004).

23. Philip Coggan, *The Money Machine: How the City Works* (New York: Penguin, 2002), 8.

24. Joseph Stiglitz, quoted in Teddy Chestnut and Anita Joseph, "The IMF and the Washington Consensus: A Misunderstood and Poorly Implemented Development Strategy," research paper, Council on Hemispheric Affairs, Washington, DC, July 17, 2005.

25. Joseph Stiglitz, interview, *Guardian,* August 11, 2008.

26. Joseph Stiglitz, quoted in Elisa Van Waeyenberge, "From Washington to Post-Washington Consensus: Illusions of Development," in *The New Development Economics: After the Washington Consensus,* ed. K. S. Jomo and Ben Fine (New Delhi: Tulika Books, 2005), 32.

27. David Loyn, "Mozambique's Lost Cashew Nut Industry," *BBC News*, September 4, 2003.

28. George Caffentzis and Silvia Federici, "A Brief History of Resistance to Structural Adjustment," in *Democratizing the Global Economy: The Battle Against the IMF and World Bank,* ed. Kevin Danaher (Monroe, ME: Common Courage Press, 2001); John Walton and David Seddon, *Free Markets and Food Riots: The Politics of Global Adjustment* (Oxford: Blackwell Publishers, 1994); Jessica Woodroffe and Mark Ellis-Jones, "States of Unrest: Resistance to IMF Policies in Poor Countries," *World Development Movement Report*, September 2000.

29. Woodroffe and Ellis-Jones, "States of Unrest"; see also the following press releases from the International Monetary Fund: "IMF Approves US$7.2 Billion Three-Year Stand-By Credit for Argentina," March 10, 2000; "Argentina Memorandum of Economic Policies," February 14, 2000; "IMF Approves Three-Year Arrangement Under the ESAF for Bolivia," September 18, 1998; "IMF Approves Second Annual PRGF Loan for Bolivia," February 7, 2000; "IMF and IDA Support US$1.3 Billion Debt Service Relief Eligibility for Bolivia Under Enhanced HIPC," February 8, 2000; "IMF Completes

First Review of Zambia Under PRGF-Supported Programme and Approves US$13.2 Million Disbursement," July 27, 2000. See also "Argentina Leader Gets Tough on Unions," *Financial Times,* January 20, 2000; "IMF Reforms Have Brought Poverty," *Zambia Post,* February 9, 2000; "IMF Faces New Round of Protests," One World News Service, April 26, 2000; "Letter from Zambia," *The Nation,* February 14, 2000.

30. Fareed Zakaria, "The Rise of the Rest," *Newsweek,* May 12, 2008.

31. Ibid.

32. Clyde Prestowitz, *Three Billion New Capitalists: The Great Shift of Wealth and Power to the East* (New York: Basic Books, 2005), 2.

33. Waeyenberge, "From Washington to Post-Washington Consensus," 29.

34. Randall Peerenboom, *China Modernizes: Threat to the West or Model for the Rest?* (New York: Oxford University Press, 2007), 12.

35. Meles Zenawi, quoted in Akwe Amosu, "China in Africa: It's (Still) the Governance, Stupid," *Foreign Policy in Focus,* March 9, 2007.

36. Prestowitz, *Three Billion New Capitalists,* 3, 32; U.S. Congress, "Testimony of Clyde Prestowitz before the 2005 Report to Congress of the U.S.-China Economic and Security Review Commission," 109th Congress, 1st sess., November 2005, Law Library Archives, U.S. Library of Congress, Washington, DC.

37. Coggan, *The Money Machine,* 3.

38. Will Hutton, *The Writing on the Wall: China and the West in the 21st Century* (Boston: Little Brown, 2007), 19.

39. Coggan, *The Money Machine,* 6.

40. Manfred Steger, *Globalization: A Very Short Introduction* (New York: Oxford University Press, 2003), 40–41.

41. Francis Fukuyama, "The End of History?" *National Interest* (summer 1989): 3–18.

42. Joel Rogers, "The Myth of Neoconservative Triumph in US Foreign Policy Debate After 9/11," doctoral thesis, Magdalene College, Cambridge, June 2007.

43. Fukuyama, "End of History?"

44. Michael Mandlebaum, quoted in Patricia Cohen, "Patricia Cohen: Does Capitalism Lead to Democracy, and How?" *International Herald Tribune,* June 13, 2007.

45. Michael Ross, "Does Oil Hinder Democracy?" *World Politics,* April 2007, 325–361.

46. Ibid., 332.

47. Ibid., 333.

48. Kiren Aziz Chaudhry, "Economic Liberalization and the Lineages of the Rentier State," *Comparative Politics* 27, no. 1 (October 1994): 8–11.

49. Fukuyama, "End of History?"

50. Timothy Garton Ash, "China, Russia and the New World Disorder: Is Authoritarian Capitalism a Stable, Durable Model? That Is Among the Greatest Questions of Our Time," *Los Angeles Times,* September 11, 2008.

51. Robert Kagan, "End of Dreams, Return of History," *Policy Review,* July 19, 2007.

52. Richard N. Haass, "The Age of Nonpolarity; What Will Follow U.S.

Dominance?" *Foreign Affairs*, May/June 2008. Mr. Haass has, inexplicably, failed to include India in this list.

53. Garton Ash, "China, Russia and the New World Disorder."

CHAPTER 3

1. "China to Boost Ties with Chad, Says Senior Chinese Official," *People's Daily Online*, October 24, 2008; "End to World Bank's Chad Oil Deal," *BBC News*, December 10, 2008.

2. Joshua Kurlantzick, "How China Is Changing Global Diplomacy," *New Republic*, June 27, 2005.

3. Declan Walsh, "Angolan Elite Accused of Squandering Oil Billions," *Independent*, August 23, 2002.

4. "Obituary: Omar Bongo, 1935–2009," *The Week*, June 20, 2009, 38.

5. Robert Kagan, *The Return of History and the End of Dreams* (New York: Knopf, 2008), 69.

6. James Mann, *The China Fantasy: How Our Leaders Explain Away Chinese Repression* (New York: Viking, 2007), 24.

7. Kurlantzick, "How China Is Changing Global Diplomacy."

8. C. J. Chivers, "China Backs Uzbek, Splitting With U.S. on Crackdown," *New York Times,* May 25, 2005.

9. Lionel Beehner, "Severing of U.S.-Uzbek Ties Over Counterterrorism," editorial, Council on Foreign Relations, September 30, 2005.

10. Ariel Cohen, "The Dragon Looks West: China and the Shanghai Cooperation Organization," *Heritage Foundation Lectures* 961 (August 3, 2006).

11. Indira Campos and Alex Vines, "Angola and China: A Pragmatic Partnership," paper presented at the conference (Prospects for Improving U.S.-China-Africa Cooperation) for the Center for Strategic and International Studies (CSIS), Chatham House, London, March 2008; "All the Presidents' Men," *Global Witness Report*, March 2002.

12. Ian Taylor, "China and Africa: The Real Barriers to Win-Win," *Foreign Policy in Focus,* March 9, 2007.

13. UN Office for the Coordination of Humanitarian Affairs, "Angola: China Entrenches Position in Booming Economy," UN Office for the Coordination of Humanitarian Affairs, April 17, 2006.

14. UN Refugee Agency, "Freedom in the World 2008—Central African Republic," Report for the United Nations Refugee Agency, July 2, 2008; "Political Scene: International Reaction to the Government Is Mixed," *Economist Intelligence Unit*, May 6, 2003.

15. "China a Reliable Friend to Central African Republic," *People's Daily Online*, January 6, 2007.

16. "Cambodia to Lose Much of Foreign Aid over Poor Governance," *Asian Political News*, December 13, 2004.

17. Yan Xuetong, quoted in Paul Marks, "China's Cambodia Strategy," *Parameters Journal* 30 (2000): 94.

18. Joshua Kurlantzick, "This Year's Model," *National Newspaper*, December 5, 2008; see also Joshua Kurlantzick, *Charm Offensive: How China's Soft Power Is Transforming the World* (New Haven, CT: Yale University Press, 2007), 172.

19. See, for example, Barbara Slavin, "Powell Accuses Sudan of Genocide," *USA Today*, August 10, 2004; Nicholas D. Kristof, "The Secret Genocide Archive," *New York Times*, February 23, 2005; Alex de Waal, "Darfur's Deep Grievances Defy All Hopes for an Easy Solution," *Guardian*, July 25, 2004; "Dozens Killed in Sudan Attack," *BBC News*, May 24, 2004.

20. Lee Feinstein, "China and Sudan," *America Abroad*, April 24, 2007; Cheryl Igiri and Princeton N. Lyman, "Giving Meaning to 'Never Again': Seeking an Effective Response to the Darfur Crisis and Beyond," Council on Foreign Relations Special Report, no. 5, September 2004, 15–17.

21. Helene Cooper, "Darfur Collides with Olympics, and China Yields," *New York Times,* April 13, 2007.

22. Carin Zissis and Preeti Bhattacharji, "Olympic Pressure on China," *Washington Post*, March 11, 2008.

23. Hilary Andersson, "China Is Fuelling War in Darfur," *BBC News,* July 13, 2008.

24. Condoleezza Rice, quoted in David I. Steinberg, "Outposts of Tyranny: Burma," *Washington Post*, April 22, 2005.

25. James Bone and David Robertson, "West Suffers Historic Defeat as China and Russia Veto Zimbabwe Sanctions," *Times* (London), July 12, 2008.

26. Abraham McLaughlin, "A Rising China Counters US Clout in Africa," *Christian Science Monitor,* March 30, 2005; Michael Wines, "Zimbabwe's Future: Made in China," *International Herald Tribune*, July 25, 2005.

27. "No Progress in Burma, Says Group," *BBC News*, September 26, 2008.

28. Mathea Falco, *Burma: Time for Change* (Washington, DC: Brookings Institution, 2004), 11; "China Grants Loan, Debt Relief to Burma," *VOA News*, November 24, 2006; Daniel Byman and Roger Cliff, *China's Arms Sales: Motivations and Implications* (Santa Monica, CA: Rand Corporation, 1999), 19–21; Myanmar Central Statistics Organization Ministry of National Planning and Economic Development, "Foreign Investment of Permitted Enterprises by Country of Origin," table, www.csostat.gov.mm/S25MA0202.asp.

29. Simon Romero, "Chávez Wins Referendum to End Term Limits," *International Herald Tribune*, February 16, 2009.

30. Hugo Chávez, quoted in Diana Markosian, "Chavez Reaffirms Russia Alliance During Visit," *CNN.com*, September 26, 2008.

31. Charlene Barshefsky and James T. Hill, eds., "US-Latin America Relations: A New Direction for a New Reality," Council on Foreign Relations, May 2008, 9.

32. Richard Lapper, "U.S.-Venezuelan Relations: Preparing for Another Term with Chavez," editorial, Council on Foreign Relations, December 1, 2006.

33. "Chavez: China to Become Top Oil Client," *South Atlantic News Agency*, March 26, 2006.

34. "Ahmadinejad: 9/11 Suspect Event," *BBC News*, April 16, 2008.

35. Anna Langenbach, Lars Olberg, and Jean DuPreez, "The New IAEA

Resolution: A Milestone in the Iran-IAEA Saga," editorial, Center for Non-proliferation Studies, Monterey, CA, November 2005.

36. Matthew Lee, "China Blocks New Iran Sanctions Talks," *Associated Press*, October 16, 2008.

37. Shirley Kan, "China and Proliferation of Weapons of Mass Destruction and Missiles: Policy Issues," Congressional Research Service, January 7, 2009.

38. Ibid.

39. Joshua Gleis, "Chinese, Russian Stall Tactics on Iran," *Boston Globe*, August 9, 2008.

40. James Phillips and Peter Brookes, "Iran's Friends Fend Off Action at the U.N. Security Council: Here's Why," *Heritage Foundation Lectures* (1071): May 11, 2006.

41. Friedrich Wu, "China Inc International," *International Economy* 3 (2005): 26–27.

42. Deborah Brautigam and Adama Gaye, "Is Chinese Investment Good for Africa?" *Online Debate*, Council on Foreign Relations, February 20, 2007, www.cfr.org/publication/12622/is_chinese_investment_good_for_africa.html.

43. Ibid.

44. Henning Melber, "The (Not So) New Kid on the Block: China and the Scramble for Africa's Resources, an Introductory Review," *Current African Issues* 33 (2007): 6.

45. Ibid., 9.

46. "China's Callous Diplomacy," editorial, *International Herald Tribune*, February 19, 2007.

47. Chris Alden, *China in Africa: Partner, Competitor or Hegemon?* (London: Zed Books, 2007), 126, 127.

48. Yoweri Kaguta Museveni, quoted in Lindsey Hilsum, "Africa's Chinese Love Affair," *Channel 4 News*, November 3, 2006, www.channel4.com/news/articles/politics/international_politics/africas%20chinese%20love%20affair/171520.

CHAPTER 4

1. Abdoulaye Wade, "Time for the West to Practise What It Preaches," *Financial Times*, January 24, 2008.

2. U.S. Congressional Research Service, *China's Foreign Policy and "Soft Power" in South America, Asia, and Africa*," (Washington, DC: U.S. Government Printing Office, 2008), 117.

3. Joshua Kurlantzick, *Charm Offensive: How China's Soft Power Is Transforming the World* (New Haven, CT: Yale University Press, 2007), 49, 96.

4. Gregory Chin, quoted in Simon Romero and Alexei Barrionuevo, "Deals Help China Expand Sway in Latin America," *New York Times*, April 15, 2009. Chin is a political scientist at York University in Toronto.

5. Daniel P. Erikson, "The New Challenge: China and the Western Hemisphere," testimony before the U.S. House Committee on Foreign Affairs, Subcommittee

on the Western Hemisphere, June 11, 2008, Law Library Archives, U.S. Library of Congress, Washington, DC.

6. Peter Rodman, interview by author, Brookings Institute, Washington, DC, March 27, 2008.

7. Kurlantzick, *Charm Offensive*, 92.

8. Thomas Lum, Wayne M. Morrison, and Bruce Vaughn, "China's 'Soft Power' in Southeast Asia," Congressional Research Service, January 4, 2008, 16.

9. "China to Promote Cooperation with Ethiopia," *ChinaGov.cn*, November 28, 2005, www.china.org.cn/english/international/150186.htm; "China, Guinea Vow to Further Parliamentary Exchange," *ChinaGov.cn*, July 14, 2008, http://lr.china-embassy.org/eng/xnyfgk/t474657.htm; "China, Gabon Vow to Boost Cooperation," *ChinaGov.cn*, February 3, 2004, www.china.org.cn/english/international/86105.htm; "Hu Jintao Holds Talks with Guinea Bissau Counterpart Vieira," *ChinaGov.cn*, September 16, 2008, www.chinaembassy-canada.org/eng/yfgk/t513302.htm; "Chinese, Malian FMs Sign Agreement on Economic Ties," *ChinaGov.cn*, January 16, 2006, www.fmprc.gov.cn/zflt/eng/zxxx/t231176.htm; "China, Namibia Reaffirm Mutual Support over Sovereignty, Territorial Integrity," *ChinaGov.cn*, February 7, 2007, www.china.org.cn/english/international/199180.htm.

10. "African Union Adhere to Principled Positions About Tibet Issue" *China-Tibet News*, November 17, 2008.

11. Reuters, "Malawi Ends Ties with Taiwan in Favour of China," Reuters, January 14, 2008; "Malawi Agonizes over Whether to Ditch Friend Taiwan in Favor of China," *International Herald Tribune*, January 1, 2008.

12. Caitlin Fitzsimmons, "A Troubled Frontier," *South China Morning Post*, January 17, 2008.

13. Keith Bradsher, "Chad, Dumping Taiwan, Forges Link to China," *International Herald Tribune*, August 8, 2006.

14. Forum on China-Africa Cooperation, "African Countries Supporting China on the Adoption of the Anti-Secession Law," Forum on China-Africa Cooperation, Ministry of Foreign Affairs, People's Republic of China, March 22, 2005, www.focac.org/eng/zt/asl/t188411.htm.

15. Chris Alden, Dan Large, and Ricardo Soares de Oliveira, "China Returns to Africa: Anatomy of an Expansive Engagement," *Real Instituto Elcano*, December 11, 2008.

16. Associated Press, "China Thanks Africans for Defeating Taiwan's Bid to Join UN," Associated Press, September 28, 2007.

17. Embassy of the People's Republic of China in the Republic of South Africa, "Joint Communiqué, the Third Session of the Bi-National Commission of the People's Republic of China and the Republic of South Africa," Beijing, September 27, 2007, www.chinese-embassy.org.za/eng/znjl/t367303.htm.

18. Joshua Kurlantzick, "How China Is Changing Global Diplomacy," *New Republic*, June 27, 2005; U.S. Congressional Research Service, *China's Foreign Policy*, 20.

19. Forum on China-Africa Cooperation, "Beijing Action Plan," Forum on China-Africa Cooperation, Ministry of Foreign Affairs, People's Republic of

China, www.focac.org/eng/zxxx/t280369.htm; David Shinn, "The China Factor in African Ethics," *Policy Innovations*, Carnegie Council, December 21, 2006.

20. Chris Alden, "Emerging Countries as New ODA Players in LDCs: The Case of China and Africa," *Gouvernance Mondiale* 1 (2007): 5.

21. Associated Press, "China Faces Charges of Colonialism in Africa," Associated Press, January 28, 2007; "South African Trade with Asia," South Africa Government Online, February 25, 2008,www.southafrica.info/business/trade/relations/trade_asia.htm.

22. Desmond Tutu, quoted in Celia W. Dugger, "South Africa Bars Dalai Lama From a Peace Conference, *New York Times,* March 23, 2009, www.nytimes.com/2009/03/24/world/africa/24safrica.html.

23. "Dalai Lama Ban Halts Conference," *BBC News*, March 24, 2009; "South Africa Bans Dalai Lama Trip," *BBC News*, March 23, 2009.

24. Richard Gowan and Franziska Brantner, "A Global Force for Human Rights? An Audit of European Power at the UN," policy paper, European Council on Foreign Relations, September 2008, 1–2, 24–25.

25. Bureau of International Organization Affairs, "Voting Practices in the United Nations, 2006," Bureau of International Organization Affairs, U.S. Department of State, April 2, 2007, 3.

26. Gowan and Brantner, "A Global Force for Human Rights?" 28.

27. Ibid.

28. U.S. House of Representatives, "China's Influence in Africa," hearing before the Subcommittee on Africa, Global Human Rights and International Operations of the Committee on International Relations, U.S. House of Representatives, 109th Congr., 1st sess., July 28, 2005, 3.

29. "Testimony of Carolyn Bartholomew, Commissioner U.S. China Economic and Security Review, Commission Hearing on China's Influence in Africa," U.S. House of Representatives, Committee on International Relations, Subcommittee on Africa, Global Human Rights and International Operations, Congressional Research Service, U.S. Library of Congress, April 2008, U.S. Government Printing Office.

30. For more in-depth analysis of Western antidumping policies toward Asia, see Jørgen Ulff-Møller Nielsen and Aleksander Rutkowski, "The EU Anti-Dumping Policy Towards Russia and China: Product Quality and the Choice of an Analogue Country," *World Economy* 28, no. 1 (January 2005):103–136.

31. "China Still Striving for 'Market Economy' Status from EU," *Electric Commerce News*, May 22, 2009; "China Still Striving for Market Economy Status from EU," *China View,* May 21, 2009.

32. Shixue Jiang, "The Panda Hugs the Tucano: China's Relations with Brazil," *China Brief* 9, no. 10 (2009), Jamestown Foundation.

33. Eugene Tang, "Venezuela, China to Build Refineries, Boost Sales," *Bloomberg*, May 12, 2009.

34. Tamara Trinh, Silja Voss, and Steffen Dyck, "China's Commodity Hunger: Implications for Africa and Latin America," *Deutsche Bank Research Brief*, June 13, 2006, 9–10.

35. "Clinton Fears China, Iran's Gains in Latin America," *ABC (Australian Broadcasting Corporation) News*, May 2, 2009.

36. Keith Bradsher, "China's Shift on Food Was Key to Trade Impasse," *International Herald Tribune*, July 30, 2008.

37. U.S. Congressional Research Service, *China's Foreign Policy*; Kurlantzick, "How China Is Changing Global Diplomacy."

38. Ian Bremmer, "State Capitalism Comes of Age," *Foreign Affairs*, May/June 2009, 42.

39. "State Capitalism," *Financial Times*, January 24, 2008.

40. Jeffrey Garten, "The Unsettling Zeitgeist of State Capitalism," *Financial Times*, January 14, 2008.

41. Bremmer, "State Capitalism Comes of Age," 42–45.

42. Ibid.; Endiama-Empresa Nacional de Diamantes de Angola (National Diamond Company of Angola), Web page, www.endiama.co.ao/default.php; Az r Enerji, "Energy of All Azerbaijan," Web page, www.azerenerji.com; Kazatomprom (state-owned nuclear holding company in Kazakhstan), Web page, www.kazatomprom.kz/; Transnationale, "Office Chérifien des Phosphates," information page, www.transnationale.org/companies/office_cherifien_des_phosphates.php; Huawei, Web page, www.huawei.com; Lenovo, Web page, www.lenovo.com; Sinopec, Web page, www.sinopec.com.cn; San Miguel Corporation, Web page, www.sanmiguel.com.ph; Novolipetsk Steel, Web page, www.nlmksteel.com.

43. Bremmer, "State Capitalism Comes of Age," 44.

44. Martin Wolf, "The Brave New World of State Capitalism," *Financial Times*, October 17, 2007.

45. Gerard Lyons, "State Capitalism: The Rise of Sovereign Wealth Funds," *Standard Chartered Global Research Paper*, October 15, 2007.

46. Edwin Truman, "Sovereign Wealth Funds: The Need for Greater Transparency and Accountability," *Peterson Institute for International Economics*, August 2007.

47. Peter Foster, "Chinese Ordered to Smoke More to Boost Economy," *Daily Telegraph*, May 4, 2009.

48. "Gazprom's Lesson," *Wall Street Journal*, January 6, 2009.

49. Ibid.

50. Martin A. Weiss, "Sovereign Wealth Funds: Background and Policy Issues for Congress," *Congressional Research Service*, September 3, 2008.

51. Joshua Aizenman, "Sovereign Wealth Funds: Stumbling Blocks or Stepping Stones to Financial Globalization?" Economic Research and Data Brief, Federal Reserve Bank of San Francisco, December 14, 2007; "Capital Markets," *Economist*, January 17, 2008.

52. Marko Maslakovic, "Sovereign Wealth Funds 2009," research paper, International Financial Services London, March 2009, 2.

53. Robert Kagan, "The Return of History and the End of Dreams," transcript from Chatham House, London, May 21, 2008.

54. The phrase *pivot power* emerged in a conversation with Dr. Ted Galen Carpenter.

55. Jocelyn Ford, "Vietnam Eyes China's Model," *Marketplace Morning Report*, American Public Media, October 24, 2005.

56. Alan Makovsky, "Syria Under Bashar al-Asad: The Domestic Scene and the 'Chinese Model' of Reform," *PolicyWatch* 512, Washington Institute for Near East Policy; Daniel Altman, "With Interest: 'China Model' Is Tough to Copy," *International Herald Tribune*, July 30, 2005.

57. Andrew Higgins, "Iran Studies China Model: To Craft Economic Map," *Wall Street Journal*, May 18, 2007.

58. Ibid.

59. Ibid.; Afshin Molavi, "Buying Time in Tehran-Iran and the China Model," *Foreign Affairs*, November/December 2004.

60. Quoted in Kurlantzick, *Charm Offensive,* 133.

61. Anonymous source (executive assistant to the foreign minister of Mongolia), interview with author, Washington, DC, April 2006.

62. William Ratliff, quoted in Rowan Callick, "The China Model," *The American*, November/December 2007.

63. Kurlantzick, *Charm Offensive,* 130–135.

64. Ibid.

65. Alden, "Emerging Countries as New ODA Players," 35.

66. Cornell Institute for Social and Economic Research, "Latinobarometro 2002," translated questionnaire, 2002, CISER Date Archive, Cornell Institute for Social and Economic Research, Cornell University, Ithaca, NY.

67. "World Poll Finds Global Leadership Vacuum," World Public Opinion poll of twenty nations, WorldPublicOpinion.org (PIPA), www.worldpublic opinion.org/pipa/pdf/jun08/WPO_Leaders_Jun08_packet.pdf.

68. Richard Holbrooke, quoted in Jonathan Tepperman, "Time of the Tough Guys," *Newsweek*, June 23, 2008.

69. Tepperman, "Time of the Tough Guys."

70. Michael Shifter, "The US and Latin America Through the Lens of Empire," *Current History* 2 (2004): 61–67.

71. Chan Heng Chee, quoted in Randall Peerenboom, *China Modernizes: Threat to the West or Model for the Rest?* (New York: Oxford University Press, 2007), 244.

72. Lee Kuan Yew, quoted in Sholto Byrnes, "The Price of Freedom," *Guardian*, July 17, 2008.

73. Peerenboom, *China Modernizes,* 248.

CHAPTER 5

1. Robert Zoellick, "Whither China? From Membership to Responsibility," remarks to the National Committee on U.S.-China Relations, New York City,

September 21, 2005, www.ncuscr.org/files/2005Gala_RobertZoellick_Whither _China1.pdf.

2. James Mann, *The China Fantasy: How Our Leaders Explain Away Chinese Repression* (New York: Viking, 2007), 2.

3. Bill Clinton, quoted in Alison Mitchell, "Clinton Launches Effort to Renew China Trade Ties," *New York Times*, May 20, 1997.

4. Bill Clinton, remarks on China, Paul H. Nitze School of Advanced International Studies, Washington, DC, March 8, 2000; "Bush's China Trip to Boost U.S.-China Ties," *People's Daily Online*, February 20, 2002.

5. Thomas J. Christensen, Deputy Assistant Secretary of State for East Asian and Pacific Affairs, "China's Role in the World: Is China a Responsible Stakeholder?" statement before the U.S.-China Economic and Security Review Commission, August 3, 2006.

6. Bates Gill, "China Becoming a Responsible Stakeholder," Carnegie Endowment, August 2006, www.carnegieendowment.org/files/Bates_paper.pdf.

7. Richard N. Haass, "China: Don't Isolate, Integrate," *Newsweek*, November 29, 2008.

8. James Mann, "The Three Futures of China," *Los Angeles Times*, February 25, 2007.

9. Will Hutton, *The Writing on the Wall: China and the West in the 21st Century* (Boston: Little Brown, 2007), 8.

10. Minxin Pei, *China's Trapped Transition: The Limits of Developmental Autocracy* (Boston: Harvard University Press, 2006).

11. STRATFOR Global Intelligence, "China's Obsession with the Zoellick Speech," STRATFOR Global Intelligence, Austin, November 9, 2005.

12. Ariana Eunjung Cha, "China Passes Germany With 3rd-Highest GDP," *Washington Post*, January 15, 2009.

13. David Sanger, *The Inheritance: The World Obama Confronts and the Challenges to American Power* (New York: Harmony, 2009), 353.

14. Joseph Fewsmith, *China since Tiananmen: The Politics of Transition* (New York: Cambridge University Press, 2001), 22–24.

15. Chen Feng, "Order and Stability in Social Transition: Neoconservative Political Thought in Post-China," *China Quarterly* 1997, 151, 593–613; June M. Grasso, Jay Corrin, and Michael Kort, *Modernization and Revolution in China: From the Opium Wars to World Power* (Armonk, NY: M. E. Sharpe, 2004), 265–267.

16. Ian Buruma, "What Beijing Can Learn from Moscow," *New York Times*, September 2, 2001.

17. David Shambaugh, *China's Communist Party: Atrophy and Adaptation* (Berkeley: University of California Press, 2008), 3–5, 43, 49.

18. Ibid., 2–3, 64, 65.

19. Zheng Bijian, "Peacefully Rising China, Firm Defender of World Peace," speech given at the East Asia Cooperation and U.S.-China Relations Conference, George Washington University, Beijing, November 2, 2003.

20. Joshua Kurlantzick, *Charm Offensive: How China's Soft Power Is Transforming the World* (New Haven, CT: Yale University Press, 2007), 37.

21. Li Jingjie, "The Historical Lessons of the Failure of the CPSU," *Sulian yu Dong-Ou Wenti* (1992): 19–25.

22. "It doesn't matter whether the cat is black or white," Deng famously announced, "as long as it catches mice." Quoted in Qin Xiaoying, "Black and White Cats? We Also Need Green Ones," *China Daily*, March 10, 2006.

23. Sanger, *The Inheritance*, 390.

24. Bruce J. Dickson, "Populist Authoritarianism: The Future of the Chinese Communist Party," paper presented at the Conference on Chinese Leadership, Politics, and Policy, Carnegie Endowment for International Peace, Washington, DC, November 2, 2005.

25. J. Stapleton Roy, quoted in Nigel Ash, "The Great Leap-Frog Forward," *CEO Magazine*, September 1, 2005.

26. For specific discussion of capitalism without democracy in Chinese thought, see Kellee S. Tsai, *Capitalism Without Democracy: The Private Sector in Contemporary China* (Ithaca, NY: Cornell University, 2007).

27. Wen Jiabao, "Number of Issues Regarding the Historical Tasks in the Initial Stage of Socialism and China's Foreign Policy," *Xinhua*, February 26, 2007.

28. "Differences Stressed Between China's NPC and Western Systems," *Xinhua*, March 9, 2009.

29. Sanger, *The Inheritance*, 372.

30. Michael Wines, "Civic-Minded Chinese Find a Voice Online," *New York Times*, June 17, 2009.

31. Sharon La Franiere, "Tiananmen Now Seems Distant to China's Students," *New York Times*, May 21, 2009.

32. Jiang Pei, interview with author, Beijing Hotel, September 14, 2007.

33. Edward Wong, "China Disables Some Google Functions," *New York Times*, June 19, 2009; Andrew Jacobs, "China Requires Censorship Software on New PCs," *New York Times*, June 8, 2009.

34. Susan Shirk, *China: Fragile Superpower* (New York: Oxford University Press, 2008), 4.

35. Peter Hays Gries, *China's New Nationalism: Pride, Politics, and Diplomacy* (Berkeley: University of California Press, July 2005), 18–19.

36. William Mellor and Allen T. Cheng, "To Get Rich Is Glorious and Risky: Capitalism Spawns Multimillionaires, but Some Disappear," *International Herald Tribune*, May 23, 2006

37. These ideas were developed in conjunction with Joel Rogers.

38. Shirk, *China: Fragile Superpower*, 62, 63.

39. Ibid., 64.

40. Paul Mooney, "Internet Fans Flames of Chinese Nationalism: Beijing Faces Dilemma as Anti-Japanese Campaign in Cyberspace Hits the Streets," *YaleGlobal*, April 4, 2005.

41. Duncan Hewitt, *Getting Rich First: Life in a Changing China* (New York: Chatto & Windus, 2007), 153–182.

42. Michael Wines, "A Dirty Pun Tweaks China's Online Censors," *New York Times*, March 10, 2009.

43. Lio Dong (Counselor), interview by author, Washington Embassy of the Peoples Republic of China, Cosmos Club, March 28, 2007.

44. Hewitt, *Getting Rich First,* 10.

45. Ibid., 6–9.

46. Ibid., 45.

47. Anne Lonsdale, interview by author, Magdalene College, Cambridge, August 2005.

48. Preeti Bhattacharji, "Religion in China," editorial, Council on Foreign Relations, May 16, 2008.

49. Brian Grim, "Religion in China on the Eve of the 2008 Beijing Olympics," Pew Forum on Religion & Public Life, May 7, 2008; William Safire, "Will They Provoke Splittism?" *International Herald Tribune,* April 27, 2008.

50. Hewitt, *Getting Rich First,* 274.

51. Andrew Scheineson, "China's Internal Migrants," editorial, Council on Foreign Relations, May 14, 2009; U.S. Congressional-Executive Commission on China, "China's Household Registration System: Sustained Reform Needed to Protect China's Rural Migrants," October 7, 2005, Law Library Archives, U.S. Library of Congress, Washington, DC.

52. "China's Household Registration (*Hukou*) System: Discrimination and Reform," Staff Roundtable of the Congressional-Executive Commission on China, June 22, 2005, Washington, DC; Fei-Ling Wang, *Organizing Through Division and Exclusion* (Stanford, CA: Stanford University Press, 2005); Kam Wing Chan and Li Zhang, "The *Hukou* System and Rural-Urban Migration in China: Processes and Changes," *China Quarterly* 160 (1999): 818–822; Li Zhang, "Spatiality and Urban Citizenship in Late Socialist China," *Public Culture* (2002): 311–315.

53. Hewitt, *Getting Rich First,* 285.

54. U.S. Congressional-Executive Commission on China, "Ministry of Public Security Reports Rise in Public Order Disturbances in 2005," January 19, 2006, www.cecc.gov/pages/virtualAcad/index.phpd?showsingle=37602.

55. Zhao Ziyang, quoted in Pei, *China's Trapped Transition,* 8.

56. BBC, "Chinese Crime 'Godmother' Jailed," *One-Minute World News,* BBC, November 3, 2009, available at http://news.bbc.co.uk/2/hi/8339773 .stm.

57. Hu Angang, ed., *China: Fighting Against Corruption* (Hangzhou Zhejiang Renmin Chubanshe, 2001), 61; Minxin Pei, "Will China Become Another Indonesia?" *Foreign Policy,* 116 (Fall 1999): 99.

58. Pei, *China's Trapped Transition,* 12–13.

59. Jonathan Watts, "Pollution Killing River They Said Was Too Big to Poison," *Guardian,* June 6, 2006.

60. Elizabeth Economy, "The Great Leap Backward?" *Foreign Affairs,* September/October 2007, 46.

61. Julianne Smith and Jesse Kaplan, "The Faulty Narrative: Fact, Fiction and China's Efforts to Combat Climate Change," in *China's Soft Power in Africa: Chinese Soft Power and Its Implications for the United States: Competition*

and Cooperation in the Developing World, ed. Carola McGiffert (Washington, DC: Center for Strategic and International Studies, 2009), 102.

62. Keith Bradsher, "China Outpaces U.S. in Cleaner Coal-Fired Plants," *International Herald Tribune,* May 10, 2009.

63. Joseph Kahn and Jim Yardley, "As China Roars, Pollution Reaches Deadly Extremes," *New York Times,* August 26, 2007; Jim Bai and Chen Aizhu, "China's Energy Efficiency Drive Loses Pace in H1," Reuters, August 7, 2008.

64. Bradsher, "China Outpaces U.S. in Cleaner Coal-Fired Plants."

65. Howard French, "Far from Beijing's Reach, Officials Bend the Rules," *New York Times,* November 24, 2007.

66. Keith Bradsher, "Choking on Growth: Trucks at Heart of China's Diesel Problems," *International Herald Tribune,* December 8, 2007.

67. Sanger, *The Inheritance,* 345–355.

CHAPTER 6

1. U.S. Senate, "Statement of Senator Hillary Rodham Clinton Nominee for Secretary of State," Senate Foreign Relations Committee, January 13, 2009, www.america.gov/st/texttrans-english/2009/January/20090113174107 eaifas0.6630213.

2. James Schlesinger, interview by author, Washington, DC, March 27, 2008.

3. International Security Advisory Board, "China's Strategic Modernisation," report, International Security Advisory Board Task Force, reproduced by the Federation of American Scientists, Washington, DC, March 14, 2009, 3, 7, 8.

4. Bill Gertz, "China Report Urges Missile Shield, Urges Development of Counter-Weapons," *Washington Times,* October 1, 2008.

5. Bill Gertz, "The China Threat," *China Confidential,* June 22, 2007; Bill Gertz, *The China Threat: How the People's Republic Targets America* (Washington, DC: Regnery Publishing, 2000).

6. Edward Timperlake, interview by author, Washington, DC, March 17, 2008.

7. Gary Schmitt and Dan Blumenthal, "Wishful Thinking in Our Time," *Weekly Standard,* August 8, 2005.

8. John J. Tkacik, Jr., "Panda Hedging: Pentagon Report Urges New Strategy for China," editorial, Heritage Foundation, Washington, DC, May 24, 2006.

9. Michael Ledeen, quoted in John B. Judis, "The China Hawks," *American Prospect,* November 30, 2002.

10. Arthur Waldron, "The Pentagon's Latest China Report," *Looking Forward,* International Assessment and Strategy Center, Alexandria, VA, May 24, 2006.

11. Robert D. Kaplan, "How We Would Fight China," *Atlantic Monthly,* June 2005.

12. Neil King, Jr., "Secret Weapon; Inside Pentagon, a Scholar Shapes Views of China," *Wall Street Journal,* September 8, 2005; Soyoung Ho, "Panda Slugger:

The Dubious Scholarship of Michael Pillsbury, the China Hawk with Rumsfeld's Ear," *Washington Monthly*, July–August 2006.

13. U.S. Department of Defense, Quadrennial Defense Review Report, February 6, 2006, www.defenselink.mil/qdr/report/Report20060203.pdf; Taiwan Relations Act, P.L. 98–6 of April 10, 1979, Section 2(b)(6).

14. Ivan Eland, "Is Chinese Military Modernization a Threat to the United States?" *Cato Policy Analysis*, January 23, 2003.

15. Qin Gang, quoted in Cui Xiaohuo, "Pentagon Report Grossly Distorts Facts," *China Daily*, March 27, 2009.

16. Office of the Secretary of Defense, "Annual Report to Congress; Military Power of the People's Republic of China; 2008," 5, www.defenselink.mil/pubs/pdfs/China_Military_Power_Report_2009.pdf.

17. Ibid.

18. Ibid.

19. Charles Freeman, interview with author, Center of the International Studies, Washington, DC, March 9, 2008.

20. "Lawmakers Seek Review of Bid for Unocal," *CNN Money*, June 25, 2005.

21. Joe Barton, quoted in "Republicans Urge White House to Review CNOOC's Unocal Bid," *Wall Street Journal*, June 29, 2005.

22. U.S. House of Representatives, "Expressing the Sense of the House of Representatives That a Chinese State-Owned Energy Company Exercising Control of Critical United States Energy Infrastructure and Energy Production Capacity Could Take Action That Would Threaten to Impair the National Security of the United States," Resolution 344, sponsored by Richard W. Pombo, Law Library Archives, U.S. Library of Congress, Washington, DC.

23. U.S. House of Representatives, "Submitted Testimony of Frank J. Gaffney, Jr., President and C.E.O., Center for Security Policy, 'CNOOCered: The Adverse National Security Implications of the Proposed Acquisition of Unocal by the China National Offshore Oil Corporation,'" House Armed Services Committee, July 13, 2005, Law Library Archives, U.S. Library of Congress, Washington, DC.

24. James Woolsey, quoted in "Security Shakeup," *Lou Dobbs Tonight*, CNN Transcripts, July 13, 2005.

25. John J. Tkacik Jr., "Say No to CNOOC's Bid for Unocal," *Briefing*, Heritage Foundation Press, Washington, DC, June 29, 2005.

26. William Reinsch, quoted in "Who's Afraid of China Inc.?" *New York Times*, July 24, 2005.

27. "The Dragon Tucks In," *Economist*, June 30, 2005.

28. "Unocal Corporation's Oil and Gas," Congressional Research Service, Report for Congress, RS22182, July 1, 2005.

29. Gary Schmitt, interview by author's research assistant, Washington, DC, March 14, 2008.

30. Robert Zoellick, quoted in "What China Knows That We Don't: The Case for a New Strategy of Containment," *Weekly Standard*, January 20, 1997.

31. Patrick J. Buchanan, *Where the Right Went Wrong: How Neoconservatives Subverted the Reagan Revolution and Hijacked the Bush Presidency* (New York: Macmillan, 2005), 129.

32. John B. Henry, interview by author, Washington, DC, March 19, 2008.

33. Naazneen Barma, Ely Ratner, and Steven Weber, "A World Without the West," *The National Interest* 90 (July–August 2007): 2.

34. Aside from the rise of Wilhelmine Germany in the era of British hegemony, other prominent examples of rising challengers often include the unification of tribes south of Lake Baikal from 1206 and Genghis Khan's challenge to the Chinese empire, or the Hohenzollern family's acquisition of the March of Brandenburg in 1415 and the rise of Prussia in Hapsburg Europe. Meanwhile, examples of acquiescence between two centers of power include the American presence in the Atlantic after the War of 1812 or coexistence between Ankara and Europe after Ottoman humiliation in the second failed siege of Vienna, which led to the Treaty of Carlowitz in 1699 and the end of Ottoman attempts to invade Europe proper.

35. For a pithy summary of these arguments, see Daniel Ikenson, "China: Mega-Threat or Quiet Dragon," *Cato Trade Policy Analysis*, March 6, 2006.

36. Bill Richardson, AFL-CIO Democratic Presidential Forum, Chicago, Augusts 7, 2007.

37. Charles E. Schumer and Lindsey O. Graham, "Play by the Rules," *Wall Street Journal*, September 25, 2006.

38. Doug Palmer, "Business Groups Scold Congress on 'Buy American,'" Reuters, February 16, 2009.

39. Burton Malkiel, "The President Should Veto 'Buy American' If He Doesn't Want to Be Remembered Like Herbert Hoover," *Wall Street Journal*, February 5, 2009.

40. "Greenspan Warns Against Anti-China Protectionism," *Fox News*, June 23, 2005.

41. Craig K. Elwell and Marc Labonte, eds., "Is China a Threat to the U.S. Economy?" Congressional Research Service, January 23, 2007, 28–31; U.S.-China Economic and Security Review Commission, "2005 Report to Congress," 109th Congr., 1st sess., November 2005, Law Library, U.S. Library of Congress, Washington, DC, 25–69.

42. Kate Bronfenbrenner and Stephanie Luce, "The Changing Nature of Corporate Global Restructuring: The Impact of Production Shifts on Jobs in the U.S., China, and Around the Globe," report submitted to U.S.-China Economic and Security Review Commission, October 14, 2004, 24–25.

43. Ibid.

44. James Fallows, "China's Way Forward," *Atlantic Monthly*, April 2009.

45. Two officials (who wished to remain anonymous) from the U.S.-China Business Council, interview with author's assistant, Washington, DC, April 18, 2008.

46. Bill Clinton, quoted in James Mann, *The China Fantasy: How Our Leaders Explain Away Chinese Repression* (New York: Viking, 2007), 3.

47. George W. Bush, "A Distinctly American Internationalism," speech, Ronald Reagan Presidential Library, Simi Valley, CA, November 19, 1999.

48. George W. Bush, quoted in Ying Ma, "China's Stubborn Anti-democracy," *Policy Review* 141 (February–March 2007).

49. Mike Huckabee, "Is China a Threat to the U.S.?" *Procon.org*, January 10, 2008.

50. Philip I. Levy, "Economic Integration and Incipient Democracy," working paper 142, American Enterprise Institute, Washington, DC, March 26, 2008, 15, 23.

51. James Mann, "The Three Futures of China," *Los Angeles Times*, February 25, 2007.

52. James Fallows, "China's Way Forward," *Atlantic Monthly*, April 2009.

53. Charles Dickens, *American Notes* (New York: Penguin Books, 2000); James Bryce, *The American Commonwealth* (Indianapolis: Liberty Fund, 1995); Wyndham Lewis, *America and Cosmic Man* (London: Nicholson & Watson, 1948); Herbert Croly, *The Promise of American Life* (New York: Capricorn Books, 1964); Waldo Frank, *The Re-Discovery of America* (New York: Charles Scribner's Sons, 1929); Dennis Brogan, *The American Character* (New York: Knopf, 1944); André Siegfried, *America Comes of Age*, trans. H. H. Hemming and Doris Hemming (London: Jonathan Cape, 1927); Thorstein Veblen, *Absentee Ownership and Business Enterprise in Recent Times* (New York: B. W. Huebsch, 1923).

54. Alexis de Tocqueville, *Democracy in America* (New York: Barnes & Noble, 2003).

55. Jed Babbin and Edward Timperlake, *Showdown: Why China Wants War with the United States* (Washington, DC: Regnery Publishing, 2006); Frank J. Gaffney and colleagues, *War Footing: 10 Steps America Must Take to Prevail in the War for the Free World* (Annapolis, MD: Naval Institute Press, 2006); Richard Bernstein and Ross H. Munro, *The Coming Conflict with China* (New York: Vintage, 1998); Steven W. Mosher, *Hegemon: China's Plan to Dominate Asia and the World* (San Francisco: Encounter Books, 2000).

56. William J. Baumol, Robert E. Litan, and Carl J. Schramm, *Good Capitalism, Bad Capitalism, and the Economics of Growth and Prosperity* (New Haven, CT: Yale University Press, 2007), 130.

57. John Micklethwait, and Adrian Wooldridge, *The Right Nation: Why America Is Different* (New York: Penguin Books, 2004), chapter 13.

58. Ning Song, "The Framing of China's Bird Flu Epidemic by U.S. Newspapers Influential in China: How the *New York Times* and the *Washington Post* Linked the Image of the Nation to the Handling of the Disease," master's thesis, Georgia State University, Atlanta, 2007, 14.

59. Robert Kaplan, "Foreign Policy: Munich Versus Vietnam," *Atlantic Monthly*, May 4, 2007.

60. "The 44th President; Renewing America," *Economist*, January 15, 2009.

61. Ibid.

CHAPTER 7

1. Winston Lord, interview by author, Washington, DC, March 26, 2008.

2. James Fallows, *Postcards from Tomorrow Square: Reports from China* (New York: Vantage Books, 2009), xiv.

3. James R. Lilley, interview by author, Washington, DC, April 2009.

4. Cyrus Chu and Ronald Lee, "Famine, Revolt and the Dynastic Cycle: Population Dynamics in Historic China," *Journal of Population Economics* (November 1994): 351–378.

5. Will Hutton, *The Writing on the Wall: China and the West in the 21st Century* (Boston: Little Brown, 2007), 44–45.

6. George Walden, *China: A Wolf in the World?* (London: Gibson Square, 2008), 257.

7. Joseph Stiglitz, "The Post-Washington-Consensus Consensus," *Policy Innovations*, August 22, 2005.

8. Ibid.

9. Ian Bremmer, "State Capitalism Comes of Age: The End of Free Markets?" *Foreign Affairs*, May–June 2009, 44–45.

10. Pew Research Center, "Global Unease with Major World Powers," 47-Nation Pew Global Attitudes Survey, Pew Global Attitudes Project, Washington, DC, June 27, 2007, 25.

11. Roger Cohen, "America Agonistas," *International Herald Tribune*, April 1, 2009.

12. Bremmer, "State Capitalism Comes of Age," 49.

13. Joshua Cooper Ramo, "The Beijing Consensus," *Foreign Policy Centre*, Spring 2004.

14. Naazneen Barma, Ely Ratner, and Steven Weber, "Chinese Ways," *Foreign Affairs*, May–June 2008.

15. Julian Borger, "David Miliband: China Ready to Join US as World Power," *Guardian*, May 17, 2009.

16. Elizabeth Economy and Adam Segal, "The G2 Mirage: Why the United States and China Are Not Ready to Upgrade Ties," *Foreign Affairs*, May–June 2009, 19–20.

17. Robert A. Pape, "Empire Falls," *National Interest*, January 22, 2009.

18. George Friedman, *The Next Hundred Years: A Forecast for the 21st Century* (New York: Doubleday, 2009), 5.

19. Leslie Gelb, *Power Rules: How Common Sense Can Rescue American Foreign Policy* (New York: Harper Collins, 2009), xiv–xv.

20. Central Intelligence Agency, "United States Economy," CIA World Factbook, May 31, 2009; Central Intelligence Agency, "Country Comparisons: Military Expenditures," CIA World Factbook, May 31, 2009.

21. Gelb, *Power Rules,* xv.

22. Ibid., 75–81.

23. Ibid., xv, 4–5, 81.

24. Ibid., 83–85.

25. Joseph Nye, *The Paradox of American Power: Why the World's Only Superpower Can't Go It Alone* (New York: Oxford University Press, 2002), xiii.

26. Ibid., introduction.

27. Economy and Segal, "The G2 Mirage," 20.

28. James Hohmann, "Scowcroft Urges US-China Cooperation," *Stanford (CA) Daily*, June 2, 2006.

29. Economy and Segal, "The G2 Mirage," 20.

30. Richard L. Armitage and Joseph S. Nye, Jr., chairs, *Commission on Smart Power: A Smarter, More Secure America* (Washington, DC: Center for Strategic and International Studies, 2007), 35.

31. Brent Scowcroft, interview by author, Washington, DC, April 12, 2008.

32. Armitage and Nye, *Commission on Smart Power*, 59.

33. Sanger, *The Inheritance*, 357.

34. Stefan Staehle, "How to Integrate China into the Global Aid Regime: Lessons from Beijing's Behaviour: In International Regimes," PowerPoint presentation, Interdisciplinary Centre of East Asian Studies, Goethe University, Frankfurt/Main, December 15, 2007.

35. Gregory Mavrides, "Keeping Face in China: Understanding the Effects of Mianzi and Guanxi in Day-to-Day Chinese Life," *Foreign Teacher's Guide to Living and Teaching in China*, 2005, www.transitionsabroad.com/listings/living/articles/keeping_face_in_china.shtml.

36. Sharon La Franiere, "Tiananmen Now Seems Distant to China's Students," *New York Times*, May 21, 2009.

37. Susan Shirk, *China: Fragile Superpower* (New York: Oxford University Press, 2007), 85.

38. Senior Pentagon official, interview by author, April 2009.

39. George Joffe, interview by author, Cambridge, April 2009.

40. Armitage and Nye, *Commission on Smart Power*, 20–23.

41. Ibid., 6.

42. Hilton Root, *The Alliance Curse: How America Lost the Third World* (Washington, DC: Brookings Institution Press, 2008), 203.

43. Jennifer Cooke, "China's Soft Power in Africa," in *China's Soft Power in Africa: Chinese Soft Power and Its Implications for the United States: Competition and Cooperation in the Developing World*, ed. Carola McGiffert (Washington, DC: Center for Strategic and International Studies, 2009), 39.

44. Thomas Lum, ed., "Comparing Global Influence: China's and U.S. Diplomacy, Foreign Aid, Trade, and Investment in the Developing World," Congressional Research Service, August 15, 2008, 164; Organisation for Economic Co-Operation and Development, *Geographical Distribution of Financial Flows to Aid Recipients* (Paris: OECD Publishing, March 2007), 260.

45. Jon B. Alterman, "China's Soft Power in the Middle East," in *China's Soft Power in Africa: Chinese Soft Power and Its Implications for the United States: Competition and Cooperation in the Developing World*, ed. Carola McGiffert (Washington, DC: Center for Strategic and International Studies, 2009), 70.

46. John Maynard Keynes, quoted in Alfred L. Malabre, *Lost Prophets: An Insider's History of the Modern Economists* (Boston: Harvard Business Press, 1994), 220.

47. Cooke, "China's Soft Power in Africa," 33.

48. Ben Simpfendorfer, "Beijing's Marshall Plan," *International Herald Trib-*

une, November 4, 2009, 6.

49. Derek Mitchell and Brian Harding, "China and South East Asia," in *China's Soft Power in Africa: Chinese Soft Power and Its Implications for the United States: Competition and Cooperation in the Developing World,* ed. Carola McGiffert (Washington, DC: Center for Strategic and International Studies, 2009), 86–89.

50. Armitage and Nye, *Commission on Smart Power,* 66–67.

51. Barcelona Forum, "The Barcelona Development Agenda," Barcelona Forum, September 24, 2004, www.barcelona2004.org/www.barcelona2004.org/esp/banco_del_conocimiento/docs/CO_47_EN.pdf.

52. Ravi Kanth Devarakonda, "Cotton Subsidies Remain Big Hurdle in WTO Doha Round," *Inter Press Service,* October 20, 2008.

53. Leslie Gelb, "Necessity, Choice and Common Sense: A Policy for a Bewildering World," *Foreign Affairs,* May–June 2009, 58.

54. Clyde Prestowitz, *Three Billion New Capitalists: The Great Shift of Wealth and Power to the East* (New York: Basic Book, 2005), 195.

55. Gelb, "Necessity, Choice and Common Sense," 58.

56. Clyde Prestowitz, "China's Industrial Policy and Its Impact on U.S. Companies, Workers and the American Economy," testimony before the U.S.-China Economic and Security Review Commission, Washington, DC, March 24, 2009.

57. Clyde Prestowitz, interview by author, Washington, DC, April 18, 2008. For more on these kinds of proposals, see Prestowitz, *Three Billion New Capitalists,* 257–269. See also Prestowitz, "China's Industrial Policy."

58. Bill Emmott, *Rivals: How The Power Struggle Between China, India and Japan Will Shape Our Next Decade* (London: Allen Lane, 2008), 284.

59. "No Pakistan-China Nuclear Deal," *BBC News,* November 5, 2003.

60. Emmott, *Rivals,* 2–4, 290.

61. Ibid., 290–291, 306.

62. Dimitri K. Simes, "Losing Russia: The Costs of Renewed Confrontation," *Foreign Affairs,* November–December 2007.

63. David Shambaugh, "When Giants Meet," *International Herald Tribune,* June 15, 2009.

64. E. Wayne Merry, "A 'Reset' Is Not Enough," *New York Times,* May 22, 2009.

65. Ibid.

66. Dimitri K. Simes, "Russia's Playing Ball—Will We?" *Los Angeles Times,* March 22, 2007.

67. Fareed Zakaria, "The Rise of the Rest," *Newsweek,* May 12, 2008.

68. Emmott, *Rivals,* 294–296.

69. Joseph Nye, "Our Impoverished Discourse," *Huffington Post,* November 1, 2006.

70. Barack Obama: "On a New Beginning," remarks at Cairo University, Egypt, June 4, 2009, www.whitehouse.gov/the_press_office/Remarks-by-the-President-at-Cairo-University-6-04-09/.

71. Helene Cooper, "Obama Says 'Justice' Is Needed for Iranians," *International Herald Tribune,* June 20, 2009.

72. Kathleen E. McLaughlin, "Iran Election: The View from Beijing," *Global Post*, June 17, 2009.

73. Jiyoung Song, "Late Chosun Philosophies and Human Rights: A North Korean Interpretation," Second Polis Annual Conference, Cambridge, England, May 28, 2009, 1–3.

74. Nye, *The Paradox of American Power*, 171.

INDEX